The Kingdom
That Turned the World
Upside Down

David W. Bercot

"They dragged Jason and some brethren to the rulers of the city, crying out, 'These who have turned the world upside down have come here too.'"
—Acts 17:6

SCROLL PUBLIS

Rod and Staff Books
(Milestone Ministries)
800-761-0234 or 541-466-3231
www.RodandStaffBooks.com

Published by Scroll Publishing Company, P. O. Box 122,
Amberson, PA 17210.

(717) 349-7033
www.scrollpublishing.com.

ISBN: 978-092-4722-177

Cover art: Albrecht Altdorfer
Cover design: Steven "Alex" Alexander II

Printed in the United States of America

Contents

Part I.
The Kingdom With Upside-Down Values

1. Holy War? 1
2. The Right-Side Up Kingdom 7
3. A Different Kind of Kingdom 10
4. Have You Made the Kingdom Commitment? 17
5. Changing Our View of Mammon 27
6. A New Standard of Honesty 38
7. The Kingdom Laws on Marriage and Divorce 48

Part II.
The Big Stumbling Block

8. Love My Enemies? 61
9. But What If ...? 70
10. But Don't the Scriptures Say ...? 84
11. What About the Kingdoms of the World? 93
12. Life under Two Kingdoms 98
13. Am I of this World? 106
14. Does this Make Us Peace and Justice Activists? . . 114
15. Has Anyone Done This in Real Life? 117
16. But Is This Historic Christianity? 121

Part III.
What Is The Gospel of the Kingdom?

17. The Jesus Road to Salvation 131
18. How to Enter the Kingdom 142
19. No Pharisees Need Apply 150
20. The Kingdom Can't Be Kept Quiet 155

Part IV.
A Hybrid Is Born

21. What Happened to the Kingdom Gospel? 161
22. The Kingdom of Theology 168
23. Was God Changing the Rules? 177
24. How Christ's Teachings Disappeared 181
25. The Golden Age That Never Happened 186
26. Augustine—Apologist for the Hybrid 195
27. Forgery in the Name of Christ! 207

Part V.
When It Was Illegal To Be a Kingdom Christian

28. The Underground Kingdom 215
29. The Waldensians 220
30. The Alternate Stream 231
31. The Waldensians Meet the Swiss Reformers 238
32. The New Zion in Geneva 243
33. The Kingdom Banner Arises Anew 250
34. The Ball Is Now in Our Court 263

Bibliography 269
Notes 272

Part I

The Kingdom With Upside-Down Values

1

Holy War?

It was Friday, July 8, 1099. The hot desert sun bore down on a ragged procession of robed clergy, carrying large crosses and relics of saints, who were marching around the outer walls of Jerusalem. The clergy were followed by 1200 emaciated barefoot Crusader knights and around 11,000 near-starved, thirsty soldiers, sailors, and workmen. The Muslim defenders of the city laughed scornfully at this procession, mocking them as they marched. The Muslims even desecrated crosses in various ways and hung them on the city walls to further insult this rag-tag band of half-crazed Christians.

Despite the insults and jeers, the Crusaders continued on their barefoot procession until they reached the Mount of Olives, where they stopped. There, one of the bishops exhorted them, saying, "Now we are on the very spot from which the Lord made His ascension, and we can do nothing more to purify ourselves. So let each one of us forgive his brother whom he has injured, that the Lord may forgive us."[1] He then reminded them of his prophecy that Jerusalem would be delivered to them the next Friday if they continued to humble and purify themselves.

If any Muslims heard the bishop's speech, they were not particularly worried. Take the city of Jerusalem in seven days? Not likely. After all, before the Crusaders had even reached the vicinity of Jerusalem, Iftikhar, the Muslim ruler of Jerusalem, had plugged or poisoned all wells outside the city walls. The Crusaders had only one intermittent spring for their source of water, and many of the Crusaders were seriously dehydrated. Furthermore, Iftikhar had moved all domestic animals inside the walls, giving the city an abundant supply of food. In contrast, the Crusaders were emaciated from hunger. Jerusalem could withstand a long siege. In fact, to conserve their food supply and protect themselves against treachery, Iftikhar had expelled all Christians from the city. Most of the Jews had also left.

So Iftikhar and his soldiers lost little sleep over the Crusaders. They knew they had plenty of water, an abundance of food, better arms, and the seemingly impregnable city walls to protect them. And they had 60,000 armed men to defend those walls! What's more, a relief force of Egyptian soldiers was on its way to lift the siege. And against all of this, what did the Crusaders have? About 1200 knights was all—supported by a poorly equipped, ragged band of 11,000 soldiers, sailors, and workmen. Altogether, the Crusaders had less than 13,000 men against 60,000 armed Muslims. Plus, the Crusaders were fighting in an unknown land and were unaccustomed to the desert heat, so different from their homeland of France. Yes, they were something to laugh at.

But the laughter stopped five days later when, to the surprise of the Muslims, the Crusaders wheeled several huge wooden siege towers towards the walls of Jerusalem. The Crusaders had been constructing these monstrous structures in secret from wood they had salvaged. Each tower was equipped with virtually everything a medieval army needed: a catapult, battering ram, drawbridge, and lofty turret from which the Crusaders could rain arrows down on the city's defenders. What's more, inside each siege tower was a small army of Frankish Crusaders, eager to pour out into the city once the walls had been breached.

Seeing the dreaded siege towers, the Muslim defenders began building up their defenses on those parts of the wall opposite the towers. However, on the night before the Crusaders attacked, they silently dismantled some of the towers and moved them nearly a mile away to parts of Jerusalem's walls that were less fortified. It was an unbelievable undertaking under any conditions. But in their weakened condition, it was an almost superhuman accomplishment. When the morning light gently bathed the Jerusalem landscape on the morning of Thursday, July 14, the Muslim defenders were stunned in disbelief. They couldn't believe that some of the towers had been moved during the night.

Having worked all night, many of the attackers were already exhausted. Nevertheless, they prayed that morning, trusting that God would give their weary bodies the needed strength. After prayer, the Crusaders launched their attack on Jerusalem. With shouts of praise to God, the Crusaders began slowly moving the ponderous towers closer to the walls of Jerusalem. As the towers inched forward, the Crusaders catapulted huge boulders against the city walls and interior houses. When some of the siege towers reached the city walls, their heavy battering rams began pounding the ancient walls of Jerusalem. From the tops of their siege towers, the Crusaders hurled flaming wooden missiles that had been dipped in tar, wax, and sulphur. These missiles set on fire the wooden fortifications inside the walls.

However, the Muslim defenders hurled their own fiery missiles back at the towers in an attempt to set *them* on fire. The defenders hammered the towers all day long with catapulted rocks. The missiles and arrows rained back and forth throughout the day. The Crusaders fought bravely, but they were unable to secure a foothold. Some of their siege towers had been battered into ruins. One of them had been burned to the ground. Both sides quit fighting when night fell.

On the morning of Friday, July 15, the Crusaders renewed their attack. This was the day that the bishop had prophesied they would take the city. But that didn't look likely. They all were exhausted from the sleepless nights and the previous day's fighting. By noon the Crusaders were greatly discouraged. They were weary, and they seemed to be making no progress. They were hopelessly outnumbered, and the walls of Jerusalem seemed impregnable.

They finally halted their operations and held council. About half of them were ready to call off the futile siege and hang the bishop who had made the false prophecies. However, while they were still talking, a knight on the Mount of Olives began to wave his shield to the others, signaling them to advance. At this signal, the men began to take heart, and they renewed their attack in earnest. The battering rams went back to work, and some of the Crusaders began climbing the walls with scaling ladders and ropes.

The city defenders had stacked a virtual mountain of hay and cotton bales inside the city walls as an additional defense. But some of the archers under the command of Godfrey of Bouillon succeeded in setting these bales on fire with their flaming arrows. When the wind changed, huge clouds of smoke blinded and choked the Muslim defenders. The shower of fire and smoke forced them from the walls.

Seizing the moment, Godfrey quickly released the long drawbridge of his tower, and his men fearlessly streamed over the walls. In mere minutes, the Crusaders secured this section of the wall, which allowed their fellow soldiers to scale the walls with their ladders. Some of the invaders reached one of the city gates and were able to open it. Waves of Crusaders swept through the opened gates.

Although they still heavily outnumbered the Crusaders, the Muslims reeled back in disbelief and confusion. Only hours before, it had appeared that the Crusaders had been defeated. But now they were swarming into the city! Stunned, the defenders fled from the Crusaders in disarray. Suddenly, the whole city was engulfed in mass panic, trying to escape from the invaders. Women screamed and children cried as the Crusaders butchered every person they met.[2]

The Crusaders saw themselves as the medieval equivalent of Jehu and his army, who slaughtered the Baal worshipers of their day. One Crusader has left us an eyewitness account of the horrible carnage:

"Piles of heads, hands, and feet were to be seen in the streets of the city. It was necessary to pick one's way over the bodies of men and horses. But these were small matters compared to what happened at the temple of Solomon, a place where religious services are ordinarily chanted. What happened there? If I tell the truth, it will exceed your powers of belief. So let it suffice to say this much, at least: that in the temple and porch of Solomon, men rode in blood up to their knees and bridle reins. Indeed, it was a just and splendid judgment of God that this place should be filled with the blood of the unbelievers! For it had suffered so long from their blasphemies. The city was filled with corpses and blood."[3]

One might think that the next day the Crusaders were filled with remorse for massacring close to 100,000 people, many of whom were little children. But not at all, for they were certain that their Lord Jesus Christ had given them their victory and was smiling down at them as their happy King. After all, the Pope himself had put out the call for all good Catholics to go and free the Holy Land from the infidels. He had assured all Catholics the complete forgiveness of sins for any who went on the Crusade. So our eye witness continues:

"Now that the city was taken, it was well worth all our previous labors and hardships to see the devotion of the pilgrims at the Holy Sepulcher. How they rejoiced and exulted and sang a new song to the Lord! For their hearts offered prayers of praise to God, victorious and triumphant, which cannot be told in words. A new day! New joy! New and perpetual gladness! The consummation of our labor and devotion drew forth new words and new songs from everyone.

This day, I say, will be famous in all future ages, for it turned our labors and sorrows into joy and exultation. This day, I say, marks the justification of all Christianity, the humiliation of paganism, and the renewal of our faith. 'This is the day which the Lord hath made, let us rejoice and be glad in it,' for on this day the Lord revealed Himself to His people and blessed them."[4]

But did Jesus view this massacre as something joyous? Had the Crusaders truly advanced the kingdom of God? Or had they done great harm to it?

After all, about 1100 years before, Jesus had planted a kingdom of *love*. His subjects were to be known for their love of each other. Not only that, they were to love their enemies as well. Their own King had described Himself as gentle and lowly in heart. The first subjects of this special kingdom had turned their world upside down—not with the sword, but with words of truth and acts of love. So what were people who claimed to be subjects of this kingdom of love and gentleness doing in a distant land, massacring the inhabitants of Jerusalem?

It's a long story. But it's one that needs to be told. Because my eternal destiny and yours are intricately bound up in this story of the kingdom that turned the world upside down.

2

The Right-Side Up Kingdom

As we shall see shortly, the kingdom that turned the world upside down is a unique kingdom. It's a kingdom of upside-down values.

In 1978, Donald Kraybill wrote a book entitled, *The Upside-Down Kingdom*, in which he explored some of these upside-down values of the kingdom of God. But to fully understand this upside-down kingdom, we must first look at a kingdom that was right-side up.

The Scriptures introduce us to this right-side up kingdom in the Book of Exodus, where God spoke to the Israelites: "Now therefore, if you will indeed obey My voice and keep My covenant, then you shall be a special treasure to Me above all people; for all the earth is Mine. And you shall be to Me a kingdom of priests and a holy nation" (Ex. 19:5,6).*

This was God's offer to the Israelites: that they could be His special kingdom of priests. And the Israelites accepted His offer. They entered into a covenant with Him at Sinai. Like most covenants, this covenant was two-sided. *If* the Israelites obeyed God's voice, then they would be to Him a "kingdom of priests and a holy nation." Like any other kingdom, the nation of Israel

---

*Unless otherwise indicated, all Scripture quotations in this work are from the New King James Version.

7

was to have a ruler and laws. However, their King, Lawgiver and Judge was to be God Himself (Isa. 33:22). The laws of the kingdom of Israel were the Mosaic Law, given directly by God.

Despite these special features, the kingdom of Israel was still an earthly kingdom. In most aspects, it was similar to the kingdoms of the world. It had a physical, geographic territory. Its people were a distinct ethnic nationality. They defended their kingdom with earthly soldiers, armed with swords, spears, and bows. Like all other earthly kingdoms, the Israelites expanded their territory through use of the sword. In the eyes of the surrounding nations, the most distinctive thing about the Israelites was that their Law forbade the use of idols.

In fact, even God's promised blessings to the Israelites were earthly, material blessings: "If you diligently obey the voice of the Lord your God, ... blessed shall be the fruit of your body, the produce of your ground and the increase of your herds. ...The Lord will command the blessing on you in your storehouses. ...And the Lord will grant you plenty of goods, in the fruit of your body, in the increase of your livestock, and in the produce of your ground. ...The Lord will open to you His good treasure, the heavens, to give the rain to your land in its season. ...You shall lend to many nations, but you shall not borrow" (Deut. 28:1-12).

But it was not only the *blessings* that would be material. If the Israelites broke their covenant, their *punishments* would likewise be earthly, physical: "The Lord will change the rain of your land to powder and dust; from the heaven it shall come down on you until you are destroyed. The Lord will cause you to be defeated before your enemies. ...You shall carry much seed out to the field but gather little in, for the locust shall consume it. You shall plant vineyards and tend them, but you shall neither drink of the wine nor gather the grapes; for the worms shall eat them" (Deut. 28:24,25,38,39).

In short, the ancient kingdom of Israel was a right-side up kingdom. Its pattern was even understandable to the other nations of the world. In fact, in many aspects, ancient Israel was modeled after the same pattern on which their nations had been built. The primary difference was that the other nations imagined it was *their* gods who had established them as a people. They believed it was *their* gods who prospered them materially when they worshipped these gods. And they believed it was *their* gods who punished them with droughts and famines when their gods were displeased with them. In many ways, the world view of the Gentile nations was quite similar to the world view of the Israelites. The primary difference was in matters of religion and morality, not in matters of state.

But the ancient kingdom of Israel, which was predominantly earthly, was not intended as an end in itself. It was meant to be a tutor leading the Israelites to something far greater—a kingdom that would truly not be of this world.

3

A Different Kind of Kingdom

The year A. D. 30 began like any other year. Jewish priests still offered daily sacrifices in the temple. Farmers worked in their fields, and women washed their clothes in the streams. Fishermen hung up their nets to dry on the shores of the Sea of Galilee. But suddenly a prophet named John burst upon the scene! Clothed in camel's hair and a leather belt, John made a striking figure. And he brought with him a startling message—the kingdom of God was at hand!

The kingdom of God was at hand? To the Jews, this meant that the Messiah was about to come. It meant the overthrow of Rome! It meant they would soon have back their independence as a nation. No wonder that John's message caught everyone's attention. People began flocking to him to find out what they needed to do to prepare for this kingdom.

However, when John identified Jesus as their long-awaited Messiah, most Jews were not excited. Jesus of Nazareth? He didn't seem at all like the Messiah they were expecting. He was obviously no warrior. And He didn't even attempt to organize an army to liberate the Jews from Rome. In fact, He didn't even *preach* against the Romans.

What did He preach about? I would like to ask you, the reader, that question. What was the theme of Jesus' preaching? Man's need for salvation? God's love for mankind? The necessity to be born again? The fact that Jesus would die as a ransom for us?

Jesus certainly spoke about all of these things. And they are all essential truths. But none of them was the *theme* of His message. The Scriptures record only one occasion on which Jesus spoke about the new birth: his private talk with Nicodemus. He mentioned His dying as a ransom for us only one time. There are only five or six passages in which He even used the word "salvation."

No, the theme of Jesus' message was the *kingdom of God*. There are nearly one hundred references to the kingdom throughout the Gospels. Furthermore, most of Jesus' parables were about the kingdom. In fact, Jesus said that the reason He was sent to earth was to preach about the kingdom: "I must preach the kingdom of God to the other cities also, because *for this purpose I have been sent*" (Luke 4:43). That's not what we're used to hearing, is it? We've all been given the impression that the primary purpose of Jesus' coming to earth was to save us from our sins. And that definitely was one of the purposes of His coming here. But it was not the only purpose.

Wherever He went, Jesus preached about the kingdom of God. "From that time, Jesus began to preach and to say, 'Repent, for the *kingdom of heaven* is at hand.' ...And Jesus went about all Galilee, teaching in their synagogues, preaching the *gospel of the kingdom*, and healing all kinds of sickness and all kinds of disease. ...But when the multitudes knew it, they followed Him; and He received them and spoke to them about the *kingdom of God*, and healed those who had need of healing. ...Then Jesus went about all the cities and villages, teaching in their synagogues, preaching the *gospel of the kingdom*, and healing every sickness and every disease among the people" (Mt. 4:17,23; Luke 9:11; Mt. 9:35).

The irony is that although the kingdom of God was the theme of Jesus' preaching, the message of the kingdom is almost totally missing from the gospel that's preached today. What's the theme of most preaching today? It's man's personal salvation, isn't it? It's not the kingdom of God.

What the Apostles Preached

You may be thinking to yourself, "Okay, maybe Jesus preached about the kingdom, but it was different with His disciples. He told them to preach about the new birth and salvation, not about the kingdom, right?" Wrong. When Jesus commissioned His disciples, He specifically told them to preach about the *kingdom*.

Notice His preaching instructions: "As you go, preach, saying, 'The *kingdom of heaven* is at hand.' ... He sent them to preach the *kingdom of God* and to heal the sick. ...Heal the sick there, and say to them, 'The *kingdom of God* has come near to you" (Mt. 10:7; Luke 9:2, 10:9). Please understand that these are not a few isolated proof texts. In nearly every passage where Jesus gave preaching instructions to His disciples, He told them to preach about the kingdom.

You no doubt remember the disciple who said he would follow Jesus, but that he first had to bury his father. What did Jesus tell him? "Let the dead bury their own dead, but you go and *preach the kingdom of God*" (Luke 9:60).

But please don't misunderstand me. I am in no way minimizing our need to be born again and to be saved. These are crucial aspects of the gospel. However, they are a means to an end—entering the kingdom of God. Jesus never intended that His followers would preach about salvation and the new birth apart from the kingdom. The kingdom is an absolutely crucial aspect of the gospel. When we tell people about salvation— but say nothing about the kingdom—we are not preaching the gospel of Jesus Christ.

And what gospel was it that Jesus said would be preached in all the world before the end? He said, "And this *gospel of the kingdom* will be preached in all the world as a witness to all the nations, and then the end will come" (Mt. 24:14). *A* gospel is being preached throughout the world today, but is it the gospel of the *kingdom*?

What Is This Kingdom of God?

Every kingdom has four basic components: (1) a ruler or rulers, (2) subjects, (3) a domain or area of rulership, and (4) laws. God's kingdom is no different. It has a ruler, subjects, domain, and laws. However, because God's kingdom is a revolutionary kind of kingdom, these four basic components take on unique aspects.

To begin with, God's kingdom has no earthly ruler. Its ruler is Jesus Christ, who reigns from heaven. Earthly kingdoms periodically change rulers and policies. In contrast, Jesus is eternal, and His policies don't change. "Jesus Christ is the same yesterday, today, and forever" (Heb. 13:8).

Who are the subjects of the kingdom of God? The Jews? No, Jesus told the Jews quite pointedly, "I say to you, the kingdom of God will be taken from you and given to a nation bearing the fruits of it" (Mt. 21:43). Who was this nation to whom Jesus said He would give the kingdom? The Romans? The British? The Americans? No, it was none of these, for the Scriptures tell us, "There is neither Jew nor Greek, there is neither slave nor free, there is neither male nor female; for you are all one in Christ Jesus. And if you are Christ's, then you are Abraham's seed, and heirs according to the promise" (Gal. 3:28,29).

So all of us who belong to Christ—all of us who are genuinely born again—we are the subjects of this kingdom. We have become the heirs of God's promise, the citizens of His new nation. In writing to Gentile Christians of his day, Peter addressed them with the following words: "You are a chosen generation, a royal priesthood, a holy nation, His own special people, that you may proclaim the praises of Him who called you out of darkness into His marvelous light; who once were not a people but are now the people of God, who had not obtained mercy but now have obtained mercy" (1 Pet. 2:9-11).

So the subjects of God's kingdom are called to be a holy nation, a kingdom of priests, just as the Israelites had been called (Exod. 19:5,6). However, the kingdom was taken from the Israelites and given to a nation that would produce the fruits of righteousness—the nation of born-again believers.

One unique aspect of the kingdom of God is that its subjects don't occupy a certain portion of the earth, like the subjects of other kingdoms. The citizens of God's kingdom are interspersed among all nations of the world. This feature has caused continual conflict for the kingdom of God. That's because its citizens always live under two different kingdoms—a kingdom of the world and the kingdom of God.

Jesus told the Samaritan woman, "The hour is coming when you will neither on this mountain, nor in Jerusalem, worship the Father" (John 4:21). God's kingdom would have no earthly capital or holy shrine.

All of this was something beyond the experience of both the Jews and the Gentiles of Jesus' day. The kingdom of the Israelites had encompassed a specific geographic area. So had all of the kingdoms of man. The Israelites had always had a physical location where their tabernacle or temple was placed. For a thousand years, that place had been Jerusalem. Every human kingdom has an earthly capital, but God's kingdom does not.

The Kingdom of God Is Within You

If all of this was not astonishing enough, Jesus told the Pharisees something even more startling: "Now when He was asked by the Pharisees when the kingdom of God would come, He answered them and said, 'The kingdom of God does not come with observation; nor will they say, 'See here!' or 'See there!' For indeed, the kingdom of God is within you" (Luke 17:20,21).

What kind of kingdom is this? A kingdom that's *within* you? Jesus was truly introducing something marvelously new—something revolutionary. This was not just a new kingdom. It was a new *type* of kingdom. It was a type of kingdom that was totally different from what anyone—Jew or Gentile—had ever heard of before. A kingdom that is "within you."

"Oh, I see," you may be thinking. "Jesus was talking about a *spiritual* kingdom, not a *real* one." No, Jesus was talking about a real kingdom. The ancient kingdom of the Israelites was definitely a real kingdom, wasn't it? It had real kings, real subjects, and real laws. The kingdom of God is just as real as the ancient Israelite kingdom. It too has a real King, real subjects, and real laws. Its domain encompasses the entire earth, even though most of the earth's population are not citizens of this kingdom.

What did Jesus mean when He said that the kingdom of God is within you? Tertullian, an early Christian writer, commented on this phrase, "Now, who is there who does not understand the phrase, 'within you,' to mean *in your hand* or *within your power*? That is, if you hear and do the commandments of God?"[1] Anybody can choose to be a citizen of the kingdom of God if he is willing to make the needed commitment. A person doesn't have to travel anywhere or pay any sum of money to become a citizen.

Now, many Greek scholars today feel that Luke 17:21 should be translated, "The kingdom of God is in your midst," rather than "within you." In other words, the King and some of His subjects were already standing there in the midst of those religious leaders who asked Jesus when the kingdom was coming. The kingdom was in their midst, but they didn't realize it.

Whichever significance Jesus intended by the phrase, "within you" or "in your midst," the principle is still the same. His kingdom has no national boundaries, no earthly king, and no military forces. His subjects live within the midst of the peoples of this world, yet the world cannot see this kingdom. Becoming a citizen of God's kingdom is within reach of everyone. In fact, what makes God's people the subjects of this kingdom is something within them—the indwelling of the Holy Spirit.

The Kingdom of God Is at Hand

A lot of Christians have the idea that the kingdom of God is something only in the future. But, no, the kingdom of God is something that is here right now. Paul wrote to the Colossians, "He has delivered us from the power of darkness and conveyed us into the kingdom of the Son of His love" (Col. 1:13). Paul speaks in the past tense. God has *already* conveyed us into His kingdom. He doesn't bring us into His kingdom after we die. He brings us into His kingdom as soon as we are born again.

Strangely, many Christians don't realize that the kingdom of God is a present reality on earth. In fact, many Christians don't even know what the kingdom of God is. Like the Pharisees, they don't *see* the kingdom of God. And so they never make the kingdom commitment.

4

Have You Made The Kingdom Commitment?

When foreigners desire to become citizens of the United States of America, they are required to take the following oath:

"I hereby declare, on oath, that I absolutely and entirely renounce and abjure all allegiance and fidelity to any foreign prince, potentate, state or sovereignty, of whom or which I have heretofore been a subject or citizen; that I will support and defend the Constitution and laws of the United States of America against all enemies, foreign and domestic; that I will bear true faith and allegiance to the same; that I will bear arms on behalf of the United States when required by the law; that I will perform noncombatant service in the armed forces of the United States when required by the law; that I will perform work of national importance under civilian direction when required by the law; and that I take this obligation freely without any mental reservation or purpose of evasion; so help me God."[1]

The United States, like most other governments, will not allow those who wish to become citizens to straddle the fence. Naturalized citizens can't claim that their loyalty and allegiance belong to the United States if they retain allegiance to some foreign government. Our government won't allow that. It wants undivided loyalty from any who apply for citizenship.

So it should come as no surprise that Jesus the King requires similar loyalty from those who wish to apply for citizenship in

His kingdom. In fact, He demands an even greater degree of loyalty: "He who is not with Me is against Me, and he who does not gather with Me scatters abroad. ...He who loves father or mother more than Me is not worthy of Me. And he who loves son or daughter more than Me is not worthy of Me. And he who does not take his cross and follow after Me is not worthy of Me. He who finds his life will lose it, and he who loses his life for My sake will find it. ...Whoever of you does not forsake all that he has cannot be My disciple" (Mt. 12:30; 10:37-39; Luke 14:33).

The United States does not require persons to forsake all they have to become its citizens. But Jesus does. In His kingdom, there can be no divided loyalties. Jesus will not be relegated to a subservient role by anyone or any thing. He requires all or nothing. In fact, that's the very reason Jesus tells us to count the cost before deciding to join His kingdom. "For which of you, intending to build a tower, does not sit down first and count the cost, whether he has enough to finish it—lest, after he has laid the foundation, and is not able to finish, all who see it begin to mock him, saying, 'This man began to build and was not able to finish.'" (Luke 14:28-30). Jesus has no desire for us to start something we won't finish. "No one, having put his hand to the plow, and looking back, is fit for the kingdom of God" (Luke 9:62).

If we truly understand the kingdom and grasp what it means, it will be more precious to us than anything we own. "The kingdom of heaven is like treasure hidden in a field, which a man found and hid; and for joy over it he goes and sells *all that he has* and buys that field. Again, the kingdom of heaven is like a merchant seeking beautiful pearls, who, when he had found one pearl of great price, went and sold *all that he had* and bought it" (Mt. 13:44-46).

Actually, in times of war, even earthly governments expect their citizens to put loyalty to their country ahead of every other loyalty, including their own families. It sometimes happens in times of war that fathers and sons fight against each other and that soldiers kill their own brothers. In fact, during war, earthly kingdoms expect their citizens to lay down their own lives if necessary for the good of their country. Any *real* government expects this type of loyalty from its citizens.

Jesus expects no less. Why? Because His kingdom is a *real* kingdom. And unlike earthly kingdoms, the kingdom of God is *always* at war (Eph. 6:12). As Jesus said, "Do not think that I came to bring peace on earth. I did not come to bring peace but a sword. For I have come to set a man against his father, a daughter against her mother, and a daughter-in-law against her mother-in-law; and a man's enemies will be those of his own household" (Mt. 10:34-36).

Jesus requires of His citizens the same level of loyalty, love and commitment that fervent patriots give their countries during time of war—if not higher. Being a citizen of the kingdom of God is not fun and games—it's serious business. "He who loves his life will lose it, and he who hates his life in this world will keep it for eternal life" (John 12:25).

Obedience

During World War II, the United States government rationed a large number of items. Rubber was the first to be rationed. Gasoline soon followed. Before long, the government began rationing sugar, coffee, meats, butter, canned goods, dried peas and beans, and a variety of other products. Eventually, the government rationed or restricted even such items as shoes and clothing.[2]

Now, what would people have thought of a person who claimed to be a zealous patriot if he were caught stealing gasoline from a local refinery so that he wouldn't have to endure the inconvenience of wartime gasoline rationing? What if the same person broke numerous other wartime laws? Would anyone have called him a true patriot? Hardly! They would have called him a hypocrite, a fraud, and even a traitor.

It's no different in Christ's kingdom. Jesus has issued various laws and commandments, and all of His laws are wartime laws. When we break His laws, we show ourselves to be traitors. We show that we have no real love for our new country. We want to enjoy the benefits of living under His government, but we don't want to incur any hardships or inconveniences. Jesus sees right through any fake patriotism for His kingdom, any artificial love for Him.

Does the Kingdom Really Have Laws?

But you may have been told that there are no laws for Christians. Many preachers say: "We no longer have commandments—that was under the Mosaic Law. We are under grace, not law." If that's the case, then please explain these statements of Jesus:

"If you love me, keep my commandments. ...He who has My commandments and keeps them, it is he who loves Me. And he who loves Me will be loved by My Father, and I will love him and manifest Myself to him. ...If anyone loves Me, he will keep My word; and My Father will love him, and We will come to him and make Our home with him. He who does not love Me does not keep My words. ...You are My friends if you do whatever I command you. ...If you keep My commandments, you will abide in My love, just as I have kept My Father's commandments and abide in His love" (John 14:15,21,23,24; 15:14,10).

We have no commandments? Just grace? Not according to Jesus! And His view is the only one that counts. Where there are no laws and no commandments—there is no kingdom. And where there is no kingdom, there is no Jesus. Any theology or any hermeneutic system that nullifies the plain words of Jesus is not of Christ. Jesus didn't spend His last night before His death repeating over and over to His disciples that they must keep His commandments—only to tell them later that He actually doesn't have any commandments after all!

Building on the Rock

Near the end of His Sermon on the Mount, Jesus forewarned us: "Many will say to Me in that day, 'Lord, Lord, have we not prophesied in Your name, cast out demons in Your name, and done many wonders in Your name?' And then I will declare to them, 'I never knew you; depart from Me, you who practice lawlessness!'" (Mt. 7:22,23). So Jesus said He would reject any professing believer who practiced *lawlessness*. My dictionary defines "lawless" as "not regulated by the authority of law."[3] Those who practice lawlessness are professing Christians who refuse either to recognize Jesus' laws or commandments or to live by them.

Jesus concluded His sermon by saying, "Therefore whoever hears these sayings of Mine, and *does them*, I will liken him to a wise man who built his house on the rock: and the rain descended, the floods came, and the winds blew and beat on that house; and it did not fall, for it was founded on the rock.

"But everyone who hears these sayings of Mine, and *does not do them*, will be like a foolish man who built his house on the sand: and the rain descended, the floods came, and the winds blew and beat on that house; and it fell. And great was its fall" (Mt. 7:24-27).

Those words are straightforward, aren't they? The only way we can build on the rock is to *do* the things Jesus taught. If we don't do what He taught, we build on the sand. It's that simple.

So I find it unbelievable that we who profess to be Bible-believing Christians throw Jesus' words right back in His face and taunt Him by singing boldly on Sunday mornings:

"My hope is built on nothing less than Jesus' blood and righteousness. I dare not trust the sweetest frame but wholly lean on Jesus' name.

"On Christ, the solid Rock, I stand. All other ground is sinking sand, all other ground is sinking sand.

"When darkness veils His lovely face, *I rest on His unchanging grace*. In every high and stormy gale, my anchor holds within the veil.

"When He shall come with trumpet sound, O may I then in Him be found. Dressed *in His righteousness alone*, faultless to stand before the throne."[4]

The only passage in Scripture that speaks of building on the rock instead of on sinking sand is the passage we just read from the Sermon on the Mount. There, Jesus made it absolutely clear that the only way we can build on the rock is to *do* what He preached in that Sermon. His grace is truly unchanging, but He extends it only to those who love and obey Him.

Yet, this popular hymn totally ignores the very words of Jesus and teaches instead that we build on the rock by simply trusting in Jesus' grace and righteousness to cover us—regardless of how we live. And guess who most professing Christians choose to believe: (1) Jesus Himself or (2) this hymn writer and others like him who preach a gospel of easy-believism?

Kingdom Values

Growing up in the Fifties, I often heard talk about "the American way." The "American way" referred to the American set of values, in contrast to the values of the Communists. Among the American values is a strong belief in freedom of religion, freedom of speech, freedom of the press, due process of law, and elected representatives who are answerable to the people.

Similarly, there is a "kingdom way." Jesus' kingdom comes with its own special set of values. In the ensuing chapters, we will look at some of the kingdom laws based on these values. Now, these kingdom values will seem upside down to most people. That's because many of them are the exact opposite of everyday human values. But the most important thing to remember about them is that kingdom values are rooted in *eternity*. And things take on entirely different characteristics when subjected to the light of eternity.

It's similar to the changing characteristics of the chemical substance H_2O at different temperatures. When this substance is above 32 degrees Fahrenheit (and below 212 degrees), we call it water. It's a liquid that will flow through a pipe. A person can drink it or swim through it. But below 32 degrees, H_2O takes on entirely different characteristics. All of its properties are suddenly turned upside down. What you could formerly drink, you can now eat. What you could formerly swim through, you can now walk on.

It's the same way with eternity. Everything—possessions, talents, activities, and values—all take on entirely new characteristics when viewed through the eyes of eternity. The things that are a blessing from an earthly viewpoint often become a curse when seen through eternal eyes. In the kingdom, eternity isn't the main thing, it's the *only* thing. Everything else is ultimately irrelevant.

And that's the whole reason why we should expect the laws and values of this kingdom to be different—to be revolutionary. These are the laws and the values of eternity. Of course they're different from those of the earth!

The Great Paradigm Shift

Living and functioning in the kingdom of God requires a radical paradigm shift. The word *paradigm* basically means a model or pattern. It can also mean an overall concept, or the sum total of our assumptions, enabling us to understand (or misunderstand) a particular event, a scenario, or life in general. We make a paradigm shift when, after thinking the reality of something is one thing, we later discover it is something else.

For example, one of the best known paradigm shifts in science occurred when Copernicus postulated that the earth and other planets revolve around the sun. Once scientists accepted Copernicus' heliocentric model, they had to shift many of their prior assumptions about the earth's movements. Similarly, when Louis Pasteur and other scientists discovered that germs cause disease, it radically altered the practice of medicine.

The writer Frank Koch gives an excellent example of a paradigm shift in a story related in *Proceedings*, the magazine of the United States Naval Institute:

"Two battleships assigned to the training squadron had been at sea on maneuvers in heavy weather for several days. I was serving on the lead battleship and was on watch on the bridge as night fell. The visibility was poor with patchy fog, so the captain remained on the bridge keeping an eye on all activities.

"Shortly after dark, the lookout on the wing of the bridge reported, 'Light, bearing on the starboard bow.'

"Is it steady or moving astern?" the captain called out.

"The lookout replied, "Steady, captain," which meant we were on a dangerous collision course with that ship.

The captain then called to the signalman, "Signal that ship: We are on a collision course. Advise you change course 20 degrees."

Back came a signal, "Advisable for *you* to change course 20 degrees."

The captain said, "Send: I'm a captain, change course 20 degrees."

"I'm a seaman second class," came the reply. *"You* had better change course 20 degrees."

By that time, the captain was furious. He spat out, "Send: I'm a *battleship.* Change course 20 degrees."

Back came the flashing message: "I'm a lighthouse."

We changed course."[5]

The paradigm shift that we must make in order to enter and remain in the kingdom is just that radical! As a new kingdom citizen, we discover that many things we thought were ships are actually lighthouses. If we are truly kingdom citizens, our whole worldview changes.

These Are Not Just Nice "Thoughts for the Day"

I want to make one final comment before we take a look at some of the ground-breaking laws and "upside-down" values of the Kingdom. Most of us have heard these teachings of Jesus so many times, that we have virtually become numb to what they actually say. The revolutionary teachings of Jesus have been reduced to clichés, trite sayings, and nice "thoughts for the day." We talk about the "Beatitudes," the "Golden Rule" and "going the extra mile." Something nice to think about, but nothing to take too seriously or too literally.

In my Bible, the first seven verses of the Sermon on the Mount (i.e., the "Beatitudes") are printed in poetic format—as though these were simply beautiful words, not meant to be taken too seriously. Poetry? Jesus wasn't reciting poetry to the crowd that came to hear Him that day. He didn't want them to go home and talk about the beautiful words He had shared. No, He wanted to challenge them to the core of their very souls. He wanted to give them a new set of values and a new set of laws—together with a new life.

In the pages that follow, we're going to be looking at a handful of the new values and challenging laws of the kingdom. But we're not going to water them down or explain them away. We're going to take them straight on. Will Jesus' laws step on some of our toes? Most definitely!

5

Changing Our View
Of Mammon

First, let's look at one of the most challenging of Jesus' revolutionary laws. It concerns the very thing that most humans seek: wealth and prosperity. Earthly governments rarely forbid their citizens to store up earthly treasures. But the government of Jesus does. Our King has commanded us, "Do not lay up for yourselves treasures on earth, where moth and rust destroy and where thieves break in and steal; but lay up for yourselves treasures in heaven, where neither moth nor rust destroys and where thieves do not break in and steal" (Mt. 6:19,20).

What? I can't accumulate treasures here on earth? Why not? Jesus explains, "For where your treasure is, there your heart will be also" (Mt. 6:21). We saw in the last chapter that Jesus will not allow His subjects to relegate Him to a secondary role in their lives. In fact, He went on to say, "No one can serve two masters; for either he will hate the one and love the other, or else he will be loyal to the one and despise the other. You cannot serve God and mammon" (Mt. 6:24).

In short, Jesus has to be our only Master. Most earthly governments don't object to our serving mammon—material things—so long as we also fulfill the obligations that they place on us. Yet, in time of war, even earthly governments expect us to put our country ahead of material concerns. The government will conscript men into the army—regardless of what effect that may have on their incomes or businesses. In such times, all things must take second place to national interests.

Again, the kingdom of God is no different—except that it requires *more*, not less, than earthly governments. And as I've said, God's kingdom is always at war. Material pursuits will *always* conflict with the commitments the kingdom requires of us.

Does that mean we're supposed to quit our jobs or leave our businesses? Not necessarily. Jesus explained:

> "Therefore I say to you, do not worry about your life, what you will eat or what you will drink; nor about your body, what you will put on. Is not life more than food and the body more than clothing? Look at the birds of the air, for they neither sow nor reap nor gather into barns; yet your heavenly Father feeds them. Are you not of more value than they? Which of you by worrying can add one cubit to his stature?

> "So why do you worry about clothing? Consider the lilies of the field, how they grow: they neither toil nor spin; and yet I say to you that even Solomon in all his glory was not arrayed like one of these. Now if God so clothes the grass of the field, which today is, and tomorrow is thrown into the oven, will He not much more clothe you, O you of little faith?

> "Therefore do not worry, saying, 'What shall we eat?' or 'What shall we drink?' or 'What shall we wear?' For after all these things the Gentiles seek. For your heavenly Father knows that you need all these things. But seek first the kingdom of God and His righteousness, and all these things shall be added to you" (Mt. 6:25-33).

Jesus didn't tell us that we couldn't provide material things for ourselves and our families. But He did say that we have to be seeking the kingdom *first*. Our jobs and our businesses have to be relegated to a secondary place if we want to remain in His kingdom.

And what does Jesus promise us if we seek His kingdom first? Material prosperity? No. He simply promises us that God will provide for our basic *needs*: food, clothing, and some type of shelter.

The Great Value Shift

When it comes to material possessions, not only does God's kingdom have different *laws*, it has a completely different set of *values*. "Blessed are you poor, for yours is the kingdom of God" (Luke 6:20). Most of us have become so deadened to the "Beatitudes," that we don't even recognize the radical, revolutionary statement that Jesus made there.

It's a blessing to be poor? How many of us believe that? I mean, *really* believe it? When we drive by a poor Christian's house, do we say in our hearts, "What a blessing! Look how God has blessed that family." Let's be honest. Very few of us do. That's because we don't really believe in our hearts that poverty is a blessing.

In contrast, I can't count how many times Christians have shown me their lovely houses and abundant possessions, saying, "Look at what the Lord has given us." The next time someone tells me that, I'm tempted to reply, "Really? Why on earth would He do that? Do you have any idea why God is cursing you?" When will we wake up and believe Jesus? He tells us, "Woe to you who are rich, for you have received your consolation" (Luke 6:24). Prosperity is a snare, not a blessing. Godly poverty is a blessing, not a curse.

This calls for a paradigm shift as radical as realizing that what we once thought was a ship is really a lighthouse. "Godliness with contentment is great gain. For we brought nothing into this world, and it is certain we can carry nothing out. And having food and clothing, with these we shall be content. But those who desire to be rich fall into temptation and a snare, and into many foolish and harmful lusts which drown men in destruction and perdition. For the love of money is a root of all kinds of evil, for which some have strayed from the faith in their greediness" (1 Tim. 6:6-10).

The Kingdom Poor Versus the Worldly Poor

So if I'm poor, does that mean I automatically have a good standing with Christ? No. Because it isn't enough simply to be poor. Just because we're poor doesn't mean that we're seeking first the kingdom. In His Sermon on the Mount, Jesus used a slightly different expression than He did in the Sermon on the Plain recorded in Luke 6. In the Sermon on the Mount, He said, "Blessed are the poor *in spirit*, for theirs is the kingdom of heaven" (Mt. 5:3). That expression, "poor in spirit," is not used anywhere else in Scripture. Many modern commentators think it means "downhearted" or "humble." Perhaps so.

However, a second century Christian elder, Clement of Alexandria, interpreted it quite differently. He understood Jesus to be saying, "Blessed are the ones who are poor *in their souls*."[1] That is, regardless of how little or how much they have, their souls are detached from material things. After all, a person can be literally poor, yet be quite covetous in spirit. In fact, the vast majority of the poor of this world are not "poor in spirit." Their souls are not focused on the kingdom, but on mammon.

Worldly poverty is not by choice. Many worldly poor have their hearts set on obtaining more material things. They envy the rich and middle classes. In fact, their desire for mammon is so strong that they typically go into debt to buy what they can't afford. Some worldly poor behave dishonestly and even steal. Typically, they are behind on payments they have agreed to make. They may skip town leaving bills unpaid, or they may declare consumer bankruptcy and leave their creditors holding the bag. The worldly poor are sometimes just as much into conspicuous consumption as are the rich. That is, they want to wear the most stylish clothes or drive an eye-catching car. The truth is that they are lovers of money, just as are the rich.

Another type of the worldly poor are those who are simply lazy or irresponsible. They may devote little time to earning mammon, which may be commendable. However, they end up being a burden on others—their church, parents, friends, or the government. (Now, I'm not speaking about persons who are unable to work, such as the elderly, sick, and disabled.) Sometimes they have no money because they squander their money on liquor, gambling, tobacco, illegal drugs, and other such things. Those of the worldly poor who profess to be Christians do very little for the kingdom. They don't work for mammon, but they don't work for Christ, either.

In contrast, kingdom poverty is by *choice*. Some of the kingdom poor are formerly wealthy Christians, but they gave their wealth away to help the needy. Others were already poor, and they remain poor by choice. The godly poor are not just poor externally, but internally as well. The plans of their hearts focus on the kingdom, not on how to acquire more mammon. The kingdom poor don't envy others who are more prosperous, for they truly believe that being poor is a blessing. So why would they envy the rich? After all, the rich are missing a blessing.

The kingdom poor are not lazy, but hardworking. Depending on their circumstances, they may have to work full time to provide for the needs of their families. They well know that the Scriptures teach, "If anyone will not work, neither shall he eat" (2 Thess. 3:10). But whether they work full or part time, they are also hard workers for the kingdom.

The kingdom poor are not covetous. They don't buy things they can't afford, and they don't buy consumer goods on credit. They honor their obligations, because their "Yes" means "Yes" and their "No" means "No." The kingdom poor may live by means of the Gospel, and that is honorable before God—so long as they work hard in their King's service. But the kingdom poor do not live off their parents, friends, or welfare agencies. They are not a burden to others.

Can a Rich Person Be "Poor in Spirit"?

Theoretically, a person can have a relative abundance of this world's goods, and yet still be "poor in spirit." That is, mammon is his *servant*, not his master. Paul is a good example of someone who was "poor in spirit." As he told the Philippians, "I have learned in whatever state I am, to be content: I know how to be abased, and I know how to abound. Everywhere and in all things I have learned both to be full and to be hungry, both to abound and to suffer need" (Phil. 4:11,12). Whether he had plenty or had little, Paul was detached from his material possessions. He had no hesitation to let go of them when the need arose.

Yet, even in his abundance, I doubt Paul was ever rich. And we should all realize that it is extremely difficult to be literally rich, but still be "poor in spirit." As Jesus said, "Where your treasure is, there your heart will be also." If we own treasure here on earth, our heart *will be* on that treasure. We will fret about maintaining it, and we will worry about losing it somehow. For that reason, Jesus said on another occasion, "It is easier for a camel to go through the eye of a needle than for a rich man to enter the kingdom of God" (Mt. 19:24).

As we saw in the previous chapter, Jesus told us quite plainly, "Whoever of you does not forsake all that he has cannot be My disciple" (Luke 14:33). Obviously, the more things we have to forsake, the harder it is to let go of them. We can fool ourselves into believing that we are still "poor in spirit," but we aren't going to fool Jesus. He knows where our treasure lies, even if we don't.

The radical teachings of Jesus on wealth should shake the souls of all American Christians. Why? Because we are the wealthiest nation on earth. In fact, the United States is the wealthiest country that has ever existed in human history. In 2002, Americans as a nation earned enough to equal $36,300 for every man, woman, and child in America.[2] Half of the families in America earn at least $56,000 per year.[3]

At the same time, the typical American family doesn't feel particularly wealthy. That's because their standard of living is about the same as other families that live around them. In fact, we Americans typically complain about how tight times are. We whine about how hard it is to make ends meet.

But usually a single trip to a third world country will open an American's eyes to the enormous wealth that we have as a nation. We Americans are truly rich, whether we recognize it or not. Throughout most of the world, any family that earned $56,000 per year would be considered extremely wealthy.

As I have mentioned, the current per capita income in the United States is $36,300 per person. In contrast, the per capita income in Romania is only $6800 per year, less than 1/5th of American per capita income.[4]

Yet, the per capita income of Romania is higher than most countries of the world. It's over twice as high as Honduras, whose per capita income is only $2600 per year.[5] But the per capita income of Honduras is over twice as high as that of Uganda, which is only $1200 per year.[6] And Uganda is more than twice as high as Somalia at $550 per year.[7] So the per capita income of Americans is over 66 times that of the Somalians. In other words, we earn in 5-1/2 days what a typical Somalian earns in a year!

So where does that put us in relation to the kingdom of God? We Americans are rich, and Jesus said it is "easier for a camel to go through the eye of a needle than for a rich man to enter the kingdom of God." Contrary to what most Christians think, the riches of America are not a blessing from God. Equating material prosperity with God's blessing is a vestige of the old value system. It shows we haven't made the necessary paradigm shift. In the kingdom of God, the poor are blessed and the rich have to struggle with getting a camel through the eye of a needle!

Are we American Christians without hope? No, for Jesus gave us the slenderest thread of hope. When His disciples heard His words on the difficulty of a rich man entering the kingdom, they were astonished and asked: 'Who then can be saved?' But Jesus looked at them and said to them, 'With men this is impossible, but with God all things are possible'" (Mt. 19:25,26).

So there is hope for the rich, thanks to God's intervention. But we Americans are only fooling ourselves if we think we're all going to squeeze through this narrow exception. If we hope to fall within this exception, we definitely need to be certain that we're in the forefront of doing what Jesus said was central to His values:

> "The King will say to those on His right hand, 'Come, you blessed of My Father, inherit the kingdom prepared for you from the foundation of the world: for I was hungry and you gave Me food; I was thirsty and you gave Me drink; I was a stranger and you took Me in; I was naked and you clothed Me; I was sick and you visited Me; I was in prison and you came to Me. ... Assuredly, I say to you, inasmuch as you did it to one of the least of these My brethren, you did it to Me'" (Mt. 25:34,35,40).

So there is one good use to which money can be put, a use with eternal value: feeding, clothing, sheltering, and visiting the sick, the poor, and the imprisoned. And if we prosperous American Christians want to remain in God's kingdom, these ministries to others need to be central to us, just as they are to Jesus.

I find it so strange that among Bible-believing Christians, serving the poor is typically viewed as a second-class ministry. If you're not out saving souls, then many consider your ministry to be essentially valueless. However, in the kingdom, we let Jesus dictate what's valuable and what's not. And He says He considers helping the poor to be a central ministry. In fact, He says it will be a prime determinant of who inherits the kingdom and who doesn't. Sharing with the poor is just as important as preaching the gospel of Jesus.

Self-Examination

Most American Christians will claim that the kingdom truly comes first in their lives. "Sure, I have considerable treasure here on earth. But none of it means anything to me. My heart is on Jesus, not on these earthly treasures." That's what most of us say, isn't it?

Perhaps that's what you yourself claim. And maybe it's the truth. But the heart of man is treacherous. That's why we all should do a thorough self-examination to determine what our hearts are really focused on. Here are some simple questions that may help you to do that.

✐ If you are a breadwinner, take a sheet of paper and write down:

1. The number of hours you spend each week in earning money, including commuting time.

2. The number of hours you devote each week to cleaning, maintaining, purchasing, and looking after material possessions.

3. The number of hours you devote each week to kingdom interests. I'm referring to activities such as witnessing, visiting the sick, feeding and clothing the poor, Bible study, prayer, fellowship, and other activities designed

to take care of your family's spiritual needs or to further God's kingdom.

Now compare the number of hours you spend each week in kingdom interests with the amount of hours you spend each week to earn and take care of material things. Where does most of your time go? Obviously, some secular work is necessary to provide for the necessities of life. But do we really think we're going to be able to convince Jesus that we are working only for the *necessities* of life—not to maintain the comfortable American lifestyle?

Which comes first when there is a conflict between our jobs and our kingdom commitments? Does our employment require us to frequently or regularly miss church? Does it leave us too tired to do anything meaningful for the kingdom of God? Do we feel we've met our Kingdom commitments if we talk 10 minutes a day to the King and His Father?

✐ If you are a homemaker, you might ask yourself the following questions:

1. Would I be content if my husband earned only the necessities of life, or does he have to provide considerably more to keep me happy?

2. Do I spend more money than what my husband earns?

3. Do I complain to my husband about the lack of money?

4. What percentage of the material possessions in our home are items that *I* am clinging to, rather than items my husband is clinging to?

A husband often bears the brunt of his wife's materialism. That's because her materialism will typically push him to work longer hours or change to a better-paying job that destroys his spiritual life. She may complain about the long hours her husband works, but *her* spending and *her* wants may drive him to work those hours?

So if you're a Christian wife, make certain that you're putting kingdom interests first. If you're truly a kingdom Christian, make certain that your husband knows that you're happy with the basic necessities of life. But don't just say it in words, *show* him this is so by how you live, how you spend, and what you ask for.

This Is Just the Beginning

Just this one teaching of Jesus requires quite a paradigm shift, doesn't it? In the kingdom, the value of material things is just the opposite of what they are in this world. But Mammon is just the start. There are many more shifts of value we must make in order to fit into God's kingdom.

Yet, don't despair. Jesus never requires anything of us except those things He knows we can do through His power.

6

A New Standard
Of Honesty

"Again you have heard that it was said to those of old, 'You shall not swear falsely, but shall perform your oaths to the Lord.' But I say to you, do not swear at all: neither by heaven, for it is God's throne; nor by the earth, for it is His footstool; nor by Jerusalem, for it is the city of the great King. Nor shall you swear by your head, because you cannot make one hair white or black. But let your 'Yes' be 'Yes,' and your 'No,' 'No.' For whatever is more than these is from the evil one" (Mt. 5:33-37).*

So Jesus told His subjects in no uncertain terms that they are not to swear and not to take oaths. Oaths open us to the real possibility of taking God's name in vain. And that is a serious sin.

Yet, there is more to Jesus' command than just the danger of taking God's name in vain. Jesus was introducing to His disciples a revolutionary standard of honesty. Swearing or making oaths was one of the distinguishing marks of ancient society—both Jewish and Gentile. People used oaths frequently, particularly in matters of commerce, religion, and government.

---

*This same teaching on oaths is repeated in James: "But above all, my brethren, do not swear, either by heaven or by earth or with any other oath. But let your 'Yes' be 'Yes,' and your 'No,' 'No,' lest you fall into judgment" (Jas. 5:12).

Why did people use them so often? Because people couldn't trust one another.

For example, let's suppose that Levi bar Joseph of first century Judea goes to the market to buy a ring. He sees a beautiful gold ring that he would like to own, but it's quite expensive. It's worth the price the merchant is asking—if it's truly solid gold. So Levi asks the merchant, "Is this solid gold?"

"Yes, it is," replies the merchant. "Pure gold."

"Hmm," Levi replies as he fingers the ring. "Are you sure?"

"Of course I'm sure."

"But are you *absolutely* sure?" Levi queries.

"Yes, I'm absolutely certain. I personally know the artisan who made the ring, and he has assured me that it's pure gold," the merchant calmly assures Levi.

Levi is still suspicious. He knows he can't trust even his fellow Jew. So he holds the ring lightly in his hand in an attempt to assess the weight. He scrutinizes the ring carefully for any scratches that might reveal a base metal underneath. At last he feels fairly confident that it's pure. But he's still not absolutely positive. So, finally, he says to the merchant, "I want you to swear by the temple that this ring is solid gold and not merely gold plated."

The merchant makes the oath that Levi requests. Now Levi can buy the ring without too much worry. No God-fearing Jew would swear by the temple if he were telling a lie.

This was everyday life in the ancient world. Few people were trustworthy. And there were no Attorneys General and no government agencies like the Federal Trade Commission to prosecute merchants making false claims. So society resorted to oaths. That's because most people were afraid to make a false oath. Even Gentiles had a reverence for oaths, for they feared retribution from the gods if they swore falsely. As a result, oaths became second nature in commerce, legal matters, business, and government. They enabled the flow of society.

Nevertheless, by its very existence, the oath system acknowledged that there were two standards of honesty. There was one standard people used in normal conversation, and there was another standard when they were under oath.

However, in His kingdom, Jesus will have no double standard of honesty. In prohibiting his subjects from swearing, Jesus was introducing a whole new standard of honesty. For His subjects, there is only one standard: let your "Yes" mean "Yes" and your "No" mean "No." A true Christian's word is as good as an oath.

Lovers of Truth

But honesty and truth are not limited to commerce, law, and government. Jesus told Pilate, "For this cause I was born, and for this cause I have come into the world, that I should bear witness to the truth. Everyone who is of the truth hears My voice" (John 18:37). Jesus will allow in His kingdom only those who are "of the truth." A love of truth must permeate every fiber of our souls. And it will—if we are truly Spirit-begotten and we continue to walk in the Spirit. For Jesus refers to the Holy Spirit as the "Spirit of truth" (John 14:17).

Yet, how many *Christians do you know who meet the kingdom standard of honesty? How many Christians do you know whose "Yes" means "Yes" and whose "No" means "No"? When a fellow Christian tells you something, do you always know that you can completely rely on the truth of it? That is, do you know for certain that it's not a lie, an exaggeration, or just

---

*When I speak of "Christians" in this book, I'm referring to persons who profess to be Christians. They may or may not be true Christians. I use the term, "kingdom Christians" to refer to Christians who live by Jesus' kingdom teachings.

a rumor? When a Christian tells you he will do something, can you absolutely count on it (barring completely unforeseeable interventions, such as a car accident)? Or does his "Yes" mean "Maybe"?

Honesty in Our Work

When a business is owned by a Christian, the whole world should know the work performed there will be completely fair and honest. It *should*, but if your experiences have been like mine, it doesn't. The sad truth is that most professing Christians aren't really kingdom people. Their honesty is little different from that of the world.

Christians regularly cheat on their taxes, lie to their employers, write worthless checks, and skip town leaving bills unpaid. I'm an attorney, and I used to have a law office on the main street of our town. I tried to serve my clients well, and nearly all of them paid me promptly. In fact, I can think of only four clients who cheated me out of my fees. And all four of them were Christians! I don't mean nominal Christians. I mean persons who were very vocal about their Christianity.

Dishonesty in Christian Literature

The dishonesty of many Christians not only shows up in their business practices, but even in the spiritual books they write. We should be able to pick up a book written by a Christian and know that we can trust the information in it. But that's not the way it really is.

Mike Warnke was (and perhaps still is!) a popular Christian comedian who wrote a book entitled, *The Satan Seller*, which was first published in 1972. The book sold millions of copies, and Mike Warnke became a Christian celebrity, appearing on shows such as *Focus on the Family* and *The 700 Club*. In his book, Warnke talks about how he had been a drug addict and later was recruited into a Satanic cult. Inside the Satanic cult, he quickly rose to the position of high priest, and he presided over bizarre rituals and orgies. Warnke further states in the book that as a Satanic priest, he had fifteen hundred followers in three cities as part of a web of clandestine Satanists. It's a fascinating book.

However, in 1992, *Cornerstone* magazine, an evangelical publication, released a cover story entitled "Selling Satan: The Tragic History of Mike Warnke." Their article was a carefully documented exposé of Mike Warnke's claims. It demonstrated that not only was Warnke's testimony fraudulent, but also that he was guilty of all sorts of serious sins. For example, he raised money for projects that never materialized. And he was involved in serious immorality while in public ministry.[1] Sadly, several figures in the Christian contemporary music industry knew about the situation but failed to take Biblical steps to resolve it.

Now, we might think that all Christians would be highly appreciative of *Cornerstone* magazine for exposing this audacious fraud. And, to be sure, many Christians did write and thank *Cornerstone* for their investigative work. However, the magazine and its editors were also flooded with letters from other Christians castigating them for their exposé. "After all," many said, "Mike's testimony—no matter how false—has led thousands of people to Christ."

For example, here are some of the letters (in condensed form) that *Cornerstone* received in response to their investigative article:

> "I was not impressed with your article on Mike Warnke—you have done no more than what the secular press does. It's bad enough what happened in Mike Warnke's life, but you went way too far! What about the scripture that says whether it's preached for the wrong reason or the right reason, nevertheless Christ is preached?

> "You talked more about condemning this man and making him out to be a fraud than saying we need to lift him up and

pray for him. Christ didn't condemn the woman caught in adultery. Is sin different because a man is on a pedestal? Or how about looking within your own life? Yes, sirs, I am angry. I am a minister and I come under fire about things. You spoke on forgiveness slightly; why not totally focus on lifting up a brother rather than condemning? Think about it! Does God condemn you even now when you mess up?"[2]

Another reader wrote:

"Why are you trying to bring down Mike Warnke? He has saved more people than you can imagine. Maybe not all his life is what you think it is. I have been to three of his concerts here in Pismo Nazarene Church, and I and two friends have reached the Lord through Mike. You know Satan will go and make up lies to bring Mike down because he is afraid of Mike. Please explain yourself to me."[3]

The response of the Christian community shocks me even more than the outrageous fraud perpetrated by Mike Warnke. Where is the love of honesty and hatred of falsehood? Obviously, if Mike is truly repentant, we need to forgive him. But this doesn't mean we sweep his dishonesty under the rug. It isn't a matter of someone simply "messing up." It's purposeful dishonesty through which Warnke made hundreds of thousands of dollars. And the case of Mike Warnke is merely one example.

In the mid-1980s, my wife and I managed a nonprofit Christian bookstore for several years. I remember a fairly popular book we carried entitled *Crying Wind*. The book contains the remarkable story of a native American woman who had converted to Christianity. The only problem was that the publisher had concluded that her testimony wasn't true, and so it had discontinued publishing the book. I eventually learned that quite a few of the remarkable testimonies and miracle stories we carried were either completely false or exaggerated.

For example, in her book, *Satan's Underground*, Lauren Stratford gives her testimony about how she left a Satanic cult and became a Christian. In her book, she describes her alleged experiences while in this cult. For example, she claims she was sexually assaulted repeatedly and that she gave birth to several babies, who were ritually sacrificed. However, persons investigating her claims were able to locate Stratford's mother (who had allegedly died), her supposedly nonexistent sister, her ex-husband, cousins and teachers—all of whom provided strong evidence that the book was a fraud.[4] As a result, the Christian publishing house that published *Satan's Underground* withdrew the book—only to then assign the publishing rights to another publisher.

These examples are just the tip of the iceberg. The fact is that today's Christianity fosters a culture of dishonesty. Cheating and falsehood seem to be woven into the very fiber of the institutional Church—from the top to the bottom. I probably don't need to say anything about televangelists, as their frauds and vices are pretty well known. However, even some pulpit evangelists seem to have accepted the principle that dishonesty can be used in the furtherance of Christ's message.

For example, even highly respected evangelists regularly plant members of their teams among their audiences. Then, when an altar call is given, those "plants" get up and come forward, pretending to be new converts. The thought is that this will make it easier for the real converts to get up the courage to come forward as well. In other words, the end justifies the means.

But that's the value system of the world. In the kingdom, the *means* by which we do something is just as important as the *end* that we accomplish. We never use the world's means to accomplish kingdom purposes. Do you think Jesus planted fakes among His audiences?

The culture of dishonesty in institutional Christianity sprouts up everywhere. Many evangelists use all sorts of tricks to be able to report back to their supporters a large number of "decisions." Lay Christians often embellish their testimonies to fit some preconceived ideal.

Fake Healing

But probably nowhere in the church is the culture of dishonesty more prevalent than in the field of miraculous healing. Jesus and his apostles healed the sick. In fact, healing was closely tied to the kingdom message. And I believe that Jesus still heals people today. However, the ministry of healing has also attracted a high number of dishonest people.

Picture this scene: An evangelist with a healing ministry stands in the front of an auditorium before a large crowd. He walks up to an elderly lady sitting in a wheelchair, and in a loud voice he commands her, "Stand up and walk!" The woman slowly arises from her chair on her feeble, quivering legs, using the wheelchair for support. At last, she lets go of the wheelchair and stands up on her own power. The audience gasps in excitement, and the auditorium reverberates with shouts of praise. But then something even more amazing happens. The woman ever so slowly takes a step—and then another step—and still another! By now, all the people are waving their hands and shouting praises to the Lord. A miracle has happened!

Or, has it? What most people don't realize is that many people in wheelchairs—perhaps most people in wheelchairs—*are* able to walk. My mother is in her late eighties, and she can walk just fine, although a bit slowly. However, when we are at a hospital or large store where she will have to do a lot of walking, we often get a wheelchair or motorized cart for her. This way, she won't be worn out from walking. If someone saw my mother get up out of a wheelchair and walk, they might think they were witnessing a miracle, but they wouldn't be.

It's no different at healing crusades. For a faith healer to order a person in a wheelchair to get up and walk is only a charade unless that healer knows for a fact that the person in the wheelchair cannot walk.

But some prominent faith healers have carried the wheelchair fraud one step further. In the 1980s, healer-evangelists, W. V. Grant and Peter Popoff, had ushers provide wheelchairs for many of the elderly people who had walked into the auditorium under their own power. These wheelchairs were all the same color, model, and make. The ushers then wheeled these persons to the front of the auditorium. So the healers knew that the people in those particular wheelchairs could definitely walk, for they all had walked into the auditorium under their own power. Yet, dishonestly these healers would call those persons to stand up and walk, and then act as though a miracle had just happened. W. V. Grant would even have these "healed" people push him in the wheelchair up and down the aisles to the cheers of the spectators.[5]

Not content with that gimmick, Peter Popoff would have his wife Elizabeth sit and chat with different members of the audience before the program began. She would take good notes and then leave the auditorium to disappear into a nearby travel trailer. The trailer was equipped with a closed circuit television and a radio transmitter. Her husband wore a tiny radio receiver in his ear, undetectable to the audience. Watching the closed circuit television broadcast of the auditorium, Elizabeth Popoff would point out different people in the audience to her husband and tell him their names, where they lived, and what illnesses they had. He would pretend that he was receiving a revelation from God as he walked down the aisles, calling out names and addresses of people God would heal that night. He was finally exposed on national television, but that didn't shut down his crusade.[6]

The saddest part of the Grant-Popoff fraud is that it was agnostics who unmasked these two prominent charlatans. It should have been Christians who exposed them. But, as I said before, modern Christianity fosters a culture of dishonesty. Christians don't *want* to unmask bogus miracles. They want desperately to believe these miracles are true, because normally these modern-day wonder-workers preach a gospel of prosperity and easy-believism. Their "miracles" bring supposed proof of the authenticity of their gospel.

No doubt, it will be these same wonder-workers and their supporters who will be saying to Jesus on Judgment Day, "Lord, Lord, have we not prophesied in Your name, cast out demons in Your name, and done many wonders in Your name?' And then I will declare to them, 'I never knew you; depart from Me, you who practice lawlessness!'" (Mt. 7:22,23).

So, according to Jesus, neither the absence nor presence of miracles has any probative value as to a person's standing with Christ. Genuine miracles have happened through authentic Christians, and genuine miracles have happened through artificial Christians. But no artificial miracle has ever been done through an authentic Christian. Genuine miracles do not prove someone's standing before God, but bogus miracles clearly prove that Christ is not behind that person's ministry. Christ never works through corruption and deception.

7

The Kingdom Laws On Marriage and Divorce

"Blessed is he who is not offended because of Me." Jesus said those words because He knew that the majority of people who heard His teachings *would* be offended by them. When people stumble over Jesus' teachings, they usually respond in one of two ways. Some simply decide they don't want to have anything more to do with Jesus, and they disappear back into the world. However, others who are offended by Jesus' teaching join a church with worldly values. They simply shop around until they find a church that teaches that Jesus really didn't mean what He said. And it's not hard to find such a church these days. In fact, it's quite difficult to find a church that *doesn't* negate Jesus' teachings.

Among the two teachings of Christ that cause the most offense today are His standards on wealth and divorce. We've already discussed Jesus' teachings on wealth. So now let's see what He said about divorce:

"It has been said, 'Whoever divorces his wife, let him give her a certificate of divorce.' But I say to you that whoever divorces his wife for any reason except sexual immorality [Gr. *porneia*] causes her to commit adultery; and whoever marries a woman who is divorced commits adultery" (Mt. 5:31,32).

That's fairly straightforward, isn't it? Whoever divorces his wife, except for sexual immorality (Gr. *porneia*), will be held accountable for being the cause of her committing adultery if she

48

remarries. For if she remarries, both she and her new husband commit adultery.

Divorce Under the Mosaic Law

To fully grasp the significance of Jesus' kingdom law on divorce, we first need to understand the practice of divorce under the Mosaic Law. Jesus began his statement on divorce by saying, "It has been said, 'Whoever divorces his wife, let him give her a certificate of divorce.'" Jesus was referring to Deuteronomy, which says: "When a man takes a wife and marries her, and it happens that she finds no favor in his eyes because he has found some uncleanness in her, and he writes her a certificate of divorce, puts it in her hand, and sends her out of his house, when she has departed from his house, and goes and becomes another man's wife, if the latter husband detests her and writes her a certificate of divorce, puts it in her hand, and sends her out of his house, or if the latter husband dies who took her as his wife, then her former husband who divorced her must not take her back to be his wife after she has been defiled; for that is an abomination before the Lord" (Deut. 24:1-4).

So under the Mosaic Law, God allowed a man to divorce his wife if he found "some uncleanness in her." But what did God mean by "some uncleanness in her"? Some teachers of the Law said that it meant almost anything. But Jesus allowed a man to divorce his wife only for sexual immorality (*porneia*).*

But what about a wife divorcing her husband? The truth is that God never allowed a wife to divorce her husband. If that is

---

*Through the centuries, there has been considerable debate among Western Christians as to the meaning of *porneia* in this passage. The Roman Catholic Church has historically interpreted it as referring to marriages that violate the Levitical laws of consanguinity or affinity. The early Christians seem to have understood it to apply to the *practice* of adultery, in contradistinction to a single act of adultery. (See Hermas, Bk. 2, Comm. 4, Chap. 1).

a new thought to you, please get out *Strongs* or some other unabridged concordance and look up "divorce." You will find that every reference to divorce in the Old Testament concerns a husband divorcing his wife. There is no exception.

The Jewish professor, Israel Abrahams, of Cambridge University, said this about Jewish divorce in the Old Testament: "Divorce was always from first to last, in Jewish law, the husband's act. The common term used in the Bible for divorce is *shilluach 'ishshah*, 'the sending away of a wife.' We never read of 'the sending away of a husband.' The feminine participle, *gerushah*, 'the woman thrust out,' is the term applied to a divorced woman. The masculine form is not found."[1]

Did Jesus Expand God's Law on Divorce?

Now, let me ask you a question, and it's not a trick question. In saying what He did to the Pharisees, was Jesus *expanding* the law on divorce, or was He *narrowing* it?

I think we all can see that He was narrowing it, can't we? Instead of allowing a man to divorce his wife because of "some uncleanness in her," Jesus allowed a man to divorce his wife only for sexual immorality. Furthermore, whereas the Mosaic law permitted a divorced woman to remarry, Jesus forbade it completely, saying, "whoever marries a woman who is divorced commits adultery" (Mt. 5:32).

So Jesus in no sense broadened what Moses had allowed. He narrowed it considerably. So one of the things I find so incredibly strange is that today's Church teaches that Jesus *expanded* the law on divorce. Really? How is that, you might ask? Because virtually every conventional church I know of teaches that a man can divorce his wife for sexual immorality <u>and</u> that a woman can divorce her husband for sexual immorality. But is that what Jesus said? Did He expand the Mosaic Law so that now wives could divorce their husbands? No, He did nothing of the sort. He didn't open the door for divorce wider. No, He almost completely shut it, leaving a narrow exception for only the husband.

Women and Divorce

"But," you may be thinking, "maybe Jesus would have permitted a wife to divorce her husband if He had lived in another culture that allowed women to divorce their husbands." Well, we don't have to speculate about that. That's because under both Greek and Roman law, a wife *could* divorce her husband. And there were plenty of Romans and Greeks living in Judea and Galilee, some of whom were Jewish proselytes.

For that reason, on another occasion, Jesus addressed the issue of a woman divorcing her husband. He said, "If a woman divorces her husband and marries another, she commits adultery" (Mark 10:12). Jesus makes no exception.

Why is this important? Because the vast majority of divorces filed today are filed by wives, not by husbands. In the United States, 67% to 75% (varying by state) of all divorces are filed by females.[2] In England, 70% of all divorces are filed by wives.[3]

However, those statistics apply to *all* divorces—whether or not there are minor children involved. When we consider only divorces involving minor children, the percentage of female-filed divorces is considerably greater.

I have practiced title law for the past twenty-two years. In the course of examining land titles, I've read the legal filings on several thousand divorce cases. I have observed that easily nine out of ten of these divorce cases were initiated by the wives. Why is the percentage of these wife-filed divorces so high, compared to the national average? The reason is that I only review divorce filings for those persons who own real property. These property owners are typically past their mid-twenties, *and most of them have minor children.*

In the article, "These Boots Are Made for Walking: Why Most Divorce Filers Are Women," Margaret Brining writes, "Children are the most important asset in a marriage, and the partner who expects to get sole custody is by far the most likely to file for divorce."[4] Women are much more willing to divorce because they rarely fear losing custody of their children.

And yet the institutional Church has closed its eyes to this wrong. Several years ago, I received a form letter from a Texas minister speaking out against our no-fault divorce laws in Texas. I was pleased to see a minister say something against divorce, as most so-called Bible-believing churches have been quite silent on this issue. But then the letter went on to say that our easy divorce laws discriminate against women and children.

Against women and children? This modern-day Don Quixote was imagining that all of the thousands of divorced women in our churches were in their situation because their husbands had divorced *them*. Without doing any research, he treated the whole subject as though men were dumping their wives by the thousands and going on their merry way.

Yet, that seems to be the general attitude of most churches toward divorce. They completely ignore the reality of today's divorces. I've heard pastors berate fathers who "dump their wives and children," as though it were fathers who typically initiate divorce. In contrast, they treat "single moms" as martyrs, heroic victims, and spiritual widows—when typically it was they who divorced their husbands.

Divorce is not a victimless sin. And the sin is no different when it is husbands who take the children from their wives. There are millions of fathers and mothers today who grieve deeply over their children who have been taken from them. Yet, very few churches have the courage to speak out against this evil fruit of divorce.

Did Paul Contradict Jesus?

Some modern Bible commentators claim that, contrary to Jesus, Paul *did* allow divorce. In fact, they contend that Paul expanded divorce even beyond the Mosaic Law, allowing wives to divorce their husbands. They base their claims on the passage at 1 Corinthians 7:10-15:

"Unto the married I command, yet not I, but the Lord: Let not the wife depart from her husband; but if she departs, let her remain unmarried, or be reconciled to her husband. And let not the husband put away his wife. But to the rest I speak, not the Lord: If any brother has a wife who does not believe, and she is pleased to dwell with him, let him not put her away. And if a woman has a husband who does not believe, and if he is pleased to dwell with her, let her not leave him."[5]

Does Paul say anything there that contradicts Jesus? Does Paul in any way authorize divorce? No, he does not. And please notice the distinction the King James Version makes between husbands and wives. It speaks of a husband "putting away" his wife, but it speaks of a wife "leaving" or "departing" from her husband.

I realize that there are a few modern Bible translations that give the reader the impression that Paul is talking here about divorce. However, most present-day translations, together with the King James Version, make it clear that Paul is talking about *leaving* a spouse, not divorcing one. But even then, he says that Christians shouldn't even leave their spouses.

The Greek word Paul uses is *aphiemi*, which is usually translated as "leave" in other passages, but never as "divorce." It is an entirely different word from *apoluo*, the term Jesus used in Matthew 5:32 when He spoke about divorce. There is no biblical or historical warrant for translating *aphiemi* as "divorce" in Paul's passage.

In the final verse of this passage, Paul says, "But if the unbeliever departs, let him depart; a brother or a sister is not under bondage in such cases. But God has called us to peace" (1 Cor. 7:15). In this final verse, does Paul authorize Christians to divorce their unbelieving spouses? No, he says nothing about divorce. Throughout this passage, Paul has been talking about *leaving* a spouse while remaining unmarried. He says the believing spouse should not be the one to leave. He concludes the passage by saying if the unbeliever departs, let him depart. The believer does not have to follow after the unbelieving spouse.

In God's kingdom, Jesus is the King and Lawgiver. His apostles *never* contradict the commandments their King has handed down. Jesus allowed only one very narrow exception for husbands, and His apostles taught accordingly.

The Two Become One Flesh

When Jesus gives us laws, He is under no obligation to explain *why* the commandment is being given. However, in one of His discussions on divorce, Jesus does give us an explanation of His strict teaching on this matter: "Have you not read that He who made them at the beginning 'made them male and female,' and said, 'For this reason a man shall leave his father and mother and be joined to his wife, and the two shall become one flesh'? So then, they are no longer two but one flesh. Therefore what God has joined together, let not man separate" (Mt. 19:4-6).

Today, I see so many Christian books on marriage that talk about the "marriage partnership." But Jesus never referred to marriage as a partnership. He referred to it as "one flesh," and that is quite different. In law, when two persons form a partnership, their separate identities still exist. If someone is negligently injured on partnership property, the injured person can sue each of the partners *individually*. The law sees the partnership as two individuals who happen to work together.

However, if two individuals create a corporation, that's different. As far as the law is concerned, when two persons incorporate, their individual identities are dissolved. If someone is injured on corporate property, he cannot normally sue the two persons who formed the corporation. He can sue only the corporation itself. The law sees the corporation as a new person. The corporation can sue or be sued as an entity of its own.

Similarly, marriage is like a corporation, not a partnership. A new entity is formed when a man and woman marry. They aren't partners; they have merged into "one flesh." The world may treat a husband and wife as partners, but Jesus doesn't. Who did Jesus say joins a man and woman together in marriage? God. So in marriage, a man and woman pass into the realm of eternity. I don't mean that marriage is eternal, but that there are eternal realities that attach to marriage. Marriage is not a human institution; it's a heavenly institution. It is God who does the joining, but it is man who tries to do the separating

Divorce Through the Centuries

What I'm sharing with you is nothing new. This is historic Christianity. It's how the early Christians understood Jesus' teachings, and it's how virtually *all* Christians understood Jesus' commandments until the time of the Reformation. Unfortunately, some of the Reformers worked to take marriage and divorce outside the jurisdiction of the church and put them in the hands of the civil magistrates. Yet, even after the Reformation, divorce among Bible believing Christians was still quite rare until the 1950s and 1960s. And then everything changed.

What happened in the Fifties and Sixties? The *world* changed its attitude and laws on divorce. Various states changed their laws to make divorces easier to obtain. Divorce no longer carried a social stigma. And when the world changed, the institutional Church changed as well. In other words, if Caesar says divorce is wrong and forbids it, then divorce is wrong. But if Jesus says divorce is wrong and forbids it—well, maybe it's not so bad after all. The churches have shown quite clearly who their real master is, and it's not Jesus.

Divorce in Today's Evangelical Church

In 1999, George Barna, president and founder of the renowned Barna Research Group, researched the incidence of divorce among various religious groups. He found that the divorce rate among born-again American Christians was higher than the divorce rate among Americans as a whole.[6] To be sure, many non-Christian couples live together without marrying. And so the divorce statistics would not take into account any break-ups of such cohabitation relationships. Nevertheless, once worldly couples vow, "until death do we part," they are as likely (or even more so!) to keep that vow as are "Bible-believing" Christians.

Although the Barna Research Group is a Christian organization, its findings drew protests and criticisms from other Christians. However, Mr. Barna has stood behind his data. He responded to his critics, "While it may be alarming to discover that born again Christians are more likely than others to experience a divorce, that pattern has been in place for quite some time."[7] Barna Project Director Meg Flammang noted: "We would love to be able to report that Christians are living very distinct lives and impacting the community, but ... in the area of divorce rates they continue to be the same."[8]

The findings of the Barna Research Group is corroborated by the statistics of government agencies. For example, the rate of divorce in the Bible Belt is higher than in any other part of America, except for the state of Nevada.[9] In fact, the divorce rate in the Bible Belt is significantly higher than it is in New England, where there are noticeably fewer fundamentalist Christians.[10]

What should really make evangelical American Christians blush is the fact that the divorce rate among so-called born-again Christians is significantly higher than it is among those Americans who categorize themselves as atheists.[11] Ironically, although the divorce rate among evangelical Christians is essentially the same or higher than that of American society, the divorce rate among Asian Americans (whether Christian or not) is significantly lower than that of American society in general.[12] And Asian-American couples rarely live together without marriage. So somehow the Asian culture can do what the indwelling of the Holy Spirit can't! Or, maybe the problem is that the Holy Spirit is not dwelling in most people who claim to be born-again Christians.

Even more shameful is that the divorce rate among evangelical Christians in the United States is over twice as high as the divorce rate of the whole nation of Canada (which is not exactly a stronghold of biblical Christianity).[13] What's worse is that the divorce rate among American evangelicals is over 6 times as high as the divorce rate of China, over 18.5 times the divorce rate of Italy, and over 33 times as high as the divorce rate in Sri Lanka![14]

Divorce is so acceptable among evangelical Christians here in the South that divorce lawyers will sometimes place the Christian fish logo by their advertisements in the Yellow Pages. That's the equivalent of a Jew running a ham shop and putting the star of David on his advertisements!

So often when I speak on the subject of divorce, Christians ask me, "But what about a situation where ...?" Yes, there are many difficult situations that can make marriage a real cross to bear. But the situation was no different in the first century, or the tenth, or the nineteenth. Why do so many twenty-first century Christians feel they are entitled to a special exception when Christians of other centuries lived by Jesus' teachings on marriage and divorce?

Have I Offended You?

I realize that the things I have been saying in this chapter are very politically incorrect. I don't doubt that many of you are so mad at me right now that you're ready to throw this book away. But before you toss out this book, please do your own honest investigation of what I've said. By that, I don't mean going out and finding a book that says divorce is okay. That will be easy enough.

No, I mean: do some *honest* research. Verify what I've said about divorce in the Old Testament. Then read all of the passages where Jesus discusses divorce. Did He expand God's law on divorce, or did He narrow it considerably?

If what I've said is true, then it's not really *me* you're offended at. It's Jesus Christ. Perhaps the Jesus you thought you were in love with is not the real Jesus. But if we don't serve the *real* Jesus, we won't inherit *real* eternal life. As He said, "Blessed is he who is not offended because of Me."

Part II

The Big
Stumbling Block

8

Love My Enemies?

As I have said, Jesus' teachings on wealth, oaths, and divorce offend most people who hear them. And those are certainly among the harder teachings of Jesus. Yet, even those three teachings aren't the main reason why the conventional churches have largely rejected the way of the kingdom.

No, the biggest stumbling block has been His teachings on 'turning the other cheek' and loving our enemies. And because these teachings are such a stumbling block, I've devoted an entire section of this book to them. Let's begin with what Jesus said about 'turning the other cheek':

"You have heard that it was said, 'An eye for an eye and a tooth for a tooth.' But I tell you not to resist an evil person. But whoever slaps you on your right cheek, turn the other to him also. If anyone wants to sue you and take away your tunic, let him have your cloak also. And whoever compels you to go one mile, go with him two. Give to him who asks you, and from him who wants to borrow from you do not turn away" (Mt. 5:38-42).

This was indeed revolutionary teaching! Not only did the Gentiles not live this way, neither did the Jews. And, sadly, neither have most professing Christians.

Nonresistance and Peacemaking

The group of commandments we've just read call for *passive* conduct. Don't resist an evil person. Turn the other cheek. If someone sues you for your tunic, let him have your cloak as well. If someone compels you to go one mile, go two instead. Give to him who asks. Putting these commandments into practice is sometimes called *nonresistance*.

But there is also a *proactive* part to Jesus' teaching: "You have heard that it was said, 'You shall love your neighbor and hate your enemy.' But I say to you, love your enemies, bless those who curse you, do good to those who hate you, and pray for those who spitefully use you and persecute you, that you may be sons of your Father in heaven; for He makes His sun rise on the evil and on the good, and sends rain on the just and on the unjust. For if you love those who love you, what reward have you? Do not even the tax collectors do the same? And if you greet your brethren only, what do you do more than others? Do not even the tax collectors do so? Therefore you shall be perfect, just as your Father in heaven is perfect" (Mt. 5:43-48).

It's not enough just to be nonresistant. We Christians must also be proactive, reaching out in love to anyone we might have formerly thought of as an enemy. If someone hates us, we should find out why. Perhaps we can clear the matter up so that the person who was our enemy becomes a friend. Jesus told us, "If you bring your gift to the altar, and there remember that your brother has something against you, leave your gift there before the altar, and go your way. First be reconciled to your brother, and then come and offer your gift" (Mt. 5:23,24).

So, as kingdom citizens, we must do all we can to make peace with others. Jesus said, "Blessed are the peacemakers, for they shall be called sons of God" (Mt. 5:9). In our everyday dealings at work and with neighbors and friends, there are always hurts, arguments, and disputes. If we are a party to such a dispute, we should be the first to offer the olive branch and make peace. Even if we're convinced we're right.

Jesus' Teachings in Everyday Life

And nonresistance absolutely goes against our fallen flesh! Nonresistance is something we have to learn. It's definitely not something we're born with.

I've realized this when watching toddlers at play. If one child has a toy, invariably the other child wants his toy. Does the first toddler say, "Yes, dear friend, you may play with my toy"? Hardly. The second child usually just grabs, and the first child resists with all his strength. Usually there's a lot of screaming and sometimes hitting and biting.

I know that when I've been called on to turn the other cheek and not to resist evil, my flesh has objected mightily. I'm certainly not nonresistant by nature. Fourteen years ago, my family and I moved to the house where we presently live. It sits out in the country on three and a half acres. Shortly after we moved in, we noticed that a number of coyotes and stray dogs roamed the woods and fields around us. We had a few goats, so we decided to build them a pen with a sturdy fence to protect them from the dogs and coyotes.

We hired a professional fencing company to build a strong five-foot high fence around the perimeter of our goat pen. Despite this, early one morning we awoke to the sound of dogs barking and goats bleating. We rushed outside to discover that dogs had somehow slipped into the pen and were attacking the goats. We ran as fast as we could to the goat pen. Seeing us, the dogs slipped back out and disappeared into the neighboring field. One of our goats died from this savage attack, and the other one was in a state of serious shock for several days, barely eating.

In the dim light of dawn, we didn't get a good look at the dogs, but we assumed they were stray dogs. So we called the county animal control officers and asked for their help. They furnished us with several humane, toothless traps that would clamp on a dog's foot and hold him, but would not damage his foot. The agency said it would pick up any dogs we caught.

We put out the traps that night, and the next morning we were once again awakened by the sound of a commotion outside. We hurriedly ran out and saw a pack of dogs outside the goat pen.

But we soon realized that these were not *stray* dogs—these were our neighbors' dogs. The dogs quickly ran off when they saw us. That is, all of the dogs but one. One of the dogs was caught in a trap and couldn't get away. The poor dog was scared to death, and he was shaking like a leaf when we approached him.

Just then I saw a pickup truck turn into our drive. It came barreling down our country drive, kicking up a trail of dust behind it. The driver jumped out and immediately sprinted toward the captured dog, which turned out to be his dog.

"Oh, is this your dog?" I asked meekly.

"Yes it is," he replied sullenly, as he helped me open the trap and free his dog. "You know," he continued, "this isn't going to do anything but cause hard feelings with your neighbors. I moved out to the country so that I could let my dogs roam free."

My first thought was to retort, "Well, I moved to the country so our goats could run free." But I didn't. I also thought about saying, "Look, I'll make a deal with you: You keep your dogs off my land, and I'll keep my goats off yours!"

However, I thought about Jesus' words to turn the other cheek. What would He do in a situation like this? There was no doubt in my mind. So I replied cheerfully, "Well, I'm open to any suggestions."

The neighbor (whom I had not met before) seemed a bit surprised at my mild response. He lost his sullen expression and replied calmly, "Well, what you could do is run an electric wire around the bottom and top of your fence. That will keep dogs out."

"I'm willing to do that," I replied, feeling a bit surprised at myself. "I'll do what you've suggested, and I'll return the traps to the county."

It seemed a bit unfair that I was having to incur extra expense so that *his* trespassing dogs wouldn't hurt my goats. But

I knew that I had handled this minor crisis the way Jesus wanted me to.

Biblical Examples

Nonresistance and loving one's enemy are perhaps the most challenging—and certainly the most revolutionary—of Jesus' teachings. They are the exact opposite of the message that the world teaches. Don't resist an evil person? Our parents, schools, governments, and churches inculcate in us just the opposite: Fight for your rights! Stand up to bullies! Don't let anyone shove you around! The heroes we're urged to emulate are rarely nonresistant persons. No, usually they're people who stood up to their enemies and resisted them.

Nonresistance is not simply a theological doctrine; it's a way of life. It touches all kinds of everyday interactions with people and companies. However, being nonresistant doesn't mean being a doormat or a Caspar Milquetoast. Jesus and Paul were nonresistant. Yet, neither of them was a doormat; neither of them was a wimp. They were both quite assertive and outspoken. But they both chose to receive injuries rather than to injure someone else. They both *spoke out* against evil, but they did not resist evil with *physical force.*

Look at how many times Paul was beaten and stoned. Paul could have armed himself and traveled with a group of hefty bodyguards. But he didn't. Paul was one of the bravest men who ever lived, but he didn't resist evil with physical force. As he later said, "Though we walk in the flesh, we do not war according to the flesh. For the weapons of our warfare are not carnal but mighty in God for pulling down strongholds" (2 Cor. 10:3). Paul was a different type of warrior—a warrior of a kingdom with upside-down values.

Lawsuits

It was often lawless mobs that beat or stoned Paul. As a Roman citizen, he could have pressed charges against those who unlawfully beat or stoned him. But he didn't. He turned the other cheek. Jesus said that if someone wanted to sue us to take our tunics, we should give him our cloaks as well. It follows that if someone simply *seizes* our tunics, we don't go to court to get them back. As Jesus said, give to him who asks.

At the same time, Paul demonstrated that it's proper for Christians to avail themselves of governmental protections when they're persecuted. For example, Paul escaped a flogging by asking the Roman centurion, "Is it lawful for you to scourge a man who is a Roman, and uncondemned?" (Acts 22:25).

Paul reiterated Jesus' teaching in his letter to the Corinthians: "Dare any of you, having a matter against another, go to law before the unrighteous, and not before the saints? ...I say this to your shame. Is it so, that there is not a wise man among you, not even one, who will be able to judge between his brethren? But brother goes to law against brother, and that before unbelievers! Now therefore, it is already an utter failure for you that you go to law against one another. Why do you not rather accept wrong? Why do you not rather let yourselves be cheated?" (1 Cor. 6:1,5-8).

Nearly twenty years ago, I saw the conflict between Jesus' teachings and the practice of trial law. If it's wrong for me as an individual Christian to take my brother to court, how can it be right for me as a lawyer to represent some other Christian who is taking *his* brother to court? The right course was quite clear.

On the other hand, this was my livelihood. If I eliminated lawsuits from my practice, what would be left? Nothing but drafting wills and deeds, and examining land titles. And these are not exactly the most exciting or financially rewarding areas of law. Due to my own limited faith, this was a hard decision for me. But in the end, I knew I had to obey Jesus. So I refused to handle any more lawsuits or any other areas of law that conflicted with Jesus' teaching.

What About War?

It's important that we understand that Jesus' instructions on nonresistance make sense only to those who have accepted His other teachings, such as "Whoever of you does not forsake all that he has cannot be My disciple" (Luke 14:33). When we have forsaken everything, there's little left to fight for, is there? Even when it comes down to our very lives, Jesus told us, "He who finds his life will lose it, and he who loses his life for My sake will find it" (Mt. 10:39).

Jesus told Pilate, "If My kingdom were of this world, My servants would fight" (John 18:36). By deduction, then, if we have a kingdom that *is* capable of being defended by physical fighting, then our kingdom *is* of the world, isn't it? Whether we're talking about personal possessions, a house, or a nation, the situation is the same. If we have a stake in this world, we're going to be sorely tempted to fight to protect it. When we try to reconcile Jesus' teachings with holding on to possessions, earthly power, and national pride, we find it's impossible. We're trying to reconcile two things that are ultimately irreconcilable.

The nineteenth century Christian author, Adin Ballou, wrote the following satirical piece to demonstrate the absurdity of trying to reconcile Jesus' kingdom commandments with the military laws of human governments:

"Jesus Christ forbids me to resist evil doers and to take from them an eye for an eye, a tooth for a tooth, bloodshed for bloodshed, and life for life.

"My government demands from me quite the opposite, and bases a system of self-defense on gallows, musket, and sword, to be used against its foreign and domestic foes. And the land is filled accordingly with gibbets, prisons, arsenals, ships of war, and soldiers.

"In the maintenance and use of these expensive appliances for murder, we can very suitably exercise to the full the virtues of forgiveness to those who injure us, love toward our enemies, blessings to those who curse us, and doing good to those who hate us. For this, we have a succession of Christian priests to pray for us and beseech the blessing of heaven on the holy work of slaughter.

"I see all this, and I continue to profess religion and take part in government, and pride myself on being at the same time a devout Christian and a devoted servant of the government. I do not want to agree with these senseless notions of non-resistance. I cannot renounce my authority and leave only immoral men in control of the government.

"The Constitution says the government has the right to declare war, and I assent to this and support it, and swear that I will support it. And because of that I do not cease to be a Christian. War, too, is a Christian duty. Is it not a Christian duty to kill hundreds of thousands of one's fellow-men, to outrage women, to raze and burn towns, and to practice every possible cruelty? It is time to dismiss all these false sentimentalities. It is the truest means of forgiving injuries and loving enemies. If we only do it in the spirit of love, nothing can be more Christian than such murder."[1]

In the last chapter, we saw that so-called Bible-believing Christians have a higher divorce rate than does the world. The pattern is the same when it comes to nonresistance. "Bible-believing" Christians are actually *more* militant than the world when it comes to resisting evil with force. When the United States ponders going to war, nowadays "Bible-believing" Christians are invariably the ones who are the most adamantly in favor of military action.

While I was writing this book, the United States entered into war with Iraq to remove from power its dictator, Saddam Hussein. Immediately, the local churches began placing American flags on the church lawns. Church billboards carried slogans such as: "God bless America," and "Pray for our troops." But I didn't see even one billboard that said, "Pray for the people of Iraq." Even though the purpose of the war was to remove Hussein from power, it was going to be the ordinary Iraqi people—men, women, children, and babies—who were going to die in the invasion. But apparently no church thought about reminding us to pray for them.

9

But What If ...?

If you're like most Christians, this whole concept of nonresistance and loving one's enemies is probably new to you. And you may be saying to yourself, "Yes, but what if ... ?" So let me address some of the "what ifs" and other questions you may have.

Q. **What if someone were to break into your house and were about to harm your wife and children? Surely you wouldn't just stand there and let them do it!**

This question naturally plays on the strong protective instinct that men have toward their families. But the answer a kingdom citizen must give to that question is the same as he would give to any other question concerning breaking the commandments of Jesus. Let me ask you, "What if your government told you to deny Jesus Christ and offer a sacrifice to Satan—or else they would violate your wife and kill your children? What would you do?" For a kingdom citizen, the answer is quite clear. Jesus has already told us that if we love our families more than Him, we cannot be His disciples. And He has also told us, "Whoever denies Me before men, him I will also deny before My Father who is in heaven" (Mt. 10:33).

Now, what if, instead of denying Christ, my government ordered me to murder my next door neighbor or to sexually assault his wife? And if I didn't, they would harm my wife and children? Would the situation be any different from offering a sacrifice to Satan? In one instance, I would be denying Christ with my mouth. In the other, I would be denying him by my actions.

What if a foreign government ordered me to drop a bomb on a United States city, or to assassinate the American president—or else they would harm my wife and children? What should I do? I think most Americans would allow their wives and children to be harmed, or even killed, before betraying their country.

So how is the situation any different when it concerns loyalty to Jesus? Jesus' teachings on nonresistance are quite clear. It's a matter of either denying Him or denying my family. To be sure, that's a very difficult choice, but I already made that choice when I gave my life to Christ.

Does that mean I would do nothing to protect my family? Of course not. I have already done the best thing that I could possibly do to ensure their safety: I have entrusted my home and family to the care and protection of Jesus. And that isn't some naive trust. There are tens of thousands of other Kingdom Christians who have similarly beat their swords into plowshares and entrusted the safety of their families into the hands of their King. And although Jesus has not promised that no harm can ever come to our families, I can say this: that, except in times of religious persecution, it's very rare for kingdom families to be harmed by ordinary criminals.

One example that comes to mind is the encounter of the desperate criminal fugitive, Stephen Roy Carr, with a nonresistant Mennonite family in Pennsylvania in May of 1988. Earlier Carr had fled from Florida, where he was wanted for grand theft. He was hiding out in the Appalachian mountains, ready to kill anyone who threatened his freedom. Before long, he met two female campers on the Appalachian Trail, and he shot them both—killing one and seriously injuring the other.

Fleeing the scene, Carr found an abandoned cement-mixing tub and used it to float down the Conodoguinet Creek to the farm of Chester and Esther Weaver. As conservative Mennonites, the Weavers had no television or radio, and so they had heard nothing about the murder. The fugitive Carr asked the Weavers for food and shelter, which they gladly provided him. Carr stayed in the Weaver home for five days—and yet he neither harmed them nor stole from them. Carr would have stayed longer, but the police finally caught up with him.[1]

Wheelbarrow Faith

It reminds me of the account given by the Christian author and speaker, Winkey Pratney, concerning the Great Blondin, an incredibly gifted tightrope aerialist of the nineteenth century. To demonstrate his abilities, Blondin stretched a 1100 foot rope above Niagara Falls. To the thrill of huge crowds, he walked across the Falls on his tightrope, performing various spectacular stunts. He even did a back somersault in the middle of the rope. Yet, Blondin had no net underneath to save him if he fell.

A newspaper reporter who had come to witness the spectacle was awe-struck. "I bet there isn't anything you can't do out there on the tightrope," he told Blondin.

"Do you think I could cross the rope pushing a wheelbarrow?" Blondin asked the reporter.

"Oh, I'm sure you could."

"Do you think I could cross the rope while pushing a wheelbarrow with a man in it?" Blondin asked the reporter.

"Undoubtedly!"

Looking the reporter straight in the eye, Blondin then asked, "Do you think I could cross the rope pushing a wheelbarrow with *you* in it?"

"Well, uh ..."

But that's what genuine faith is all about—getting into the wheelbarrow for Christ. Any other kind of faith is not really faith. It's just words. Most Christians will readily acknowledge that God is all-powerful. They will proclaim that God is in charge of the universe. They say nothing can happen outside of God's active or permissive will. They'll plaster bumper stickers on their cars saying, "His angels are watching over me!" But, no, they won't get into the wheelbarrow. They won't entrust their family's safety to God.

Sadly, every year Christian families suffer death and injury *from their own weapons* because they didn't put their trust in God. One of the most heartbreaking episodes occurred a few years ago when a man and his wife returned home from a trip. Their daughter was staying at a friend's house. However, the daughter thought she would surprise her parents by coming home early and hiding in their bedroom closet. When her parents came home, they heard a noise in their closet. Thinking it was a burglar, her father got out his loaded pistol and slowly approached the closet. When the closet door suddenly burst open, her father instinctively pulled the trigger. He immediately realized it was his daughter, but it was too late. She murmured, "I love you, Daddy," and fell over dead.

This was not some rare occurrence. A gun kept in the home is 22 times more likely to kill a family member or a friend than to kill or wound an intruder.[2] Evil can be confronted with less dangerous methods than guns.

A number of years ago, some Christian friends of mine, Decio and Olivia, were staying at a motel in Atlanta. There had been a number of armed robberies and murders in the city. In these robberies, the assailants had ordered their victims to lie face down on the floor and then shot them in the backs of their heads. So Decio was on his guard.

It was a mild October evening, and Decio and Olivia had momentarily left their motel door open for a friend. Suddenly two teenage thugs appeared in the doorway with guns. They ordered everyone down on the floor. Decio hesitated and then knelt down, praying and trying to think of a way to foil the robbery.

His wife, Olivia, thinking it was a Halloween prank, remained seated on the bed. So one of the young robbers waved his gun at her and ordered her to lie on the floor. Instead, she started singing out loud "Jesus Loves Me," as she got up from the bed and slowly walked over to the two young men. One of them raised his pistol, pointed it at her face, and cocked it. But when she continued singing and walking toward him, he suddenly yelled to his partner, "These are a bunch of Jesus nuts! Let's get outta here!" And with that, the two young men vanished into the dark.

Over the years, I have heard and read many other accounts of how a prayer, a hymn, or a testimony effectively disarmed a would-be burglar or assailant. There's no point singing "Our God Is an Awesome God," if we don't really believe that He is.

Q. **"But what about Hitler?" I'm often asked.**

Actually, that's *my* question to Christians who reject nonresistance: "But what about Hitler?" You see, if all Christians had practiced what Jesus taught, Hitler would never have been able to do the things he did. Why? Because most of the soldiers in Hitler's army were professing Christians. They had voluntarily joined or had been conscripted into the German army, and they were serving their country just as were the British and American Christian soldiers who fought against them. If Christians had stood by the commandments of Jesus, the evil of Hitler would never have happened. He would have had few soldiers to carry out his plans.

If all Christians stood by Jesus' teachings, perhaps there would be no wars. This is no idle dream. The Pax Romana demonstrated this. The Pax Romana is the name given by secular historians to the period of peace enjoyed by the Roman Empire from 27 B. C. to A.D. 180. The Pax Romana was the most peaceful period the Roman Empire had ever known. In fact, it's the longest period of peace that the Mediterranean world has known from the beginning of European civilization to the present day. During the Pax Romana, the Empire did not suffer even one successful invasion of its frontiers. There were a few domestic uprisings, such as those of the Jews. But there were no civil wars between Romans.

What brought about the Pax Romana? The mighty armies of Rome? No, those mighty armies of Rome were still around in the fourth and fifth centuries when there was no peace. And it was in the fourth and fifth centuries that the barbarians finally were able to successfully invade the Empire.

Was the Pax Romana a result of good rulers? To be sure, there were certainly a number of very able emperors during this period, such as Caesar Augustus and Marcus Aurelius. Yet, there were also madmen and moral monsters such as Caligula, Nero, and Domitian. Still, even during the reigns of these madmen, the Romans had peace.

So what really was different about the period of the Pax Romana? Secular historians have no clear answer. However, I believe the difference was that God had introduced peace into the Mediterranean world into which His Son, the Prince of Peace, was to be born. I believe God brought about that peace without the help of any human armies. And I believe that Christians later maintained that peace—not by using the sword to defend the Empire—but by their nonresistant, peaceful lives and by their prayers.

But this is not merely my own personal belief. The early Christians who lived near the time of the Pax Romana were also firmly convinced that the Pax Romana was the result of God's intervention. For example, Origen told the Romans, "How was it possible for the Gospel doctrine of peace, which doesn't permit men to take vengeance even on their enemies, to prevail throughout the earth, unless at the coming of Jesus a milder spirit had been introduced into the order of things?"[3]

Another early Christian writer, Arnobius, wrote, "It would not be difficult to prove that (after the name of Christ was heard in the world), wars were not increased. In fact, they actually *diminished* in great measure by the restraining of furious passions. ...As a result, an ungrateful world is now enjoying—and for a long period has enjoyed—a benefit from Christ. For by His means, the rage of savage ferocity has been softened and has begun to withhold hostile hands from the blood of a fellow creature. In fact, if all men without exception...would lend an ear for awhile to His salutary and peaceful rules,...the whole world would be living in the most peaceful tranquillity. The world would have turned the use of steel into more peaceful uses and would unite together in blessed harmony, maintaining inviolate the sanctity of treaties.[4]

Defending a Country by Nonresistance

Today, many professing *Christians* criticize kingdom Christians for not taking up arms and defending their country. Interestingly, the *pagans* made the same criticism of the early Christians, who refused to defend the Roman Empire with swords. In reply to these pagan critics, Origen wrote:

"Our prayers defeat all demons who stir up war. Those demons also lead persons to violate their oaths and to disturb the peace. Accordingly, in this way, we are much more helpful to the kings than those who go into the field to fight for them. And we do take our part in public affairs when we join self-denying exercises to our righteous prayers and meditations, which teach us to despise pleasures and not to be led away by them. So none fight better for the king than we do. Indeed, we do not fight *under* him even if he demands it. Yet, we fight on his behalf, forming a special army—an army of godliness—by offering our prayers to God.

" And if he would have us 'lead armies in defense of our country,' let him know that we do this too. And we do not do it for the purpose of being seen by men or for vainglory. For in secret, and in our own hearts, our prayers ascend on behalf of our fellow-citizens, as from priests. So Christians are benefactors of their country more than others."[5]

Total dependence on God worked! It had powerful results. It brought about the longest period of peace in the Mediterranean world that has existed since the beginning of civilization. If it could work there against all of the warlike peoples of the ancient Mediterranean world, it would have worked to stop Hitler. In fact, as we've discussed, Hitler would have never even come into power.

But someone may object, saying, "Have you never heard that 'the only thing needed for evil to prevail is for good men to do nothing'?" Ah, that's the crux of the whole problem. Regardless of our pious words about faith and trust, most Christians view prayer as essentially 'doing nothing.' Whether they admit it or not, most Christians believe that if we don't take up our guns and stop evil, nothing else will.

But what if all professing Christians today were to live nonresistantly and love their enemies? What if the entire church truly put its faith in God as the Protector of mankind and really believed in the efficacy of prayer? The whole church did this in the first three centuries, and the world they lived in had peace as a result. I have no doubt that we would have a new Pax Europa or Pax Americana if the Church did the same today.

Evil can never be defeated by evil, nor can error ever be corrected by error. Satan cannot be cast out by Satan's means. Following Christ's teachings is the only effective resistance to evil.

Q. **But don't Jesus' words apply merely to private retribution—not to state-sponsored actions?**

Some Christians maintain that if we pay back evil for evil as *individuals*, it's wrong. However, if we do it under *state* authority, it doesn't violate Jesus' teaching. This argument makes me think of the pamphlet that Adin Ballou wrote, entitled "How Many Men Are Necessary to Change a Crime into a Virtue?" In it, he asked:

"How many does it take to annul the commandments of God, and render something lawful that He has forbidden? How many does it take to metamorphose wickedness into righteousness? One man must not kill. If he does, it is murder. Two, ten, one hundred men, acting on their own responsibility, must not kill. If they do, it is still murder.

"But a state or nation may kill as many as they please, and it is not murder. It is just, necessary, commendable and right. Only get enough people to agree to it, and the butchery of myriads of human beings is perfectly innocent. But how many does it take? This is the question.

"Just so with theft, robbery, burglary, and all other crimes. Kidnapping is a great crime in one man, or a very few men only. But a whole nation can commit it, and the act becomes not only innocent, but highly honorable. So a whole nation can rob on the largest scale, and perpetrate burglary on an entire city by martial power, without crime. They can do all these things with impunity, and call on the ministers of religion to say prayers for them. Verily there is magic in numbers! The sovereign multitude can out-legislate the

Almighty, at least in their own conceit. But how many does it take?"[6]

If the state orders me to worship idols, would that make it right? In other words, is it wrong for me to worship idols as an *individual*, but perfectly right to worship idols if I do it under the authority of the *state*? Is it wrong for me to practice divination as an individual, but acceptable if I do it under state authority? Is it wrong for me to commit adultery as an individual, but not a sin if the state orders me to do so? Is divorce wrong for me as an individual, but perfectly legitimate if the state authorizes me to divorce my spouse?

Or suppose a Christian lives in a country where the government orders women to obtain abortions for the good of the country. Perhaps the country is overcrowded, and the government thinks the most feasible way to end the overcrowding is by reducing the birth rate. Does that make it lawful for a Christian woman to kill her baby through an abortion? If not, why is it different when the same government orders its citizens to kill others in a war?

When Jesus gave His commandments on nonresistance and loving our enemies, did He make any distinction between private actions and state-sponsored actions? Not at all. In fact, His teaching was supplanting an Old Testament law that itself pertained to state actions, not private ones. As you remember, Jesus began His message on nonresistance by saying, "You have heard that it was said, 'An eye for an eye and a tooth for a tooth.' But I tell you not to resist an evil person" (Mt. 5:39). Now, where had his listeners heard "an eye for an eye and a tooth for a tooth"? They had heard it from the Mosaic Law, where it appears three times.

The first passage where that expression occurs is in Exodus, which says, "If men fight, and hurt a woman with child, so that she gives birth prematurely, yet no harm follows, he shall surely be punished accordingly as the woman's husband imposes on him; and he shall pay as the *judges* determine. But if any harm follows, then you shall give life for life, eye for eye, tooth for tooth, hand for hand, foot for foot" (Exod. 21:22-24). Please note that the judges were involved in this action; it was not private vengeance.

The second passage is found in Leviticus, concerning an incident where a man with an Egyptian father and an Israelite mother had blasphemed God. When the Israelites inquired of the Lord as to what they should do, God replied, "Whoever blasphemes the name of the Lord shall surely be put to death. *All the congregation* shall certainly stone him. ...Whoever kills a man shall surely be put to death. ...If a man causes disfigurement of his neighbor, as he has done, so shall it be done to him—fracture for fracture, eye for eye, tooth for tooth; as he has caused disfigurement of a man, so shall it be done to him. ...Then Moses spoke to the children of Israel; and they took outside the camp him who had cursed, and stoned him with stones" (Lev. 24:16-23). Is this passage talking about private actions? Hardly! The whole congregation of Israel was to be involved in meting out the punishment.

The final passage is in Deuteronomy: "If a false witness rises against any man to testify against him of wrongdoing, then both men in the controversy shall stand before the Lord, before the *priests* and the *judges* who serve in those days. And the *judges* shall make careful inquiry, and indeed, if the witness is a false witness, who has testified falsely against his brother, then you shall do to him as he thought to have done to this brother; so you shall put away the evil from among you. And those who remain shall hear and fear, and hereafter they shall not again commit such evil among you. Your eye shall not pity: life shall be for life, eye for eye, tooth for tooth, hand for hand, foot for foot" (Deut. 19:16-21). Once again, this passage does not refer to a private form of justice. Both the priests and judges were involved.

So the context of Jesus' teaching on nonresistance concerned national and judicial retribution, not private vengeance. After all, that's what the "eye for an eye" standard was all about. And Jesus' teaching replaced that standard.

Q. **But can't we wear two hats? When I'm in an army uniform and am part of the U. S. Army, it isn't *me*, the individual, doing the killing. It's the United States government. And the United States government has been entrusted with the sword by God, according to Romans 13.**

This argument seems plausible only because most Christians are still unable to think of the kingdom of God as a real, existing government.

To illustrate, suppose an American citizen were living in Germany in the 1930s. And further suppose that the German army drafted him. (Yes, governments have the power to conscript residents who are non-citizens.) Let's say that this American accepted being drafted into the German army and that he later killed his fellow Americans during one of the battles of World War II. Further suppose that he was eventually captured by American forces and was put on trial.

Suppose that at his trial, this American presented the following defense: "I know it would have been wrong for me, an individual American, to take up arms against my fellow citizens. However, I was drafted into the German army and so it was no longer me, the American citizen, who killed other Americans. It was the German government conducting lawful warfare against the United States."

Do you think the people and government of the United States would accept that plea? Of course not! So why do we imagine that Jesus will accept such a plea?

Actually, a real-life situation similar to my illustration recently happened. A few years ago, the United States conducted a war against the Taliban regime of Afghanistan. In the course of the war, the U. S. Army captured an American citizen named John Walker Lindh, who had joined the Taliban fighters. Now, let's suppose that Mr. Lindh had made the following defense at his trial:

"I, John Walker Lindh, as an individual American citizen, would never do anything to harm another American. Yes, it's true that I joined the Taliban army. But at the time I joined, they were not at war with the United States. Whatever actions I took after that were not mine—they were the Taliban government's actions. I did not fight against the United States as an individual. I only fought as a unit of the Taliban government. Therefore, I am innocent."

Do you think an American jury would have accepted that? I think not.

Christians who reject nonresistance, in effect, want Jesus to subjugate Himself to Caesar. They want Jesus to acknowledge that His laws can be broken if Caesar requires people to do so. But would Caesar be willing to do the reverse? Will Caesar allow us to break Caesar's law if Jesus requires it?

In answer to that question, let's suppose that Mr. Lindh had made this defense: "I, John Walker Lindh, *the American citizen*, would never do anything to harm another American. Of course that would be wrong! If I fought against the United States in Afghanistan, I did so purely as John Walker Lindh, *the Muslim*. My allegiance to Allah requires me to kill all infidels. Therefore, as a member of Islam, I killed Americans. But I did this only as part of the Islamic international community—not as an individual nor as an American. Therefore, I am innocent."

What do you think? Would that defense have worked? Of course not. The United States government will not allow its citizens to kill one another, regardless of their religious beliefs. If someone kills another American, he will be charged with murder. The fact that his religion required it will be no excuse.

If our government will not allow its citizens to slaughter one another because of their *religious* differences, why do we imagine that Jesus will allow His citizens to slaughter one another because of their *political* or *national* differences?

10

But Don't The
Scriptures Say ...?

Over the years, Christians who are uncomfortable with nonresistance have asked me about various Scripture passages that seem to contradict nonresistance. So let's look at some of these passages.

Q. **Jesus said that He didn't come to bring peace on earth, but a sword. In saying that, wasn't He authorizing war?**

It's true that Jesus said, "Do not think that I came to bring peace on earth. I did not come to bring peace but a sword" (Mt. 10:34). Looking at that one statement alone, it might sound as though Jesus were saying that His followers would need to take up the military sword to fight for the kingdom. However, when we read the entire passage, it becomes quite clear that this is not what Jesus was talking about.

Actually, Jesus' statement was part of the instructions that He gave the twelve apostles when He sent them out to preach. Let's look at the whole passage:

"Behold, I send you out as sheep in the midst of wolves. Therefore be wise as serpents and harmless as doves. But beware of men, for they will deliver you up to councils and scourge you in their synagogues. ...Now brother will deliver up brother to death, and a father his child; and children will rise up against parents and cause them to be put to death. And you will be hated by all for My name's sake. But he who endures to the end will be saved.

"When they persecute you in this city, flee to another. ...And do not fear those who kill the body but cannot kill the soul. But rather fear Him who is able to destroy both soul and body in hell. ...Therefore, whoever confesses Me before men, him I will also confess before my Father who is in heaven. But whoever denies Me before men, him I will also deny before My Father who is in heaven.

"Do not think that I came to bring peace on earth. I did not come to bring peace but a sword. For I have come to set a man against his father, a daughter against her mother, and a daughter-in-law against her mother-in-law; and 'a man's enemies will be those of his own household.' He who loves father or mother more than Me is not worthy of Me. And he who loves son or daughter more than Me is not worthy of Me. And he who does not take his cross and follow after me is not worthy of Me. He who finds his life will lose it, and he who loses his life for My sake will find it" (Mt. 10:16-39).

When we read the entire passage, we can readily see that Jesus is hardly authorizing His apostles to take up arms and fight holy wars against those who oppose the kingdom. It's just the opposite. He told His apostles that He was sending them out as sheep among wolves. Sheep don't carry swords, and they don't slay wolves. Rather, it's the wolves that do the slaying. Jesus was telling His apostles that they needed to be ready to die for Him. If they weren't ready to die for Him, they weren't worthy of Him. The only thing He authorized His disciples to do in the face of violence was to flee to another location if they could.

In ancient times, a sword served two purposes. The use we normally think of was in warfare, where the sword was used for killing. However, a sword was also a tool for cutting or dividing.

The Scriptures speak of the Word of God as "sharper than any two-edged sword, piercing even to the *division* of soul and spirit" (Heb. 4:12).

In Matthew 10:34, isn't Jesus actually speaking of the sword of division? For He said, "I have come to set a man against his father, a daughter against her mother, and a daughter-in-law against her mother-in-law; and 'a man's enemies will be those of his own household.'"

Was Jesus saying that mothers and daughters would take up the sword of warfare against each other and kill one another? Was He authorizing Christians to kill their parents and children? Or, instead, was Jesus saying that the gospel of the kingdom would cause family divisions?

I think most of us can see that He was talking about the latter. Our own family may disinherit and persecute us. Yet, if we put them ahead of our Lord, we are not worthy of Him.

Now, let's reflect for a moment on what Jesus said in Matthew 10 concerning priorities. He said, "He who loves son or daughter more than Me is not worthy of Me." If He won't allow us to love even our own children more than Him, why do we imagine that it's acceptable to love our country more than Him?

Q. **What about the soldiers who came to see John the Baptist? John didn't tell them to lay down their swords or leave the army.**

Let's read that passage together. It says, "Then tax collectors also came to be baptized, and said to him, 'Teacher, what shall we do?' And He said to them, 'Collect no more than what is appointed for you.' Likewise the soldiers asked Him, saying, 'And what shall we do?' So He said to them, 'Do not intimidate anyone or accuse falsely, and be content with your wages'" (Luke 3:14).

The Greek word that the New King James translates as "intimidate" is *diaseio*, which literally means "to shake violently."[1] The King James Version translates this word as "do violence to." So the King James Version renders this passage: "And the soldiers likewise demanded of him, saying, And what shall we do? And he said unto them, Do violence to no man, neither accuse any falsely; and be content with your wages" (Luke 3:14). So perhaps John actually *was* telling the soldiers not to assault or kill others.

Nevertheless, regardless of how we interpret *diaseio*, the fact remains that John was a prophet of the old order, not the new. John wasn't even a citizen of God's new kingdom. We know this because Jesus told His disciples, "I say to you, among those born of women there has not risen one greater than John the Baptist; but he who is least in the kingdom of heaven is greater than he" (Mt. 11:11). And again, Jesus said, "The Law and the Prophets were until John. Since that time the kingdom of God has been preached" (Luke 16:16).

In short, John was a forerunner, preparing the way for Jesus. Although His message of repentance foreshadowed many of the things that Jesus preached, he was the last *Jewish* prophet, not the first *Christian* prophet. God did not send John to explain the gospel of the kingdom.

Q. **What about the Roman centurion? Jesus didn't tell him he had to leave the army. Or what about Cornelius? The Bible doesn't say he left the army after his conversion.**

First, let's take a brief look at the passage concerning the centurion: "Now when Jesus had entered Capernaum, a centurion came to Him, pleading with Him, saying, 'Lord, my servant is lying at home paralyzed, dreadfully tormented.' And Jesus said to him, 'I will come and heal him.' The centurion answered and said, 'Lord, I am not worthy that You should come under my roof. But only speak a word, and my servant will be healed. ...Then Jesus said to the centurion, 'Go your way; and as you have believed, so let it be done for you.' And his servant was healed that same hour" (Mt. 8:5-13).

The truth is that Jesus said absolutely nothing about this man's profession. He expressed neither approval nor disapproval. In fact, the point of the passage was not that this man was a *centurion*. Rather, it was that he was a *Gentile*. That's why Jesus remarked, "Assuredly, I say to you, I have not found such great faith, not even in Israel!" (Luke 8:10). This incident foreshadowed the fact that the Gentiles later proved more responsive to the gospel than had Israel.

Jesus' encounter with the Roman centurion is quite similar to his meeting with the Samaritan woman at the well. She was living with a man to whom she was not married. Yet, Jesus did not tell her to leave this man, did He? Does that mean Jesus approved of cohabitation without marriage?

As for Cornelius, the Scriptures say nothing—one way or the other—about what he did after his conversion. There is no evidence that Cornelius continued to use the sword after he became a Christian.

In reality, the Scriptures give us relatively few accounts of what new converts did after becoming Christians. I think most of us assume that if new converts were engaged in unscriptural occupations they changed their livelihoods after their conversions. For example, many prostitutes believed in Jesus. We rightfully assume that they left their harlotry, but the Scriptures are silent about the matter (Mt. 21:31,32).

Q. **Yes, but didn't Jesus whip the money-changers and forcibly drive them out of the temple?**

Let's read that account: "Now the Passover of the Jews was at hand, and Jesus went up to Jerusalem. And He found in the temple those who sold oxen and sheep and doves, and the money changers doing business. When He made a whip of cords, He drove them all out of the temple, with the sheep and the oxen, and poured out the changers' money and overturned the tables. And He said to those who sold doves, 'Take these things away! Do not make My Father's house a house of merchandise!'" (John 2:13-16).

So on whom or what did Jesus use the whip? The account doesn't say, does it? Sheep will normally follow only their own shepherd. So how was Jesus going to get the sheep and oxen to leave the temple courtyard? Absent a miracle (which He chose not to perform on this occasion), the most reasonable way to get the animals out of the temple was to drive them out with a whip. There's absolutely no evidence that Jesus used His whip on *people.*

Nevertheless, this account does shed important light on nonresistance. Jesus demonstrated that being nonresistant doesn't mean that a person cannot be assertive or speak out against sin. Of course, being God's Son, He had much more authority than you or I have. The apostles never cleared the money changers out of the temple.

Q. **Perhaps Jesus' teachings on nonresistance were temporary. Didn't He later tell His disciples to buy swords?**

The passage referred to is Luke 22:35,36: "And He said to them, 'When I sent you without money bag, knapsack, and sandals, did you lack anything?' So they said, 'Nothing.' Then He said to them, 'But now, he who has a money bag, let him take it, and likewise a knapsack; and he who has no sword, let him sell his garment and buy one.'"

At first glance, it's easy to see how someone might think this passage is counteracting Jesus' earlier teachings on nonresistance. But when we read the rest of the chapter, we see that this was not the case. Immediately after telling His apostles to buy a sword, Jesus explained: "For I say to you that this which is written must still be accomplished in Me: 'And He was numbered with the transgressors.'" (Luke 22:37). So Jesus Himself explained His words. The purpose of the swords was simply to fulfill the prophecy in Isaiah 53:12, which said that Jesus would be numbered with the transgressors.

The next verse sheds further light: "So they said, "Lord, look, here are two swords.' And He said to them, "It is enough" (Luke 22:38). Obviously, Jesus was not telling his apostles to prepare themselves for an armed conflict. After all, two swords were not sufficient to defend twelve men. Rather, the two swords were enough to fulfill the Old Testament prophecy.

The remainder of this passage in Luke, concerning Jesus' arrest, clarifies the matter even further: "When those around Him saw what was going to happen, they said to Him, 'Lord, shall we strike with the sword?' And one of them [Peter] struck the servant of the high priest and cut off his right ear. But Jesus answered and said, 'Permit even this.' And He touched his ear and healed him" (Luke 22:49-51). So, in the end, Jesus did *not* permit His disciples to use the two swords for self-defense. He even undid the evil effect of the sword.

Jesus used this episode with the swords to teach an object lesson. The worst crime in human history was about to take place. The innocent Son of God was about to be falsely arrested, tortured, and killed. If there was ever a time for Christians to use the sword, this was surely it! But Jesus wouldn't permit His disciples to use the sword to defend either Him or themselves. When He had told them not to resist evil, that's exactly what He meant! Even when the crime of all crimes was being committed.

Matthew's account adds one more detail about what Jesus told Peter, "But Jesus said to him, 'Put your sword in its place, for all who take the sword will perish by the sword. Or do you think that I cannot now pray to My Father, and He will provide Me with more than twelve legions of angels?" When God wants to protect us, His angels are sufficient. As Tertullian later put it, "in disarming Peter, [the Lord] disarmed every soldier."[2]

What did Jesus mean when He said, "All who take the sword will perish by the sword"? That statement is very similar to Jesus' earlier words, "He who finds his life will lose it, and he who loses his life for My sake will find it" (Mt. 10:39). If we put our trust in military arms and in the world's power, we will ultimately perish in that trust.

We never again read of Jesus' disciples having swords or fighting to defend themselves. The Book of Acts graphically details the nonresistance of the apostles and other Christians. Christians were set upon by mobs, Jewish authorities, and Gentile rulers. But in no instance did they offer physical resistance. Stephen did not defend himself from the mob that seized him. And even at his death he showed his love for his enemies, saying, "Lord, do not charge them with this sin" (Acts 7:60).

Acts tells us that immediately after the death of Stephen, "a great persecution arose against the church which was at Jerusalem" (Acts 8:1). So what did Jesus' disciples do? Arm themselves and fight back? No. Luke tells us, "And they were all scattered throughout the regions of Judea and Samaria, except the apostles" (Acts 8:1). The only action that Jesus had authorized His followers to take in the face of persecution was to flee. And that's what they did.

The Permanence of Jesus' Teachings

At the end of the Sermon on the Mount, which contains so many of the laws of the kingdom, Jesus told His hearers: "Whoever hears these sayings of Mine, and does them, I will liken him to a wise man who built his house on the rock: and the rain descended, the floods came, and the winds blew and beat on that house; and it did not fall, for it was founded on the rock" (Mt. 7:24,25).

When we think of a rock as a foundation, we think of permanence. The Law of Moses had lasted for fifteen hundred years, but it was eventually fulfilled. It proved to be temporary. But Jesus' teachings are permanent. After all, it wouldn't be much of a rock if Jesus or His apostles had abrogated His teachings within a few years after He gave them. No, His teachings don't change. They apply to us just as literally and just as absolutely as they applied to Jesus' first hearers.

As I have quoted before, "Jesus Christ is the same yesterday, today and forever" (Heb. 13:8).

11

What About the Kingdoms Of the World?

I've talked a lot about the kingdom of God, but so far I've said very little about the kingdoms of the world. So let's talk about them for awhile.

Actually, the Scriptures reveal only a little about God's governance of the kingdoms of the world. In the Old Testament, we see God's interaction with kingdoms that had dealings with the Israelites, such as Egypt, Assyria, and Babylon. But the Bible tells us little or nothing about other kingdoms of the world during this period, such as ones in China, India, Japan, Africa, and the Americas.

We can surmise that God raised up the Roman Empire to make the spread of Christianity easier throughout the Mediterranean world. After all, the Romans built good roads throughout the Empire, and they made the Mediterranean safe for travel. But why did the Han dynasty arise in China? Or the Aztec kingdom in Mexico? Why did the Sunga dynasty come into power in India, and why were the Mauryan rulers there overthrown? We don't know. In fact, the truth is that we know relatively little about God's governance of the kingdoms of the world. The fact that a nation prevails in war in no way indicates that God approves of them as a nation.

However, the Scriptures do reveal five principles of God's governance over the kingdoms of the world:

- God is in ultimate control of these kingdoms.

- All earthly rulers derive their power from God.

- God's oversight of earthly kingdoms is separate and distinct from His governance of His kingdom.

- All earthly kingdoms are only temporary.

- Satan has considerable involvement in the kingdoms of the world.

1. God is in ultimate control of the kingdoms of the world. This fact was brought home to King Nebuchadnezzar in a powerful way when God temporarily took away both his sanity and his kingdom. The Scriptures explain why God did this: "In order that the living may know that the Most High rules in the kingdom of men, gives it to whomever He will, and sets over it the lowest of men" (Dan. 4:17).

So God is in ultimate control. That's why kingdom Christians don't worry about the Hitlers of this world. God never lets their evil go unchecked. They may rule for awhile, but only as long as God permits them. Christians who truly believe that God is in control know that prayer is the most effective weapon against evil.

2. All earthly rulers derive their power from God. When Pilate warned Jesus that he had the power to crucify Him, Jesus calmly replied, "You could have no power at all against Me unless it had been given you from above" (John 19:11). Or as Paul said, "There is no authority except from God, and the authorities that exist are appointed by God" (Rom. 13:1).

So the kingdoms of men have legitimate, God-given authority. But why has God given them this authority? Paul explains, "Rulers are not a terror to good works, but to evil. Do you want to be unafraid of the authority? Do what is good, and you will have praise from the same. For he is God's minister to you for good. But if you do evil, be afraid; for he does not bear the sword in vain; for he is God's minister, an avenger to execute wrath on him who practices evil" (Rom. 13:3,4).

So God has given power to the kingdoms of men because of the sinfulness of mankind. Even evil rulers are almost always better than anarchy. In the recent war with Iraq, the western coalition forces quickly defeated the armies of Saddam Hussein of Iraq. However, there was a gap of several days between when the government of Hussein collapsed and when the American occupying forces established an interim government in Baghdad, the capital of Iraq. During those few days, anarchy reigned. Looters ransacked store after store, armed thugs hijacked cars, and people executed vendettas against their enemies. As evil as was the regime of Saddam Hussein, even his regime was better than no government at all.

When Paul said that the ruler is "God's minister," the man who was ruling the Roman Empire was Nero—a thoroughly wicked man. So let no one imagine that Paul meant that the ruler is in partnership with God or that he is even a friend of God. The word Paul used here for "minister" is *diakonos*. The normal meaning of this word in Greek is "servant." Paul is not saying that the ruler is God's willing agent or partner. He is saying that the ruler is God's *servant*, because God is the Master.

Like Nero, most kings and rulers have not acknowledged God's authority over them. More often than not, they have worked against God and His people. This was true in the days of ancient Israel, and it's been true since the days of Jesus. Rulers nearly always try to exercise more power than what God has allotted them. They're not satisfied with "Caesar's things." They want "God's things" as well.

3. God's oversight of earthly kingdoms is separate and distinct from His governance of His kingdom. Jesus explained this to Pilate, saying, "My kingdom is not of this world. If My kingdom were of this world, My servants would fight, so that I should not be delivered to the Jews; but now My kingdom is not from here" (John 18:36).

All earthly governments are "of this world." This puts them in contrast, and usually in opposition to, the kingdom of God. No earthly kingdom can ever be a partner with the kingdom of God. The essence of one is totally opposite the essence of the other. To try to bond one of the kingdoms of men with the kingdom of God would be like trying to bond modeling clay to plastic. They will not bond, because their natures are too different.

Bible-believing American Christians typically mix patriotism with their Christianity, and they imagine that the United States is somehow in partnership with God's kingdom. They talk of America as a "Christian nation." But the United States is just as much a kingdom of the world as is France, Germany, or China. The United States may imprint "In God We Trust" on its coins, but it does not trust in God. It trusts in its armies, tanks, and missiles.

4. All earthly kingdoms are only temporary. The opposing nature of the kingdom of God to the kingdoms of the world is made clear in Daniel's prophecy: "In the days of these kings the God of heaven will set up a kingdom which shall never be destroyed; and the kingdom shall not be left to other people; it shall break in pieces and consume all these kingdoms, and it shall stand forever" (Dan. 2:44).

Daniel didn't say that the kingdom of God would bond together with one or more of the earthly kingdoms. He didn't say that some of them were in partnership with God's kingdom. No, he said God's kingdom would break every one of these kingdoms into pieces and consume them. That includes the United States. The kingdoms of the world are only temporary entities that will eventually be destroyed.

5.   Finally, we must always remember that Satan has considerable involvement in the kingdoms of men. This should be quite obvious from the way governments have acted through the centuries. But the point was brought home more directly when Satan tempted Jesus: "The devil took Him up on an exceedingly high mountain, and showed Him all the kingdoms of the world and their glory. And he said to Him, 'All these things I will give You if You will fall down and worship me.' Then Jesus said to him, 'Away with you, Satan! For it is written, 'You shall worship the LORD your God and Him only you shall serve'" (Mt. 4:9,10).

It's important to note that Jesus didn't dispute Satan's power to give Him all of the kingdoms of the world. After all, it wouldn't have been much of a temptation if Satan had been offering Jesus something he couldn't deliver on anyway. In fact, Jesus later referred to Satan as the "ruler of this world" (John 12:31). Centuries before the birth of Christ, Daniel's prophecies revealed that the earthly kingdoms are controlled by ungodly spiritual forces (Dan. 10:13,20).

Of course, Satan would have no power over the governments of the world if God did not permit it. The ultimate authority of the kingdoms of men comes from God, not Satan. But normally, the kingdoms of the world follow the path of Satan, not of God.

12

Life Under Two Kingdoms

Being a citizen of God's kingdom is not easy. What makes it especially difficult is that—unlike all other kingdoms—God's kingdom doesn't have exclusive occupation of any geographic area. So its citizens will always be living under two governments: the kingdom of God and a kingdom of the world. Which government are Christians to obey?

The situation is not that different from a citizen of the United States who lives in a foreign country. Suppose that Joe American, a United States citizen, were to move to Germany and take a job there. Would the fact that he was a United States citizen exempt him from obeying the laws of Germany? Not at all. If he breaks the German traffic laws, he won't be excused because he is a foreigner. If Joe robs a bank, he'll be prosecuted under German laws. And he will face imprisonment in Germany. Furthermore, even though Joe is a United States citizen, if he works in Germany, he will have to pay German taxes.

At the same time, even though he is a foreigner, Joe American also has various *rights* under German law. He's entitled to police protection, the same as a German citizen. He can file a petition in the German courts. If he works in Germany, he comes under the protection of the same workplace safety provisions as does a German citizen.

Our situation as citizens of the kingdom of God is virtually identical to Joe's situation. Although we are citizens of God's kingdom, we have to obey the laws of the land where we reside. The Scriptures make that quite clear: "Submit yourselves to every ordinance of man for the Lord's sake, whether to the king as supreme, or to governors, as to those who are sent by him for the punishment of evildoers and for the praise of those who do good. For this is the will of God, that by doing good you may put to silence the ignorance of foolish men" (1 Pet 2:13-15).

Even though we are citizens of God's kingdom, we do not view earthly governments as illegitimate, hostile forces. This is because we realize that the kingdoms of the world ultimately derive their authority from God. The Scriptures make this clear: "Let every soul be subject to the governing authorities. For there is no authority except from God, and the authorities that exist are appointed by God. Therefore whoever resists the authority resists the ordinance of God, and those who resist will bring judgment on themselves" (Rom. 13:1,2).

One of the seeming ironies of being a citizen of God's Kingdom is that to be obedient to *Christ*, we first must be obedient to *Caesar*. In fact, citizens of God's kingdom are usually more conscientious about obeying the laws of the earthly governments than are those people whose *only* citizenship is here on earth.

A Conflict of Kingdoms

But now let's return for a moment to our illustration about Joe American who lives in Germany. What if the laws of Germany conflict with the laws of America? For example, what if, in order to obey the laws of Germany, Joe would have to commit an act that would be disloyal to America? In that situation, Joe would have to decide where he wants his permanent citizenship to be. Because when a conflict arises, he will not be able to obey *both* governments. He will have to choose.

To illustrate, suppose that Germany and the United States enter into a war against each other. Would the United States have the power to draft Joe into the armed forces even though he lives in a foreign land? Absolutely. Does Germany have the power to draft Joe, even though he is not a German citizen? Yes, it does. Can Joe allow himself to be conscripted into the German army and give a military oath to Germany? Not if he wants to remain an American citizen! He can't serve two masters. He will have to decide which government is going to be his absolute master, and which one will receive only relative obedience.

Rendering God's Things to God

From reading the passages above from Romans 13, some persons have imagined that the earthly governments under which we live have the *ultimate* claim over us. They imagine that we owe our allegiance—and even our lives—to the nation in which we live. But the Scriptures never say that.

We must never forget Jesus' answer when the Pharisees and Herodians asked Him whether it is lawful or not to pay taxes to Caesar. He told them, "Render therefore to Caesar the things that are Caesar's, and to God the things that are God's" (Mt. 22:21).

Please note that the Pharisees and Herodians hadn't asked Jesus about God. They had only asked about taxes. By bringing God into the equation, Jesus demonstrated that his interrogators had too narrow a focus. Their hearts were fixated on issues of this world, not on matters of eternity. Yes, to be sure, they were to pay Caesar's taxes to him. Why? Because his image was on their coins. God didn't mint those coins. Caesar did. So give him back what belongs to him.

But what about us humans? Whose image is stamped on us? Caesar's? Hardly. God created us in *His* image. We belong to Him. As a result, God has the ultimate call on our lives. Caesar has rights only to the things that he has created. He has created neither our bodies nor our souls. So he has no right to either.

In Romans 13, Paul told us to subject ourselves to the higher powers or governing authorities. But he then goes on to delineate the areas of subjection of which he is speaking: "Render therefore to all their due: taxes to whom taxes are due, customs to whom customs, fear to whom fear, honor to whom honor. Owe no one anything except to love one another, for he who loves another has fulfilled the law" (Rom. 13:1-8).

Please notice that Paul lists only *earthly* things: taxes, customs (i.e., duties levied against transported goods), fear, and honor. All these things are in the sphere of Caesar. Quite noticeably, Paul didn't list military service as one of the things owed to the governing authorities.

As I've previously remarked, most earthly governments aren't content to have merely Caesar's things. They want God's things as well. They believe they are entitled to the absolute, unqualified allegiance of all of their citizens. They even imagine that they own the lives of their citizens, and, to a large degree, their souls. But as Tertullian asked, "What will be God's if all things are Caesar's?"[1]

Indeed, what do most professing Christians have left to give to God? They've typically risked their lives and given their money, their youth, their souls and their unqualified allegiance to Caesar. What do they have left to give to Christ's kingdom? Nothing but some leftover crumbs—their tithes and a few hours a week of their time. And they imagine that this will be acceptable to Jesus!

When Caesar Wants God's Things

So what are we to do if the laws of Caesar and the laws of God conflict? Well, we are essentially in the same position as Joe American in our illustration. He has to decide which country has his ultimate allegiance—Germany or the United States. He cannot give his ultimate allegiance to both. Similarly, citizens of God's kingdom have to decide whose kingdom has their ultimate allegiance, God's or Caesar's.

The apostles were put to this very test. Jesus had commanded them to preach the good news of the kingdom. However, the Jewish authorities had them arrested and commanded them not to preach about Jesus any more. Now, these Jewish authorities were not some renegades usurping governmental authority. They included the high priest, whose position had been directly established by God. And the Roman government accepted their authority in matters of the Jewish religion.

But none of that changed things. The apostles had their orders from Jesus, whom they recognized as their King and to whom they gave their ultimate allegiance. So they answered the Jewish authorities, "Whether it is right in the sight of God to listen to you more than to God, you judge. For we cannot but speak the things which we have seen and heard" (Acts 4:20). And the apostles went right back out on the streets and continued preaching.

So the authorities soon called them back, saying, "Did we not strictly command you not to teach in this name?" But Peter and the other apostles answered them, "We ought to obey God rather than men" (Acts 5:28,29).

What should we learn from their example? We should learn that if we want to become a citizen of God's kingdom and *remain* one, His kingdom has to have our primary allegiance. There can be no hesitation as to whom we must obey when the commandments of our heavenly King conflict with those of earthly rulers. The answer is always the same: we must obey God rather than men. If we want to be a citizen of the kingdom of God, then we have to recognize that it is the dominant kingdom.

The relationship of the kingdoms of the world to God is very similar to the relationship of a corporation to the state. A corporation exists by the power of the state. It would have no authority if the state hadn't given it authority. Does this mean that the state endorses everything a corporation may do? No.

Does this make the corporation a partner with the state? Not in the least. Yet, because the state has empowered the corporation, employees of the corporation are bound to obey the corporation so long as they are employed there.

However, this obedience is relative. If the corporation orders its employees to do something illegal, the state will expect them to disobey the corporation. Otherwise, they will face criminal liability. The fact that the corporation ordered them to do something illegal won't protect them.

In the same way, the kingdom of God is the dominant estate when there is a conflict between God's laws and man's laws. Man's laws must give way to God's laws—not the other way around. Jesus will not excuse disobedience to His laws just because some earthly ruler was presumptuous enough to order his subjects to do something that Jesus has declared illegal.

It's similar to the relationship of state laws to the U. S. Constitution. Each state has authority to pass laws concerning a wide range of subjects. And persons who reside in that state must obey those laws. But what if a state law conflicts with one of the provisions of the Constitution? In that situation, the Constitution overrules the state law. It's never the other way around. Likewise, God's laws always overrule conflicting laws of man. If Caesar says to do one thing but God says to do another, God's law prevails—not man's. That is one of the cardinal rules of the kingdom of God.

Loving Our Enemies

Aside from religious persecution, Caesar's laws and Christ's laws probably most often conflict in the area of nonresistance. For example, an earthly government often tells a young man that he must be enrolled in the armed forces, take up arms, and kill others who are enemies of his country. However, our King has already commanded us to love our enemies, not to hate them. Whether they are Buddhists, Muslims, or atheists, we can hardly slaughter them and yet claim that we love them. So we cannot obey both Christ and Caesar.

If Christ's laws do not allow us to kill *unbelievers*, how much more so do they prohibit us from killing our fellow *Christians*. Yet, in nearly every war fought by Americans or Europeans in the past 1700 years, there have been professing Christians on both sides. If a foreign government ordered an American to fight against and kill his fellow Americans, most Americans would refuse to do so. However, if an earthly government orders a Christian to fight against and kill his fellow Christians, most professing Christians *will* do so.

Our ultimate allegiance cannot belong to two different kings. When a Christian kills a fellow citizen of God's kingdom simply because some earthly ruler has ordered him to, he's acknowledging that his ultimate allegiance belongs to his earthly ruler. He will put his country's welfare above the welfare of the kingdom of God and the brotherhood of Christ.

But, again, a Christian's refusal to take up arms doesn't apply only to wars involving other Christians. Jesus told us to love our *enemies*. If we refuse to take up arms only against our fellow citizens of the kingdom, we aren't that different from the world. They likewise refuse to take up arms against their fellow citizens. Joining God's kingdom means we go one step further than the world—we love our enemies as well as our comrades.

Honoring the Government

In light of Jesus' teachings on nonresistance and loving our enemies, some Christians have the mistaken idea that Christians should oppose and belittle soldiers and police officers. But that's not the case at all. Jesus and His apostles were always respectful toward the soldiers with whom they interacted. The Scriptures tell us that God has entrusted the governments of this world with the sword. Whereas God's kingdom needs no military forces, the governments of this world normally do. Jesus' teachings are for

His kingdom. He didn't pretend that a government of this world could operate without the sword of power.

For that reason, I try to always show courtesy and respect to soldiers and police officers. In fact, I think one of the genuine social injustices in our society is the low pay that soldiers receive. They endure all sorts of hardships, and they risk their very lives on behalf of their fellow citizens. Yet, they are near the bottom end of the economic pay scale. In 2003, the base salary for an American soldier with one year of service was only $15,480. This is only slightly higher than the average pay of American theater ushers ($14,144) and street crossing guards ($15,080).[2]

Naturally, I would like to see all soldiers enroll in the army of God's kingdom instead of in the armies of this world. However, that is a decision they must come to for themselves. But as long as they are serving the people of their country on behalf of their government, they deserve respect, not ridicule. And they deserve to be paid by their government commensurately with the sacrifices they are called to make.

13

Am I of This World?

A short while ago, we looked at Jesus' words to Pilate: "My kingdom is not of this world. If My kingdom were of this world, My servants would fight, so that I should not be delivered to the Jews; but now My kingdom is not from here" (John 18:36).

If there had been any doubt in Pilate's mind about the revolutionary nature of Christ's kingdom, there should have been none after he heard those words. It was a kingdom that would not—in fact, *could* not—be defended with the sword. Pilate had nothing to fear from Jesus. Jesus' kingdom was not going to overthrow the Empire that Pilate served—at least, not in his lifetime and not with earthly swords. Jesus' kingdom was not of this world. It depended solely on supernatural power for its preservation—not on earthly might.

Not only is Christ's kingdom not of the world, but His subjects are not of the world, either. Shortly before He was arrested, Jesus had prayed about his subjects: "I have given them Your word; and the world has hated them because they are not of the world, just as I am not of the world. I do not pray that You should take them out of the world, but that You should keep them from the evil one. They are not of the world, just as I am not of the world. Sanctify them by Your truth. Your word is truth. As you sent Me into the world, I also have sent them into the world" (John 17:14-18).

So if we're going to be subjects of Jesus Christ, we have to be "not of the world." Does this mean that we retreat to some inaccessible mountain peak or desert sanctuary? Not at all. For

Jesus said that He was sending us into the world. Not away from it, but *into* it.

So if we have been sent into the world, how do we avoid being "of the world"? John explains: "Do not love the world or the things in the world. If anyone loves the world, the love of the Father is not in him. For all that is in the world—the lust of the flesh, the lust of the eyes, and the pride of life—is not of the Father but is of the world. And the world is passing away, and the lust of it; but he who does the will of God abides forever" (1 John 2:15-17).

So being "not of the world" means that we live in the world but we are dead to all of its attractions. We are simply pilgrims passing through the world but not making it our home. As John tells us, there's no point talking about how much we love Jesus, if we love the world. We gain nothing by plastering Jesus stickers all over our cars and homes—if we love the world. Because if we love the world, we don't love Jesus.

As James puts it, "Adulterers and adulteresses! Do you not know that friendship with the world is enmity with God? Whoever therefore wants to be a friend of the world makes himself an enemy of God" (Jas. 4:4).

For this reason, neither Jesus nor His disciples ever talk about such a thing as a "Christian nation." The term is actually an oxymoron, like the phrase "thunderous silence." The word "Christian" of necessity must always apply to persons and things that are "not of this world." On the other hand, unless we are referring to God's kingdom, the word "nation" necessarily refers to something that is always "of this world."

Throughout the New Testament, God gives His people instructions on how they are to act in various spheres of authority. He gives instructions to both husbands and wives. He gives instructions to both masters and servants. He gives instructions to both parents and children. He gives instructions to both pastors and to members of the flock they shepherd. However, when it comes to earthly governments, it's quite different. The New Testament gives instructions only to Christian *subjects*—never to Christian rulers. If God had intended for there to be Christian rulers, why were no instructions given to them?

The Dye of the World

Of course, every church claims it loves Jesus. No church advertises that it's a friend of the world. But words are easy. It's not what a church says, but what it does. On Judgment Day, Jesus will commend us with "Well *done* good and faithful servant," not with "Well *spoken* good and faithful servant" (Mt. 25:21).

Many banks use dye packs to help foil robberies. If a robbery occurs, the bank employees surreptitiously place thin dye packs in each bundle of cash handed over to the robber. About ten minutes later, when the robber is fleeing the bank, the dye packs explode, spraying red dye all over the stolen cash and usually on the robber.

In 1999, in Wilmington, Delaware, a not-too-clever crook held up a local bank, fleeing with a considerable amount of cash. However, moments after the robber left the bank, the dye packs exploded, spraying dye all over the money and all over the robber's right hand. The crook made it only a few blocks before he noticed a policeman in hot pursuit. So he leaned up against an apartment building, put the money sack behind his back, and stuck his hands in his pockets.

He was standing there nonchalantly when the police officer came running by, searching for the bank robber. The thief immediately recognized the policeman as an acquaintance. So he took his right hand out of his pocket and waved to the officer. Oops—that was the hand with the dye. And that was the end of his brief criminal career.[1]

Just like that dye pack, the world leaves an identifying mark on its friends. When friends of the world lift their hands to worship Jesus, what He sees are the red dye marks left by the world. Regardless how loudly a church protests otherwise, that mark is there to identify it.

How can we tell if the church we attend is stained with the dye of the world? When a church is stained with the world's dye, whatever social mores, attitudes, and movements go through the world will likewise move through that church. In contrast, Jesus is "the same yesterday, today and forever." His attitudes, values, and commandments never change. A church that is not of the world will have the same values and live the same lifestyle as the New Testament church. Its moral standards don't change every decade or two.

However, ever since the time of Constantine, the institutional Church has been locked in step with the world. For example, it had been acceptable to the Romans to burn people at the stake, so it became acceptable for the Church to do so. The ancient Romans saw torture as a perfectly acceptable way to obtain evidence from accused criminals. So the Church accepted torture. The Romans had looked down on various "barbarian" people groups, so the Church did so as well.

The post-Constantinian Church continued to profess its love for Jesus Christ, but its guilty hands were covered by the world's dye. The Church loved the world, so it adopted many of the world's values and mores. And typically, the Church has continued to practice these evils—until the *world* finally recognizes them as wrong. For example, when the world lost its stomach for burning people at the stake, so did the Church. When much of the world finally recognized torture as a hideous evil, the Church quit using it.

Fifty years ago, here in the South, white persons who belonged to the world wouldn't eat in the same restaurants, sleep in the same motels, or socialize in the same auditoriums with blacks. Did the Church take a different stand? No, white Christians acted no differently from the world. They even refused to worship alongside blacks. But today, southern whites eat in the same restaurants, sleep in the same motels, and sit in the same auditoriums with blacks. The world finally recognized racism as wrong. And guess what? Now most churches recognize racism as wrong. In most, but not all, Southern churches, blacks can now worship alongside whites. But the world had to change before white Christians were willing to practice loving those of a different skin color. Somehow Jesus' teachings never pierced the hearts of white Southern Christians, but the *world* finally got through to them.

Earlier, we talked about divorce. Seventy-five years ago, virtually every church prohibited divorce. Today, hardly any church does. What changed? Jesus certainly didn't. No, the world changed, and the Church with its dye-stained hands changed right along with it.

One of the most significant social movements of the past forty years has been feminism. As feminism began to influence nearly every institution of the world, it likewise began to influence the institutional Church. Suddenly the Church became ashamed of what Jesus Christ and His apostles taught concerning the two genders. As a result, the Church has "re-interpreted" almost every passage of Scripture pertaining to men and women.

Although feminism mouths the slogan of equality, in reality, it has promoted an enormous double standard between the sexes. If persons say anything that could even remotely be interpreted as derogatory to women—no matter how fair and accurate—they are immediately shouted down, disregarded, and labeled as sexist. However, persons can freely denigrate men—whether it is fair and accurate or not—and that is perfectly acceptable.

Even so-called Bible believing Christians have adopted wholesale the world's double standard. Male-bashing in sermons is now quite typical. What's more, virtually every passage of Scripture that contains a special commandment for women has been neutralized or abrogated. In contrast, every passage of Scripture that contains a special commandment for men has been emphasized and often amplified.

For example, few pastors today talk about wives submitting to their husbands in everything, as the Scriptures teach. Or, if they do speak about it, they interpret it in such a fanciful way that the commandment means nothing. However, many pastors typically preach at length about husbands loving their wives. And they interpret that commandment in such a way that it's a heavy, nearly impossible burden to fulfill.

Another example is the Scriptural teaching on the head covering: "Every man praying or prophesying, having his head covered, dishonors his head. But every woman who prays or prophesies with her head uncovered dishonors her head, for that is one and the same as if her head were shaved. For if a woman is not covered, let her also be shorn" (1 Cor. 11:4,5).

From the early days of the New Testament church up through the mid-nineteenth century, virtually every church obeyed the Holy Spirit in this matter. Men took their hats off when praying or when in church. Women covered their heads with a veil when praying or when in church. But then the first feminist movement of the 1800's swept through society—and through the Church. In many churches, women quit wearing any type of prayer covering. In most churches, women still wore coverings, but the coverings changed from veils or bonnets to stylish hats. Until the sixties, women in many churches still wore hats when in church. But hats quickly disappeared with the new feminist movement of the Sixties.

The irony is that virtually all churches today still apply the first part of Paul's instructions—the part where he says that men must pray with their heads uncovered. Men still are told to take off their hats when they come into church, or when a prayer is being offered. I remember being at a prayer meeting once, and a couple of men came in with hats on. The preacher immediately called them down, and told them to take off their hats. Yet, I've never seen a preacher tell a woman to cover her head in church or before prayer. The world has a new double standard toward the sexes, and so does the Church.

At first glance, it may seem that today's Church is doing women a great favor. However, in truth, they are practicing the worst form of sex discrimination against women possible.

I used to work as a corporate attorney, answerable directly to the president and other officers of the corporation. Those officers depended upon me to correctly inform them on matters of law. What sort of a lawyer would I have been if I had told the officers that certain conduct was lawful, when in fact it wasn't? When they ended up in jail, would they have thanked me for not being straightforward with them? I think not.

It's exactly the same with Jesus' laws. The laws and teachings He has given to each gender—either in person or through His apostles—remain the same "yesterday, today, and forever." When Christian authors and preachers tell Christian women that they don't have to obey Jesus, they are setting these women up to be disqualified from the kingdom.

Right Wing Is Just as Worldly as Left Wing

Many Bible-believing Christians today pride themselves in being separate from the world because they reject today's liberal views on homosexuality, abortion, and other social and political issues. They somehow imagine that following a right-wing Republican agenda is being different from the world. But the Republican Party *is* the world, or at least part of it. In fact, it tends to be more militaristic and more supportive of war than the liberal parties. Its political platform is no more built on the teachings of Jesus than is the Democratic platform. However, to its credit, the Republican Party is usually slower than the Democratic Party to throw out traditional and Biblical morality.

Jesus doesn't care which segment of the world we're friends with. If we're friends with *any* part of it, we're His enemies.

14

Does this Make Us Peace And Justice Activists?

From what I've said so far, you might be thinking that I'm saying we should all be "peace and justice" activists. Perhaps all of us should be picketing nuclear power plants and munitions factories. But that's not at all what I'm saying.

"Peace and justice" activism is merely the reverse side of "God and country" activism. Both sides imagine that the kingdoms of the world are part of God's kingdom—or, at least, that the kingdoms of the world can be run by Jesus' teachings. But did Jesus try to "Christianize" the world? When Jesus stood before Pilate, did He lecture Pilate about various social wrongs within the Roman Empire? Did the New Testament Christians work to end capital punishment and torture throughout the Roman Empire?

The Inconsistency of "Peace and Justice" Activists

"Peace and justice" Christians imagine that they are other-worldly, in contrast to right-wing, redneck fundamentalists. They imagine that they alone are standing up for Jesus' teachings. But the truth is, they are just as worldly as right-wing fundamental-ists. They merely align themselves with a different sector of the world—the liberal left. Yet, like the Republican Party, the Democratic Party *is* the world.

Like their right-wing counterparts, "peace and justice" Christians practice a pick-and-choose approach to Jesus' commandments. They somehow manage to pick only the teachings that are politically correct in left-wing circles. They speak out fervently against the sins of war and economic greed. But they are usually silent when it comes to other sins, such as divorce, abortion, and homosexuality. They imagine that they can be an active citizen of God's kingdom and yet never have to be politically incorrect.

But Jesus is never politically correct. He wasn't politically correct in the first century, and He hasn't been in any century since. He didn't come to preach a message about changing the governments and kingdoms of this world. He sought to transform *individuals*, not to transform the world. He came to invite us all to join *His* kingdom.

His message wasn't: Let's make the rich take care of the poor by taxing them heavily. No, his message was, "David Bercot, you give up *your* comforts to help the poor." He and His apostles didn't band together in a political action committee to force Zacchaeus to care for the poor with all of his money. No, Jesus changed Zacchaeus, so that Zacchaeus *wanted* to care for the poor.

"Peace and justice" Christians speak out vociferously against capital punishment, which kills a hundred or so Americans every year.[1] Yet, most of them are totally silent about abortion, which kills more than a *million* Americans every year.[2] "Peace and justice" Christians protest discrimination against women, but they are quite mute when it comes to discrimination against men. They speak out against the persecution of left-wing revolutionaries, but they rarely say anything about the persecution of Christians in leftist dictatorships. Like the "God and country" Christians, they let the world dictate their agenda.

Are Kingdom Christians Anti-American?

Many "peace and justice" Christians imagine that nearly all of the evils in the world are caused by America. They continually lash out against the sins and policies of America. Yet they close their eyes to the evils and oppressions of other governments.

America is not "God's country," any more than is any other kingdom of this world. It has its inconsistencies, pride and selfishness, like all other countries. It has used its enormous wealth and military power primarily to further its own selfish interests. It rarely uses its money and power to help a poor, powerless nation—unless that nation is important to American self-interests.

At the same time, America is certainly one of the most benevolent world powers that has ever existed. It has not used its might as cruelly as most past world powers, such as Russia, Spain, Rome, Babylon, and Assyria. Furthermore, it has been friendly to Christianity—and not just to worldly Christianity. It has been quite tolerant of kingdom Christianity as well. Kingdom Christians can be thankful for the freedoms that the American government gives them. Today, most European countries offer the same freedoms, but America was the first to do so.

The narrow way of the kingdom excludes political activists of both the right and the left. Kingdom Christians honor and obey their governments. But they don't imagine that their country is somehow "God's country" or a partner of God's kingdom. They know that God's kingdom is not of this world.

15

Has Anyone Done This in Real Life?

Jesus didn't merely *teach* us how a kingdom Christian should live. No, He lived the kingdom life Himself, leaving us a real-life pattern of kingdom living. And God chose the perfect time to send His Son to earth—a time that would precisely illustrate the very things Jesus would be teaching. To appreciate God's timing, we first have to understand some of the historical background leading up to the birth of Jesus.

Most of us remember how the Jews had been taken captive and exiled in Babylon. After the Persians overthrew Babylon, a remnant of Jews returned to Judea and rebuilt the temple. However, they were not an independent nation. The Persians continued to rule them for more than two hundred years. However, in 335 B.C., the Greeks defeated the Persians, and they became the new rulers over the Jews.

Finally, in 142 B.C., under Simon Maccabee, the Jews gained their independence. For the first time since the Babylonian Captivity, the Jews no longer had to submit to any foreign king. What a time of rejoicing that brought!

The Rise of Rome

While the Jews were struggling against the Greeks, Rome was slowly rising to become the dominant world power. Since Greece was the mutual enemy of both Rome and Judea, the Jews had signed a treaty of friendship with the Romans. In this treaty,

Rome affirmed that Judea was an independent nation, and it warned the Greeks not to try to reconquer Judea.[1]

Despite this treaty, in 66 B.C., the Romans took control of Judea themselves. And they soon began taxing the Jews quite heavily. And what were those taxes used for? To benefit the Jews? No. To support the very armies that were keeping the Jews subjugated.

The Jews had been a free people for over seventy-five years, and they weren't about to submit meekly to Rome. So at the time that Jesus was born, Jewish nationalism ran high. In fact, by the time Jesus reached manhood, there already had been a number of Jewish uprisings against the hated Romans. But Rome had brutally suppressed them all.

Jewish Traitors

However, not all Jews hated the Romans. In fact, some Jews profited from Rome. This was because the Romans did not personally collect the taxes they levied against the Jews. Rather, they farmed the job out to other Jews. After all, it was easier for a Jew to collect Jewish taxes than it was for a Roman. A Jew would be wise to the tricks and schemes his fellow countrymen might use to evade taxes. Furthermore, he lived right in the midst of them. He knew what was going on—who was prospering and who wasn't.

Traitors! Turncoats! The Jews detested the men who served as tax collectors for the hated Romans. "Just wait until we get our independence, and we'll hang you from the highest gallows," was surely what most Jews were thinking.

Naturally, most of the Jewish nation yearned eagerly for the coming of the promised Messiah. They firmly believed that surely *he* would lead the Jews in a victorious war of liberation against Rome. If the Maccabean family had been able to overthrow the Greeks, how much more so would the Messiah overthrow the Romans!

But then here comes this carpenter's son named Jesus, and He tells them to *love* their enemies. Love the Romans? That borders on treason! And what's this? If a Roman soldier commands you to carry his pack for one mile, carry it two miles instead? That's not only treason, that's insanity! Pay all of the onerous taxes that Caesar demands? Surely this can't be the long-awaited Messiah. And what's worse, this Jesus actually befriends the traitorous tax collectors and eats with them. (Luke 7:34).

If there was ever a time and place when a patriot was needed by his country, it was in first-century Judea. The Romans had no legal right to be in Judea. And the only way to get them out was going to be with the sword. To His fellow countrymen, Jesus was a coward and a traitor. Not only would He not join their cause, He treated the Romans like friends.

Why didn't Jesus help the Jews in their struggle for independence? Because He was simply a sojourner here on earth. He *lived* in Judea, but his *citizenship* was in God's kingdom. God's kingdom rendered Jewish national affairs irrelevant. What difference would it make to the kingdom of God whether the Jews obtained independence from Rome? Struggles for earthly power and earthly independence are meaningless in the realm of eternity. Earthly patriotism has no place in God's kingdom.

What Did the Disciples Do?

Some Christians make the claim that Jesus didn't get involved in the Jewish struggle for independence only because He had come to lay down His life as a ransom for mankind. But if this were the case, then surely His disciples—who were nearly all Jews—would have been closely involved with that struggle.

However, Jesus' disciples ignored the Jewish fight for freedom, just as Jesus had. In fact, from reading Acts and the Epistles, a person would never even know that such a struggle was going on. Acts and the Epistles never even mention it—even though most of the New Testament writers were Jews. That's how irrelevant the Jewish struggle for independence was to the kingdom of God.

In fact, history shows that Christian Jews didn't join the fight for Jewish independence. Rather, the Christians *abandoned* Jerusalem after the Jews had freed it (briefly) from the Romans. Instead of helping their countrymen, they fled to the city of Pella, outside Judea.[2] Like Jesus, the Jewish Christians in Judea weren't Jewish patriots. They didn't care if Judea was ruled by Romans or by Jews, for they had no interest in promoting *any* earthly kingdom—Jewish or Gentile!

Does that sound unpatriotic? Indeed, it was. The banner of Jesus' disciples wasn't "God and country!" It was God *or* country. Either a person's heart is entirely devoted to God's kingdom, or it's devoted to the kingdoms of this world. We can't have a divided heart or serve two masters. The love of country that the first century Jewish Christians had once had for Judea was now transferred to the kingdom of God.

It was the same for Roman Christians. Like their Jewish brethren, they didn't care whether Judea was ruled by Romans or Jews. They didn't take part in the war against the Jews, and there was no rift between Jewish and Roman Christians over the issue of Judea's independence.

As I have said, obtaining citizenship in the kingdom of God is similar to obtaining citizenship in the United States. To become a United States citizen, a person must transfer his allegiance from his former country to America. He can't maintain allegiance to both. It's no different when we seek citizenship in the kingdom of God.

16

But Is This Historic Christianity?

The things I've shared with you so far have probably spiritually stretched you a bit. In fact, they may have offended you. I realize that all of this is new territory for most Christians. But it's important that you realize that what I've been sharing with you isn't the personal viewpoint of David Bercot. This isn't another one of those books where the author says that everyone else through the centuries has misunderstood the Bible, and he is the only one finally to get it right. There's no shortage of such books, and I have little use for them.

No, what I have been sharing with you about war, nonresistance, and government is actually the *historical* position of the Christian church. These were the original teachings of the church, and they remained the universal or near-universal view of all Christians until the time of Constantine in the fourth century.

But I don't want you to take my word for this. I want you to hear this right from the horse's mouth. So on the pages that follow, I'm going to share with you the testimony of those Christians who lived closest to the time of the apostles. Please understand that these are not special proof-text quotations. I haven't carefully selected certain quotations from the early Christians, while leaving out ones that support a different view. I have made the early church my special field of study for the past twenty years, and I know of no one before the time of

Constantine who expressed a view different from what is presented below.

Living as Foreign Residents

When the church was still close to the time of the apostles, Christians truly lived in this world as strangers and foreign residents. They lived by kingdom values, which made them noticeably different from the world around them. Because their focus was on Jesus Christ and His kingdom, the public affairs of this world were essentially irrelevant to them.

Hermas, who wrote around the year A.D. 150, or perhaps earlier, from the city of Rome, had this to say:

"You know that you who are the servants of God dwell in a strange land. For your city is far away from this one. If, then, you know your city in which you are to dwell, why do you here provide lands, and make expensive preparations, and accumulate dwellings and useless buildings? He who makes such preparations for this city cannot return again to his own. ...Do you not understand that all these things belong to another, and are under the power of another? ...Take note, therefore. As one living in a foreign land, make no further preparations for yourself except what is merely sufficient. And be ready to leave this city, when the master of this city will come to cast you out for disobeying his law."[1]

Tatian, who lived in the Middle East, wrote a defense of Christianity around A.D. 160. In it, speaking on behalf of all Christians, he proclaimed: "I do not wish to be a king. I am not anxious to be rich. I decline military command. I detest fornication. I am not impelled by an insatiable love of [financial] gain to go to sea. I do not contend for chaplets. I am free from a mad thirst for fame. I despise death.. ...Die to the world, repudiating the madness that is in it! Live to God!"[2]

Clement of Alexandria was a Christian instructor in the church in Alexandria, Egypt. His writings, which date to around

A.D. 195, express the early Christian detachment from the politics, patriotism, and events of this world. He summed up the early Christian spirit when he wrote, "We have no country on earth. Therefore, we can disdain earthly possessions."[3]

Tertullian, who wrote between the years A.D. 195 and 212, was a fiery author who belonged to the church in Carthage, North Africa. Like his fellow Christians of that age, he testified that Christians have no interest in the political and governmental affairs around them:

"All zeal in the pursuit of glory and honor is dead in us. So we have no pressing inducement to take part in your public meetings. Nor is there anything more entirely foreign to us than the affairs of state. We acknowledge one all-embracing commonwealth—the world. We renounce all your spectacles. ...Among us, nothing is ever said, seen, or heard that has anything in common with the madness of the circus, the immodesty of the theater, the atrocities of the arena, or the useless exercise of the wrestling ground. Why do you take offense at us because we differ from you in regard to your pleasures?"[4]

Addressing his fellow Christians, Tertullian wrote, "As for you, you are a foreigner in this world, a citizen of Jerusalem, the city above. Our citizenship, the apostle says, is in heaven."[5]

Origen was one of the most brilliant men of his day. For several decades, he served as a teacher in the church in Alexandria. Later, he moved to Caesarea, where he was ordained as an elder or presbyter. One of Origen's most valuable works was his reply to Celsus, a pagan critic of Christianity:

"Celsus also urges us to 'take office in the government of the country, if that is necessary for the maintenance of the laws and the support of religion.' However, we recognize in each state the existence of another national organization that was founded by the Word of God. And we exhort those who are

mighty in word and of blameless life to rule over churches.
...It is not for the purpose of escaping public duties that
Christians decline public offices. Rather, it is so they may
reserve themselves for a more divine and necessary service in
the church of God—for the salvation of men."[6]

Cyprian served as bishop of Carthage around the year A.D.
250. He left a considerable body of correspondence with other
Christians and with other churches, which gives us valuable
insight into the beliefs of Christians in his day. Corroborating
what his fellow Christians were saying, he wrote, "We should
ever and a day reflect that we have renounced the world and are
in the meantime living here as guests and strangers."[7]

Nonresistance

Not only did the early Christians distance themselves from
government and other affairs of this world, they followed the
teachings of Jesus on nonresistance quite literally. Here are some
representative passages from the same writers I quoted from
above:

Clement of Alexandria wrote, "Christians are not allowed to
use violence to correct the delinquencies of sins."[8]

Tertullian confirmed this, saying, "For what difference is
there between provoker and provoked? The only difference is
that the former was the first to do evil, but the latter did evil
afterwards. Each one stands condemned in the eyes of the Lord
for hurting a man. For God both prohibits and condemns every
wickedness. In evil doing, there is no account taken of the order.
...The commandment is absolute: evil is not to be repaid with
evil.[9]

Again, Tertullian wrote, "The Lord will save them in that
day—even His people—like sheep. ...No one gives the name of
"sheep" to those who fall in battle with arms in hand, or those
who are killed when repelling force with force. Rather, it is given

only to those who are slain, yielding themselves up in their own place of duty and with patience—rather than fighting in self-defense."[10]

Lactantius was a well-educated Christian who wrote in the early part of the fourth century, saying, "When we suffer such ungodly things, we do not resist even in word. Rather, we leave vengeance to God."[11] And again, "The Christian does injury to no one. He does not desire the property of others. In fact, he does not even defend his own property if it is taken from him by violence. For he knows how to patiently bear an injury inflicted upon him."[12] And, "We do not resist those who injure us, for we must yield to them."[13]

Another early Christian writer to whom I have not introduced you is Athenagoras. He wrote a defense of Christianity around A.D. 175, in which he said, "We have learned not to return blow for blow, nor to go to law with those who plunder and rob us. Not only that, but to those who strike us on one side of the face, we have learned to offer the other side also."[14]

Christians in the Army

There is no evidence in either Christian or secular Roman writings that any Christians served in the Roman armies prior to A. D. 170. However, despite the early Church's condemnation of war and killing, the testimony of history clearly reveals that after A.D. 170, there were some Christians in the Roman army. Some writers have pointed to this fact, and from it they have tried to argue that the early Christians were not opposed to war after all. However, that's not an honest presentation of history, since the unanimous testimony of all the early Christian writers is that all Christians refused to engage in killing.

So how do we reconcile this seeming contradiction? An early Christian work entitled *The Apostolic Tradition,* compiled by Hippolytus around A. D. 200, clarifies the matter. In describing how the church should handle applicants for baptism, Hippolytus states: "A soldier of the civil authority must be taught not to kill men and to refuse to do so if he is commanded, and to refuse to take an oath. If he is unwilling to comply, he must be rejected for baptism. A military commander or civic magistrate who wears the purple must resign or be rejected. If an applicant or a believer seeks to become a soldier, he must be rejected, for he has despised God."[15]

It appears, then, that after A.D. 170 or so, the general policy of the church was that, if a soldier was converted to Christ, he did not have to leave the army to be baptized. Rather, he had to agree never to use the sword or take an oath. However, if a Christian civilian voluntarily joined the army, or if a discharged soldier willingly returned to the military, that person was put out of the church. Even as late as the early fourth century, this was still the general policy of the church.[16]

Why did the Church not require newly converted soldiers to leave the army before they could be baptized? Because normally a soldier enlisted for 25 years. Usually, his only way out of the military was either by death or by the completion of his commission. Remaining in the army without using the sword wouldn't have been as difficult as it might seem to us today. It should be remembered that the Roman Empire was at relative peace during this early period of Christianity, so it was quite feasible that a Christian could spend his entire life in the army and never be required to shed blood or use violence against anyone. In fact, during the period of early Christianity, soldiers primarily served in the capacities of civil peacekeepers and engineers—building roads, city walls, and aqueducts.

In fact, the earliest record of Christians being in the army (c. A.D. 170) specifically states that the Christians refused to use their swords, but only prayed. God answered their prayers by bringing a heavy rain that caused the invaders to retreat without any battle.[17]

Please understand that I'm not saying that the position of the early church after A.D. 170 toward newly converted soldiers was necessarily the correct position. I'm only saying that the church's position represented neither an acceptance of war nor an express rejection of nonresistance.

When Kingdoms Clash

Because it is not of this world, God's kingdom typically clashes with the kingdoms of this world. Like Peter and the apostles, the early Christians refused to break any of Jesus' commandments—even when Caesar demanded it.

Origen wrote, "What if the law of nature—that is, the law of God—commands what is opposed to the written law? Does not reason tell us to bid a long farewell to the written code ... and to give ourselves up to the Legislator, God. This is so even if in doing so it may be necessary to encounter dangers, countless labors, and even death and dishonor."[18]

Lactantius added, "When men command us to act in opposition to the law of God, and in opposition to justice, we should not be deterred by any threats or punishments that come upon us. For we prefer the commandments of God to the commandments of man."[19]

In short, nonresistance and separation from the world were the historic practices of Christianity.

Part III

What Is The Gospel
Of the Kingdom?

17

The Jesus Road to Salvation

"This gospel of the kingdom will be preached in all the world as a witness to all the nations, and then the end will come," Jesus had prophesied (Mt. 24:14). We have talked about some of the important values and commandments of the kingdom. But what exactly is the *gospel* of the kingdom?

The gospel of the kingdom is basically the *historic* Christian faith. It's what the Christians of the first few centuries believed and practiced. The kingdom gospel takes the totality of what Jesus and His apostles say on every subject. It's not built on proof-texts, and it doesn't depend on anything outside Scripture.

You've probably heard of the "Romans road to salvation." Well, in a sense, the gospel of the kingdom is the *Jesus* road to salvation. Its foundational beliefs are the direct teachings of Jesus Himself—not the writings of Paul. To be sure, Paul's writings are inspired by the Holy Spirit and are therefore inerrant and true. But Paul was building on the foundational teachings of Jesus. He wasn't starting a whole new gospel. In contrast, popular theology today—the gospel of easy-believism—begins with Paul. And, ignoring the context of Paul's letters, it interprets Paul in such a way as to make Jesus' teachings heretical.

"Come on! Now you're going too far," you may be thinking. "How does modern theology make Jesus' teachings *heretical*?" Well, what would happen if I went into most Bible-believing churches today and preached:

- The sins you commit each day will not be forgiven unless you forgive other people their sins (Mt. 6:15).

- To be saved, a person must *live* by the teachings of Jesus (Mt. 7:24,25).

- If we do not feed the hungry and clothe the poor, we will not see heaven (Mt. 25:32-46).

I know I would be called a heretic if I preached those things in most evangelical churches. But the kingdom gospel says: "I can believe Jesus! I can take Him at His word." That might sound like a truism for a Christian. Yet, most popular theological systems today require a Christian *not* to believe Jesus.

The Centrality of the Kingdom

Unlike most theological systems, the gospel of the kingdom centers on the kingdom of God, not on man's personal salvation. We cannot separate salvation from the kingdom. And we cannot be devoted to Jesus if we're not devoted to His kingdom.

Actually, all of Scripture looks toward this kingdom. From the beginning, God had purposed to establish a special kingdom. In fact, He prophesied about it during the Old Testament period. One of the most significant of these Old Testament prophecies is found in the second chapter of Isaiah:

"Now it shall come to pass in the latter days that the mountain of the Lord's house shall be established on the top of the mountains, and shall be exalted above the hills; and all nations shall flow to it. Many people shall come and say, 'Come, and let us go up to the mountain of the Lord, to the house of the God of Jacob; he will teach us His ways, and we shall walk in His paths.' For out of Zion shall go forth the law, and the word of the Lord from Jerusalem. He shall judge between the nations, and rebuke many people; they shall beat their swords into plowshares, and their spears into pruning hooks; nation shall not lift up sword against nation, neither shall they learn war anymore" (Isa. 2:2-4).

Most Christians read this passage as though it's talking about events after Christ returns to earth. And while it certainly applies to that time as well, its fulfillment is going on right now. In fact, it's been going on since Christ began His ministry. Jesus inaugurated His kingdom when He came to earth and invited His hearers to enter it.

At first, it was only the Jews who were invited to enter the kingdom, but then the way was open to everyone. And people from all nations began to "flow to it." Those who entered this kingdom "beat their swords into plowshares and their spears into pruning hooks." They no longer lifted up sword against each other, and they forgot war forever.

Jesus has made a covenant to bestow a kingdom upon those who walk in His ways: "You are those who have *continued with Me* in My trials. And I bestow upon you a kingdom, just as My Father bestowed one upon Me" (Luke 22:28,29). And again, "To him who overcomes I will grant to sit with me on My throne, as I also overcame and sat down with My Father on His throne" (Rev. 4:21).

Who Can Enter the Kingdom

God has opened to all humans the opportunity to be citizens of His kingdom. He didn't arbitrarily select a certain portion of mankind and destine them for the kingdom, while consigning the rest to eternal punishment. What would have been the purpose of that? If being in the kingdom was a matter of arbitrary choice, God would have chosen *everyone* to be in the kingdom, for He "is not willing that any should perish but that all should come to repentance" (2 Pet. 3:9).

God's selection of his eternal subjects is anything but arbitrary. No, God wants to fill His kingdom with that small minority of humankind who really love Him. The kingdom is for those who truly want to walk in His ways. And He wants in His kingdom only those who believe that He will do what He has promised. He wants only those who have faith that His laws and His ways are always right, good, and the best for His subjects.

And how does God determine who meets these requirements? He tests us. Did you notice Jesus' words above: "You are those who have continued with Me in My *trials*" and "To him who *overcomes*." There will be testing and trials for those who enter His kingdom. As Paul expressed it, "We must through many tribulations enter the kingdom of God" (Acts 14:22).

In fact, God has *always* tested mankind—even before His eternal kingdom had been announced. One of the first things He did after creating the first humans was to give them a test. He tested Noah by commanding him to build an ark. He tested Abraham by telling him to offer up Isaac as a sacrifice. As the Scriptures tell us, "The Lord tests the righteous" (Ps. 11:5). And again, "The refining pot is for silver and the furnace for gold, but the Lord tests the hearts" (Prov. 17:3). And, "The righteous God tests the hearts and minds" (Ps. 7:9).

The Three Principal Tests

There are three principal tests that God uses to weed out those who are unfit for His kingdom.

Test No. 1: Faith. The kingdom is invisible to anyone who has not been born again. "Unless one is born again, he cannot *see* the kingdom of God" (John 3:3). So it requires considerable faith for persons to even *want* to join a kingdom they can't see. Secondly, most of the promised blessings pertaining to the kingdom take place in the future. So a person has to have faith that God will actually do what He has promised.

This test of faith weeds out most of mankind. Most people don't have sufficient faith to believe in a kingdom they can't see and to count on promises that will be fulfilled only after they die.

Test No. 2: Commitment. As we have previously discussed, Jesus requires us to lay down *everything* for His kingdom. Our primary and ultimate allegiance has to be to our King, Jesus Christ, and His kingdom. Jesus requires our loyalty to Him and His kingdom to surpass even our loyalty and affection for our parents, children, spouse, country, and even our own lives.

The only kind of people Jesus wants in His kingdom are those who realize that "the kingdom of heaven is like treasure hidden in a field, which a man found and hid; and for joy over it he goes and sells all that he has and buys that field. Again, the kingdom of heaven is like a merchant seeking beautiful pearls, who, when he had found one pearl of great price, went and sold all that he had and bought it" (Mt. 13:44-46).

The majority of people who pass the test of faith stumble over the test of commitment. Sure, they'll believe in an invisible kingdom and eternal rewards—but only if it doesn't cost them much. To give up *everything*, based only on promises? No way.

Because few persons pass the test of commitment, we would reasonably assume that we're left with hardly anybody in the kingdom. However, Jesus indicated that many would enter His kingdom without ever making the needed commitment. He told His disciples, "Most assuredly, I say to you, he who does not enter the sheepfold by the door, but climbs up some other way, the same is a thief and a robber" (John 10:1). So a lot of people symbolically climb over the walls and try to steal kingdom citizenship that way.

Jesus again pointed this out in His parable of the wedding feast. "Those servants went out into the highways and gathered together all whom they found, both bad and good. And the wedding hall was filled with guests. But when the king came in to see the guests, he saw a man there who did not have on a wedding garment. So he said to him, 'Friend, how did you come in here without a wedding garment?' And he was speechless.

Then the king said to the servants, 'Bind him hand and foot, take him away, and cast him into outer darkness; there will be weeping and gnashing of teeth.' For *many* are called, but *few* are chosen" (Mt. 22:10-14).

So the people who pass the test of faith but fail the test of commitment are of a different breed than those who don't believe, the ones who refuse the wedding invitation altogether. Those who have no faith usually reject Jesus' claims and promises outright. They don't believe there even *is* a kingdom, and they make no effort to enter it.

However, those who fail the test of commitment often *do* believe Jesus' claims and promises. But they don't want to make the commitment that Jesus requires. In effect, they try to accept Jesus' invitation to the kingdom feast, while rejecting all of His conditions. How do they do this? They find someone who's giving out kingdom invitations without any conditions. So they figuratively climb over the wall in throngs.

According to Jesus, in the end the gate-crashers will comprise the majority of those in His kingdom. They are the "many" who are called, but they are not among the "few" who are chosen. They've never made any commitment to Christ or to His kingdom. They may believe that Jesus is their Savior, but they do not truly accept Him as their Lord.

Test No. 3: Obedience. In the previous chapters, I have talked about some of the laws of the kingdom. These laws help to take us from the values and mindset of this world to the values and mindset of God. They also serve as a test. Some of the believers who pass the tests of faith and commitment later become disobedient. Fortunately, many of these Christians later repent and return to the kingdom life.

However, others lose their love for Christ altogether. They no longer obey Him because they no longer love Him. In the end, they, too, will be weeded out of the kingdom: "The Son of Man will send out His angels, and they will gather out of His kingdom all things that offend, and those who practice lawlessness, and will cast them into the furnace of fire. There will be wailing and gnashing of teeth" (Mt. 13:41,42).

So, in the end, Jesus will have left in His kingdom only those who truly believe His promises and accept His conditions. These are those who love Him more than anything on earth and will gladly lay down their lives for Him. These are the ones that Jesus wants to spend eternity with.

That, in a nutshell, is the gospel of the kingdom.

Relationship with Our King

In the next chapter, we're going to be discussing how a person enters the kingdom of God. But before we do that, it's important that we understand that the essence of the kingdom gospel is *relationship*. To be sure, there are necessary theological doctrines, but theology isn't the *essence* of the gospel, nor the essence of Christianity.

When we become citizens of the kingdom, we enter into an ongoing relationship with our King. But this relationship is quite different from the type of relationship talked about in the modern gospel of easy believism. Jesus Himself explained the type of relationship He wants: "I am the true vine, and My Father is the vinedresser. Every branch in Me that does not bear fruit He takes away; and every branch that bears fruit He prunes, that it may bear more fruit. You are already clean because of the word which I have spoken to you. Abide in Me, and I in you. As the branch cannot bear fruit of itself, unless it abides in the vine, neither can you, unless you abide in Me" (John 15:1-4).

What does Jesus mean when He talks about our bearing fruit? Here are some examples of how this term is used in the New Testament:

"The fruit of the Spirit is love, joy, peace, longsuffering, kindness, goodness, faithfulness, gentleness, self-control. Against such there is no law. And those who are Christ's have crucified the flesh with its passions and desires. If we live in the Spirit, let us also walk in the Spirit.

"Bear fruits worthy of repentance. ...Every tree which does not bear good fruit is cut down and thrown into the fire. ...Now may He who supplies seed to the sower, and bread for food, supply and multiply the seed you have sown and increase the fruits of your righteousness, while you are enriched in everything for all liberality.

"And this I pray, that your love may abound still more, ... that you may be sincere and without offense till the day of Christ, being filled with the fruits of righteousness which are by Jesus Christ, to the glory and praise of God" (Gal. 5:22-25; Luke 3:8,9; 2 Cor. 9:10; Phil. 1:9-11).

These are the "fruits of righteousness" that will grow on us when we are attached to the vine of Jesus. They dovetail nicely with the kingdom values we have been talking about. But this fruit does not grow automatically. We have to *abide* in Christ and let His Father prune us. We must continue to walk in the Spirit. If we don't produce fruit, the Father will cut us off of the Vine. That's why citizenship in the Kingdom is relational. It depends on our abiding with Christ and yielding to Him and His Father.

But *how* do we abide with Christ? Jesus told us quite plainly: "If you keep My commandments, you will abide in My love, just as I have kept My Father's commandments and abide in His love" (John 15:10) So we abide in Jesus Christ, not by singing His praises, but by *obeying* Him. And what happens if we choose not to obey Him? He tells us quite frankly: "If anyone does not abide in Me, he is cast out as a branch and is withered; and they gather them and throw them into the fire, and they are burned" (John 15:6).

So our relationship with Jesus is not just *any* relationship, real or imagined. It's an obedient love relationship. Actually, the phrase, "obedient love relationship," is redundant. Because it's impossible to love Jesus without obeying Him. We can publicly proclaim how much we love Him, but, without obedience, it's all empty words. For He Himself said, "He who has My commandments and keeps them, it is he who loves me. And he who loves Me will be loved by My Father, and I will love him and manifest Myself to him" (John 14:21). So if we don't obey Jesus, we don't love Him. It's that simple. (He said it, not me!)

Fake Obedience

Now, when Jesus talks about obedience, He means real obedience—not the phony obedience that is so popular today. His real commandments are the ones *written* in the New Testament. But today's gospel of easy-believism says that we can ignore His written commandments. Most Christians treat His commandments as though they were merely suggestions. What really counts, according to this popular gospel, are the *subjective* impulses that come into our minds. These are supposedly the real commandments of Jesus, the ones to which we need to be obedient. And since these are supposedly revealed to each Christian personally, each person is the sole judge of what God has told him to do or not to do.

It's like a giant game of the Emperor's New Clothes. Millions of Christians pretend they're walking obediently to Christ, when the truth is that they ignore and trample on His teachings. In fact, they find many of His commandments quite odious. But they obey subjective impulses that come into their mind, so they delude themselves into thinking that they're obeying Jesus.

To be sure, Jesus *does* give personal direction to prophets and to those who are close to Him. But who did He say He would manifest Himself to? "He who loves Me will be loved by My Father, and I will love him *and manifest Myself to him*" (John

14:21). As we read earlier, those who love Him are those who keep His commandments. Jesus had already told His disciples, "He who is faithful in what is least is faithful also in much; and he who is unjust in what is least is unjust also in much" (Luke 16:10). If we can't be faithful in the *basic,* written directions that apply to all Christians, we're only kidding ourselves if we think Jesus is going to give us additional *special* directions.

If we aren't abiding on the vine, bearing fruit, then Jesus isn't manifesting Himself to us. In such a case, the special relationship we imagine we have with Christ is as deceptive as the relationship that many Catholics imagine they have with Mary.

It's Not the Mosaic Law All Over Again

However, when we talk about Jesus' commandments, please don't think that we accumulate brownie points by obeying Jesus' teachings or that we earn our salvation by doing so. As I said earlier, the only relationship acceptable to Him is a love relationship. Nor is this the Mosaic Law all over again. Jesus didn't fulfill that Law just to give us another long list of similar regulations in its place.

Jesus described what the Christian life is like when we love Him, saying, "Come to Me, all you who labor and are heavy laden, and I will give you rest. Take My yoke upon you and learn from Me, for I am gentle and lowly in heart, and you will find rest for your souls. For My yoke is easy and My burden is light" (Mt. 11:28-30).

But how can that be? Elsewhere, Jesus said that we had to forsake everything for Him. And He even said, "He who does not take his cross and follow after Me is not worthy of Me. He who finds his life will lose it, and he who loses his life for My sake will find it" (Mt. 10:38,39). That doesn't sound like an easy yoke.

Ah, now we come to the Kingdom Paradox. When viewed from the flesh, Jesus' statements seem contradictory. But in the

Spirit, they are completely harmonious. The kingdom life was never intended to be lived in the flesh. It is not a new Talmud. It was intended to be relational, lived in the Spirit. And it's only when we bury our life into Jesus Christ that His yoke can be easy and His burden light. His burden is light only when we detach ourselves from every entanglement of this life and lose ourselves in devoted service to our Lord.

It's only when our hearts are free from the cares and concerns of life in this world that we can say with John, "For this is the love of God, that we keep His commandments. And His commandments are not burdensome" (1 John 5:3). His commandments are easy when our only kingdom is the kingdom of God, and our souls have let go of everything else. On the other hand, Jesus' commandments are quite heavy and burdensome when we want to stay attached to this world and our earthly possessions, powers, and freedoms—but still try to serve Jesus.

kingdom were free gifts. They were saved by grace, not by their own righteousness.

What the New Birth Does

What happened to the crowd at Pentecost who believed and were born again? Many things—marvelous things! All of their past sins were forgiven and washed away. They had a clean slate before God. Furthermore, they were reborn as new creatures. That is, they underwent a supernatural, spiritual transformation. They became citizens of the kingdom. And these new citizens of the kingdom became a branch on the vine of Jesus (John 15:5). If they had died right then, they would have gone on to Paradise.

The Two Aspects of Salvation

According to the gospel of easy believism, that was the end of the matter. According to this popular gospel, every sin a person has ever committed, *plus* every sin they will commit in the future is forgiven when he or she is born again. This popular gospel declares that salvation is a one-time step. Once persons are born again, their salvation can be spoken of only in the past tense.

But Jesus never said any of those things. The gospel of easy believism is not the gospel of the kingdom. The gospel of the kingdom recognizes that there is both a *past* aspect of our salvation and a *future* one. Unless a person understands these two stages, he can never understand the gospel of the kingdom or the New Testament teaching on salvation.

A number of passages in the New Testament speak of salvation in the **past** tense. For example, the Scriptures say, "And the Lord added to the church daily those who *were* being saved. ...For by grace you *have been* saved through faith, and that not of yourselves; it is the gift of God. ... For we *were saved* in this hope" (Acts 2:47, Rom. 8:24, Eph.2:8).*

---

*These quotations are from the New King James Version. In the original KJV, these passages are all in the present tense.

So, when we are born again, we *have been* saved. We have been taken out of the world. We enter the kingdom of God right then. At that moment, our names are written in the Book of Life. When writing to the Philippians, Paul referred to his fellow workers as those "whose names are in the Book of Life" (Phil. 4:3).

But the Scriptures also refer to a **future** aspect of salvation. Jesus said, "You will be hated by all for My name's sake. But he who endures to the end *will be* saved" (Mt. 10:22). So there is a *future* aspect of salvation. We must endure to the end of our life for our salvation to be final. Again, Jesus made this quite clear in his illustration of the vine: "I am the vine, you are the branches. He who abides in Me, and I in him, bears much fruit; for without Me you can do nothing. If anyone does not abide in Me, he is cast out as a branch and is withered; and they gather them and throw them in the fire, and they are burned. ...Every branch in Me that does not bear fruit He takes away" (John 15:5,6,2).

This passage demonstrates the two aspects of salvation—past and future. Only those who have been born again, who have been saved, can be branches on this vine. That's the *past* aspect of salvation. Nevertheless, just because we're a branch on Jesus' vine doesn't mean that we are going to *stay* on the vine. If we don't maintain our obedient love relationship, God will lop us off of the vine. That's why we must also talk of the *future* aspect of salvation.

Because of this future aspect of salvation, Jesus told the Christians in Sardis, "He who overcomes shall be clothed in white garments, and I will not blot out his name from the Book of Life; but I will confess his name before My Father and before His angels" (Rev. 3:4,5). So just because our names were written in the Book of Life at our new birth, we can't presume that our names will stay there. In fact, Jesus' words to the church in Sardis sound like He was going to blot out the *majority* of their names. For He said, "You have a *few* names even in Sardis who have not defiled their garments; and they shall walk with me in white, for they are worthy" (Rev. 3:3,4).

It's because of this future aspect of salvation that Jesus told the Christians in Thyatira, "Hold fast what you have till I come. And he who overcomes, and *keeps My works until the end*, to him I will give power over the nations" (Rev. 2:25,26). And it's because of this future aspect of salvation that the Scriptures tell us:

- "Take heed to yourself and to the doctrine. Continue in them, for in doing this you *will save* both yourself and those who hear you" (1 Tim. 4:16).

- "*If we endure*, we shall also reign with Him. If we deny Him, He also will deny us" (2 Tim. 2:12).

- "For if, after they have escaped the pollutions of the world through the knowledge of the Lord and Savior Jesus Christ, they are again entangled in them and overcome, the latter end is worse for them than the beginning. For it would have been better for them not to have known the way of righteousness, than having known it, to turn from the holy commandment delivered to them" (2 Pet. 2:20,21).

Sometimes We Miscommunicate

It pains me to hear kingdom Christians argue with each other about salvation, not acknowledging that there are both past and future aspects. I've heard or read exchanges between kingdom Christians who resemble Christian No. 1 and Christian No. 2 in the following scene:

Christian No. 1 is a kingdom Christian who loves Jesus and lives by His teachings. But he belongs to a church that empha-sizes the *future* aspect of salvation. Christian No. 2 likewise loves and obeys Jesus, but he belongs to a church that empha-sizes the *past* aspect of salvation. Unfortunately, even though both churches in reality believe in both aspects of salvation, neither church places an *equal* emphasis on the two aspects. As a result, their members often have exchanges similar to the following:

Christian No. 2: "Brother, have you been saved?"

Christian No. 1: "What do you mean, 'have I *been* saved.' Of course not! It would be presumptuous for anyone to say that he is already saved. Jesus will make that determination once I die."

Christian No. 2: "Well, if you don't know now that you have already been saved, it will be too late when you die. You're holding to a false gospel."

Christian No. 1: "No, you're the one holding to a false gospel—a gospel of presumption!"

It might sound like these two Christians are light years apart in their beliefs. And perhaps they truly are. But often their beliefs are quite similar. If they are truly kingdom Christians, each of their churches probably hold to both the past and future aspects of salvation. Yet, because each church emphasizes one aspect almost to the exclusion of the other, their members have a confused understanding of salvation. And they cannot clearly articulate the gospel of the kingdom, even though they hold to it in their hearts.

Asking someone, "Have you been saved?" is like asking a person, "Have you quit stealing from your employer?" An honest employee can't answer that question with a simple yes or no, can he? He can only thwart this deceptive question by replying, "I have never stolen from my employer, so there's nothing to quit."

The salvation question is just as deceptive, although unintentionally so. A simple yes or no will not suffice. Someone who understands the gospel of the kingdom must counter the inherent deceptiveness of the question by responding, "Yes, I was saved when I was born again. However, my final salvation will not be determined until I have endured to the end."

Before leaving this subject of salvation, I want to add a quick statement about security. We kingdom Christians don't live in constant anguish and insecurity. No, we live in joyous anticipation of the promises that Jesus has made. And we know that Jesus' grace will enable us to stay on the vine—so long as we continue to love and obey Him. However, at the same time, we must not become overconfident and presumptuous. Nor should we ever lose our fear of our Lord. Yes, we enjoy true security, but it's conditional security.

Salvation by Theology?

Please understand that, to be saved, a person doesn't have to be able to articulate the various things I've discussed in the last two chapters. Jesus is not that interested in what we say. He's primarily interested in what we *do*. He made this clear in one of His parables: "A man had two sons, and he came to the first and said, 'Son, go, work today in my vineyard.' He answered and said, 'I will not,' but afterward he regretted it and went. Then he came to the second and said likewise. And he answered and said, 'I go, sir,'" but he did not go. Which of the two did the will of his father? They said to Him, 'The first'" (Mt. 21:28-31). It's what we *do*, not what we *say*.

Jesus' teachings were designed to be understandable by the simplest of people. No education was necessary. If our theology requires someone to study for years to master it and be able to teach others, something is seriously wrong. Neither Jesus nor His apostles founded any seminaries, because none are needed for the gospel of the kingdom. Kingdom Christians rarely establish seminaries. And when they do, they invariably end up losing the kingdom gospel.

The kingdom gospel is so simple, so unattached from complicated theology, that for the first 300 years of Christianity, the following statement of faith sufficed:

"I believe in God the Father Almighty, Maker of heaven and earth. And in Jesus Christ his only Son our Lord; who was conceived by the Holy Ghost, born of the virgin Mary, suffered under Pontius Pilate, was crucified, dead, and buried; he descended into hell [Hades]; the third day he rose again from the dead; he ascended into heaven, and sits at the right hand of God the Father Almighty; from thence he shall come to judge the quick and the dead. I believe in the Holy Spirit; the holy catholic [universal] church; the communion of saints; the forgiveness of sins; the resurrection of the body; and the life everlasting.[2]

This simple statement of faith usually is known as the Apostles Creed. To be sure, the early Christians had teachings and views that went beyond that simple statement of faith. But that was all the theology a Christian *had* to believe. If some Christians wanted to dig further, they were welcome to, so long as they didn't take themselves too seriously and go beyond the things handed down.

If the Apostles Creed was adequate theology for the first three centuries of Christianity, it was adequate theology for the centuries that followed. And it's still adequate theology for today. The institutional Church didn't grow into a better understanding of Christ once it abandoned the gospel of the kingdom. Rather, it has grown further and further from the real Christ.

Texas Railroad Commission in Austin. It probably sounds strange to a non-Texan, but in Texas the state agency that regulates oil and gas production is the Railroad Commission. Anyway, we had a hearing about changing the field rules for a particular gas field. Because our company had its own helicopter, we decided to fly down to Austin. On the way down, we stopped and picked up a petroleum engineer and a geologist from Fina, who also were going to the same hearing.

The meeting in Austin went fine. During the trip back, I sat up front with the pilot and was watching him fly the helicopter. I said to myself, "That doesn't look very hard; I can probably do that myself." So I asked the pilot if he could let me man the controls for awhile, and he readily agreed. I asked him what I needed to do, and he showed me a little ball on the instrument dial. "All you have to do is to keep that ball in the center of the dial," he explained to me. Well, that sounded easy enough. So I told him I was ready, and he handed me the controls.

However, I soon found out that keeping the ball on the center was anything but easy for a novice. The controls were so sensitive that the slightest move sent the helicopter reeling in one direction and then back the other direction when I tried to correct my error. So we went zig-zagging across the Texas skies as I tried desperately to keep that little ball in the center of the dial. Finally, the engineer from Fina in the backseat, who was feeling nauseous, shouted, "Get that lawyer away from the controls!" The pilot lost no time in taking the controls back over. When we dropped the two Fina men off, they both gave me nasty looks.

In fact, it turned out that we had to return to Austin for a second hearing a month later. So we called up Fina to see if their engineers wanted to ride with us again. They politely declined, saying they would just drive down and meet us there. I think they were afraid that I might be at the controls again.

Living the Christian life is a lot like trying to fly a helicopter. We have to keep in the center of the road. And it isn't easy to do that, because the road is narrow. The confines of this road don't allow us to go zig-zagging along. We must not zig into the chasm of worldliness or zag into the chasm of self-righteousness. We have to keep straight on course.

Can We Speak Against Sin?

Jesus told us not to judge others. But He didn't tell us that we can't speak out against sin. Paul, James, Peter, and other New Testament writers spoke out against sin in the church. Not self-righteously, but in obedience to Jesus.

This book is being written to tell Christians and unbelievers about the kingdom gospel—a gospel that is hardly preached any more. And in this book, I point to a lot of shortcomings of today's Church and to some of the deviant turns the Church has made through the centuries. I talk about the "gospel of easy-believism." I contrast "kingdom Christians" with those who are merely professing Christians.

But I can assure you that I'm not writing this book in a spirit of self-righteousness. For I well know that David Bercot needs this message as much as any of his readers. My only prayer is that reading this book will challenge my readers as profoundly as writing this book has challenged me. I honestly do not judge individuals or presume to know their final standing with Christ. Yet, I am quite concerned about the state of Christianity today. And that's why I'm writing this book.

At the same time, I know some of my readers will feel I shouldn't even use the term "Christian" when I talk about those who love the world, those who hold to serious theological errors, and those who have committed gross evils in the name of Christ. So I again want to make it clear that when I use the term "Christian" throughout this book, I am referring to those who *profess* to be Christians. The authenticity of their Christianity is certainly open to question, but I will leave that up to Jesus.

I should also explain that I use the term, "kingdom Christians," to refer to Christians who are serious about being a citizen of God's kingdom and who abide in Christ through an obedient love relationship. However, by using that term, I do not mean to imply that everyone else is categorically assigned to judgment. Again, that's Jesus' decision to make, not mine.

Finally, I should clarify that when I use the term "Church" (with a capital "C"), I'm referring to the *institutional* Church. I'm talking about all of the bodies of professing Christians. Once again, to what extent the institutional Church coincides with the body of genuine Christian believers, I'm quite content to leave in Jesus' hands.

Other Laws of the Kingdom

The four or five laws of the kingdom that we've examined certainly are some of the more challenging teachings of Jesus. But they are only a small portion of the laws our King has given us. The rest of His laws and teachings are contained throughout the New Testament. The fact that I haven't discussed these other laws doesn't mean that they're not just as important as the ones on which we've focused.

The largest single collection of kingdom commandments is found in the Sermon on the Mount. If you're serious about being a kingdom Christian, I urge you to read the Sermon on the Mount afresh, pondering each teaching and evaluating your own life as measured by these teachings.

20

The Kingdom Can't Be Kept Quiet

When we join something that's going to cause the world to hate us, it's natural to want to keep it quiet. Why stir up trouble? Let's keep everything hush-hush. But our King won't let us keep His kingdom a secret: "Whatever I tell you in the dark, speak in the light; and what you hear in the ear, preach on the housetops" (Mt. 10:27).

We must remember that a person can't even see the kingdom of God unless he's born again. So how is anyone even going to know about this kingdom—unless we who are born again tell them? Jesus hasn't hired an advertising agency to get the word out about His kingdom. Instead, He has commissioned all of his citizens to be news-spreaders.

As soon as Jesus returned from the wilderness after His baptism, He immediately began preaching. And what did He preach? Matthew tells us: "From that time Jesus began to preach and to say, 'Repent, for the kingdom of heaven is at hand'" (Mt. 4:17). Jesus lost no time traveling throughout Galilee, preaching the "gospel of the kingdom." And He quickly began recruiting others to join His kingdom.

Jesus not only taught His disciples about the kingdom of God, but He also gave them specific training on how to preach the gospel of the kingdom to others. Right after He selected His twelve apostles, Jesus sent them out to preach. And what were they to preach? "As you go, preach, saying, 'The kingdom of heaven is at hand'" (Mt. 10:7). Later, Jesus trained seventy disciples and sent them throughout the land in groups of two. Again, He told them that after they entered a city, they were to "heal the sick there, and say to them, 'the kingdom of God has come near to you'" (Luke 10:9).

Before His death, Jesus prophesied, "This gospel of the kingdom will be preached in all the world as a witness to all the nations, and then the end will come" (Mt. 24:14). And among the last things He said to His apostles was: "Go therefore and make disciples of all the nations, baptizing them in the name of the Father and of the Son and of the Holy Spirit, teaching them to observe *all* things that I have *commanded* you" (Mt. 28:19,20).

So kingdom preaching was not going to end when Jesus left the earth. His disciples were to preach all of the things He had taught them about the kingdom. They were to recruit other citizens for the kingdom. The whole world would hear the good news about this upside-down kingdom! And with God behind them, nobody could stop them!

Just Keep Quiet and We'll Leave You Alone

Not surprisingly, it was this noisy aspect of the kingdom that caused most of the problems. If the disciples had retreated to some desert oasis and started a spiritual community there away from the world, there probably would have been no clash with the governmental authorities. After all, neither the Jewish nor the Roman governments bothered the Qumran community by the Dead Sea (until the Jewish war of independence). If the disciples of Jesus had followed the same pattern, they might have lived long and peaceful lives.

But that wouldn't have been acceptable to the King. He, too, could have lived a long and peaceful life if He had just kept quiet. But the Father had sent Jesus *into* the world, not away from it. And Jesus had done the same with His disciples. Their mission was to spread the news about the kingdom, not to hide it!

So no sooner had the Spirit fallen on the apostles than they were out preaching Jesus Christ and telling their fellow Jews about His kingdom. Up to now, the Jewish authorities had left the apostles alone. But this was too much. So they arrested the apostles and told them to quit teaching the people about Jesus. But the apostles fearlessly replied, "Whether it is right in the sight of God to listen to you more than to God, you judge. For we cannot but speak the things which we have seen and heard" (Acts 4:19,20). Later, they told the authorities, "We ought to obey God rather than men" (Acts 5:28,29).

Soon after that, the Jewish authorities put to death Stephen, one of the disciples. And they began imprisoning as many Christians as they could find. But even that didn't slow down the kingdom. The Christians who fled from Jerusalem preached the word everywhere they went (Acts 8:4). Kingdom Christians just won't keep quiet! When the gospel of the kingdom reached Thessalonica, the Jews there protested to the authorities, "These who have turned the world upside down have come here too!" (Acts 17:6).

Kingdom Preaching

One basic aspect of the kingdom is that it can't be kept secret. It must be proclaimed! It must continue to bring in new subjects. Whenever a group of kingdom Christians are silenced, whenever they lose interest in witnessing, they begin to deteriorate spiritually. It's like a stream of water that's no longer moving. Pretty soon algae begins to grow. Eventually, the water becomes brackish and smells putrid. Likewise, stagnant Christians can become a stench to their King.

Part IV

A Hybrid Is Born

21

What Happened To The Kingdom Gospel?

So far, we've seen what Jesus and His apostles taught, and we've seen how the church for nearly three hundred years followed Jesus' teaching quite literally. Yet, these teachings aren't practiced by most Christians today. So what happened?

During the last forty years of the third century (from approximately A.D. 260 to 300), the church enjoyed an unprecedented time of peace. There was sporadic local persecution, but no empire-wide persecution. This seemed like a blessing to the wearied, beleaguered church, which had survived wave after wave of vicious persecution from the time it had been planted.

However, the church was beginning to lose its first love. As a result, it forgot that Jesus said it's a blessing when we're persecuted. The church let its guard down. With persecution off their minds, Christians began to bicker with one another. Theology (beyond the basics) had always been a secondary thing to the church, but now it came to the forefront. Theological battles raged across the Empire.

Christians also forgot Jesus' words about ecclesiastical power: "You know that the rulers of the Gentiles lord it over them, and those who are great exercise authority over them. Yet it shall not be so among you; but whoever desires to become great among you, let him be your servant. And whoever desires to be first among you, let him be your slave" (Mt. 20:25-27). Instead of desiring to be servants of all, the bishops of the major cities of the Empire—Rome, Antioch, and Alexandria—began jockeying among themselves for power. The bishop of Rome began claiming that he was the successor of Peter and that he had jurisdiction over all the other churches.

Christians also began to lose their separation from the world. Discipline became lax, particularly in Rome. For the first time, Christians began assuming governmental positions. Nevertheless, the church of A.D. 300 was still far more disciplined and more separated from the world than the vast majority of churches today. But it had backslidden considerably from what it once had been.

Then, suddenly, the peace of forty years ended, catching most Christians off guard. In the year 303, Emperor Diocletian initiated the most sweeping persecution the church had ever experienced. Christian prayer houses everywhere were burned down, and the Scriptures were assigned to bonfires. Soldiers dragged men and women into prison and tortured them with every kind of hideous torment of which twisted minds could think. Although many Christians compromised during this persecution, the church as a whole stood firm. Although they had lost some of their kingdom zeal, Christians were still quite ready to die for their King.

The persecution continued blazing against the Christians for eight long years, but the government could not destroy the church. In the end, the kingdom of God prevailed. It had not been an easy battle, but Christians had shown Satan that he could not defeat the kingdom through brute force. Exhausted, Emperor Diocletian issued the Edict of Toleration in 311— which ended the persecution. In admitting defeat, the emperor asked the Christians for their prayers. He then retired from office and later committed suicide. Satan had been defeated![1]

Or had he? What the church didn't realize is that Satan had one more weapon in his arsenal: guile. If he and the world couldn't defeat the kingdom, they would *join* it. Or rather, they would cunningly entice the Christians to join *them.*

The Edict of Milan

In 312, Christians received some more good news. Constantine, one of the co-regents who replaced Diocletian, had defeated his rival, Maxentius, at Rome. This was good news because Constantine was favorably disposed toward Christians. In fact, during the Diocletian persecution, Christians who lived in the regions under Constantine's control had been protected from most of the persecution.

The year 313 brought even more good news. Constantine and his co-ruler, Licinius, issued a new edict that put Christianity on an equal level with all other religions. This edict, known as the Edict of Milan, said: "[We resolve] to grant both to the Christians and to all men freedom to follow the religion which they choose, so that whatever heavenly divinity exists may be favorably inclined to us and to all who live under our government."[2] Other decrees of Constantine and Licinius went further. Any property confiscated from Christians during the Diocletian persecution was to be returned to them. Furthermore, all of the prayer houses that had been burned down or otherwise destroyed during the persecution would be rebuilt at public expense.

The Edict of Milan did not make Christianity the state church. It merely instituted freedom of religion in the Roman Empire. However, soon afterward, Constantine adopted a decidedly pro-Christian policy for the portion of the Roman Empire that he governed. (Licinius, his co-ruler, still governed much of the eastern Empire.) The fourth century church historian, Eusebius—who was completely taken in by all of this—describes Constantine's actions:

"The pious emperor, glorying in the confession of the victorious cross, proclaimed the Son of God to the Romans with great boldness of testimony. ...All, indeed, with one voice and one mouth, declared that Constantine had appeared by the grace of God as a general blessing to mankind. ...

"The emperor also personally sought the company of God's ministers. He distinguished them with the highest possible respect and honor. He showed them favor in both word and deed as persons consecrated to the service of his God. Accordingly, they were admitted to his table. ...He also made them his travel companions, believing that God would thus help him, since they were His servants."[3]

"Blessing" the Church

So in a matter of a few years, Christians went from being a persecuted minority to being the court favorites. Unfortunately, this governmental favor did not come unfettered. When a government decides to help Christianity in some way, that help usually comes with some degree of government involvement in the church.

For example, I've mentioned that Constantine had decreed that the prayer houses destroyed in the persecution were to be rebuilt at public expense. Since the state was furnishing the funds, Constantine naturally felt that the state was entitled to some say as to how the new prayer houses should look.

Constantine genuinely desired to promote Christianity throughout the empire. Yet, he was an unregenerated man of the world. So, naturally the only way he knew to promote Christianity was through human means. He felt quite certain that the previous prayer houses of the Christians would be insufficient to accommodate the large numbers of people who would be coming to the church now that he, the emperor, was promoting Christianity. So he issued a statute that *required* places of Christian worship throughout the Empire to be substantially enlarged. Not only that, he put the construction of these new church buildings under the oversight of the Roman provincial governors.[4]

In fact, Constantine decided that the buildings should not merely be larger—but that they should also be more magnificent. Why should the Christian places of worship be mere houses or simple buildings, when pagan temples were so ornate? Shouldn't it be the other way around? Shouldn't the true religion have the most impressive buildings? Following this human reasoning, Constantine directed the new church buildings to be adorned with impressive colonnades and vaulted ceilings. He arrayed many of them with beautiful fountains and elegant marble floors. Constantine wanted it to be difficult for an unbeliever to walk past a church building without being tempted to peer inside to see more of its beauty.

Constantine racked his brain to think of other ways he could "bless" the church. For he sincerely believed that if he blessed the church, God would bless the Empire.

Before long, Constantine noticed that most of the Christian bishops and elders lived in poverty. He didn't think this was at all suitable for the representatives of the one true God. So he began paying salaries to the bishops and elders out of state funds. He even gave one of his residences, the Lateran Palace, to the bishop of Rome and his successors. Constantine also exempted all the bishops, elders, and deacons from taxation, and he exempted all church buildings from property taxes. Since Roman taxes were quite high (and they got even higher during Constantine's reign), these tax exemptions were a considerable benefit.

And the best part of it was that no strings were attached to these salaries and tax exemptions. Or so it seemed.

The Donatists

In North Africa, there had been a rift in the church over the question of church leaders who had compromised during the Diocletian persecution. Those Christians who refused to have anything to do with the leaders who had compromised were eventually known as Donatists. The others were known as Catholics. As a result of this rift, there were two bishops, two sets of elders, and two bodies of believers in Carthage, North Africa—the Donatist and the Catholic. Each claimed to be the legitimate church in that city.

In the past, this controversy would have been purely an internal church matter. But Constantine's "blessings" to the church created a whole new issue. Which bishop would receive the handsome salary offered by the state? Which bishop and which group of presbyters would receive tax exemption? Which bishop would have charge of the magnificent new church building that had been rebuilt at state expense?

Constantine's government initially recognized Caecilian, the Catholic bishop, as the rightful bishop of Carthage. So Caecilian was provided with a state salary, and he and all of his clergy were exempted from taxes. Outraged by this, the Donatists filed a complaint with the Roman proconsul of Africa, saying that they were the lawful church of Carthage. The proconsul forwarded the complaint to Constantine. Not knowing what to think, Constantine appointed the bishop of Rome to hear the case. Not surprisingly, the lax bishop of Rome sided with the Catholic bishop, Caecilian, who was his friend.

Feeling that this was not a fair trial, the Donatists asked Constantine to appoint someone more impartial to hear their case. So Constantine called for a council of bishops in the province of Gaul (modern-day France) to hear the case. The council met at Arles in 314, and they once again sided with the Catholics. So the Donatists appealed one last time to Constantine. This time, he personally heard the case, and he also ruled in favor of the Catholics.

The Donatist controversy set the precedent for the Roman emperor to convene church councils and even to personally adjudicate church matters. The wall between church and state had largely crumbled. Christians were now willing to mix the affairs of God's kingdom with the affairs of this world.

Constantine, the New Bishop

Constantine appointed Christians to high government posts because he believed that God would bless his rulership if his government was staffed with Christians. Ironically, just a few years before, Lactantius had said: "God might have bestowed upon His people [i.e., the Christians] both riches and kingdoms, as He had given previously to the Jews, whose successors and posterity we are. However, He would have Christians live under the power and government of others, lest they should become corrupted by the happiness of prosperity, slide into luxury, and eventually despise the commandments of God. For this is what our ancestors did."[5]

As Lactantius had unwittingly predicted, once Christians came into power, they did become corrupted, they slid into luxury, and they eventually despised the commandments of God.

By now, Constantine viewed himself as the "bishop of those outside the church." In other words, the church bishops were responsible to shepherd those in the church, and Constantine was responsible to be the spiritual shepherd of those outside the church. As the secular bishop, Constantine issued a decree that prohibited government officials from offering sacrifices to idols or practicing divination.

But before long, Constantine even began to see himself as the governor or "universal bishop" of those *inside* the church.

22

The Kingdom of Theology

The year 325 found the church embroiled in a heated controversy over the nature of the Son of God and His Father. The main
two proponents in this dispute were Alexander, the bishop of
Alexandria, and Arius, an elder or presbyter in that same city.
Viewing himself as a sort-of universal bishop, Constantine took
it upon himself to convene a worldwide council of bishops in the
city of Nicaea in order to resolve this dispute. He even presided
over the council.

Let me give you some background understanding about the
nature of the Arian heresy discussed at the council.

Understanding "Nature" and "Order"

Ever since the first century, the church had held to some basic
understandings about the Father and the Son. These beliefs were
well-grounded in Scripture. To grasp the church's historic
teachings about the Father and Son, a person has to understand
the difference between "nature" and "order." In theology,
"nature" or "substance" refers to the essence or class to which a
person or creature belongs. All humans are of the same nature or
substance. No man or woman is any less human than anybody
else. However, humans differ from one another as to order or
positions of authority. The President has authority over the Vice-
President. These two persons are the same in *nature*, but they
differ in *order*.

Now, the church has always taught that the Father and the Son are of the same nature or substance. The Son is not something foreign to the Father. He does not have the nature of the angels, but rather He possesses the same nature as the Father. Both the Father and the Son are equally Divine. The Son possesses true Godhood, just as does the Father.

However, there is a difference of *order* or authority between the Father and Son. Equality of nature does not mean equality of order. Just as there is a hierarchy of order between a husband and wife, there is a hierarchy of order within the Trinity. Paul explained this, saying, "I want you to know that the head of every man is Christ, the head of woman is man, and the head of Christ is God" (1 Cor. 11:3). The Father has authority over the Son. The Son is sent by the Father. The Son does the will of the Father. And the Son sits at the Father's right hand. This hierarchy of order cannot be reversed. But this difference in order in no way diminishes the Son's Divinity.

When Christians do not understand the difference between nature and order, they end up with a confused understanding of the Trinity. And that was the problem with the fourth century elder, Arius. He confused nature and order. Because there is a hierarchy of *order* in the Trinity, Arius mistakenly believed that there is also a hierarchy of *nature* or substance. So he maintained that the Son is not of the same nature as the Father. Rather, he said the Son is somewhere between the angels and the Father.

Constantine's Solution

As we have already seen, to clear up this matter, Constantine convened a worldwide council in the city of Nicaea. However, when the Council of Nicaea first convened, the supporters of Arius soon saw that they were going to lose the debate, for they were heavily outnumbered. At that point, they made liberal concessions and asked for tolerance in light of the incomprehensible nature of the issues under discussion. They even agreed to use no language or expressions that are not found in Scripture.

However, instead of reaching out to Arius and his supporters in love, working to end this theological division in the Church, the orthodox bishops received with contempt their concessions and their proposals for reconciliation. In fact, the bishops purposefully sought a solution that would force an irreconcilable wedge between the two parties.

Yet, no orthodox bishop was willing to suggest that the council do what had previously been unthinkable: adding something to Scripture. So the council was at an impasse. At this point, Constantine again intervened to "help" the church. He suggested that the bishops change the simple creed that had served the church for 300 years and add to it the word *homoousian* (of the same nature)—saying that the Father and Son were *homoousian*. The bishops soon accepted Constantine's solution and adopted this new creed.

As a succinct statement of the Divinity of Christ and of the relationship of the Father to the Son, I think the Nicene Creed is one of the best. It accurately encapsulates what Christians had believed about the Son of God from the days of the apostles up through the time of Constantine.[1]

Nicaea: A Major Turning Point for the Church

Nevertheless, Nicaea marks a major turning point in Christian history—a turn for the worse. That's because it introduced four new corruptions into the Church that took the Church further and further from the kingdom of God and from original Christianity:

1. The Persecuted Become the Persecutors

After the Council of Nicaea, the Church rightfully excommunicated Arius, who was a divisive man teaching erroneous doctrines. In the first three centuries of Christianity, the matter would have ended there. However, Constantine went further and banished Arius from his home city of Alexandria to the province of Illyricum, across the Mediterranean Sea. Constantine then ordered all of the writings of Arius to be burned. But worst of all, he declared that anyone found with Arius' writings would be put to death.[2] Instead of protesting these measures, the bishops applauded them.

Fourteen years before, Christians were the *persecuted*. Now they were the *persecutors*. Constantine came to believe that the most important duty of the civil magistrate was to preserve and support the "catholic" faith. To Constantine, any heretics or schismatics who opposed his commands were nothing but obstinate criminals. He eventually began taking almost verbatim the language from the decrees of Diocletian (who had inaugurated the last great persecution against Christians) and applying that language to various decrees intended to suppress heretics.[3]

This new type of persecution was far more poisonous in its effects than anything pagan Rome had previously wrought. This new persecution didn't target everyone who believed in Jesus as their Lord and Savior, the way the pagan persecution had. Rather, it targeted only those who the institutional Church labeled as heretics. To be sure, the Arians were heretics. But that didn't justify persecuting them. Moreover, many of those the Church persecuted thereafter were not heretics at all—but were instead genuine kingdom Christians.

This new persecution not only frequently targeted innocent kingdom Christians, but it also bloodied and defiled the hands of the Christian persecutors themselves, dragging them down to the depraved conduct of the world. Christians began to imagine they could use the tools of Satan if they did so for a "godly" purpose. This new persecution made it harder for the Church ever to be reformed or restored to its original purity. That's because any potential reformers were soon singled out as heretics and then silenced.

By instituting Church-sponsored persecution, the Council of Nicaea undid any good that would have otherwise come from the Council.

2. Going Beyond Scripture

In many ways, the impact the Nicene Council had on *theology* was even more serious than its impact on persecution. That's because the Nicene Creed made orthodoxy turn on a word that doesn't even appear in Scripture: *homoousian*. This Greek word means "of the same nature," and it accurately describes the relationship of the Son of God to the Father, as we have discussed. I have no objection to the use of the word.

However, in making a word that is never used in Scripture the touchstone of orthodoxy, Nicaea opened a Pandora's box. That's because basically the Nicene Council was saying that Scripture is inadequate. It was saying that there are essential truths—without which we cannot be saved—that are not stated with the needed specificity in Scripture. Instead of trusting God and believing that His Scriptures were adequate, the bishops at the first Council of Nicaea had resorted to a human solution to resolve the Arian dispute. And the fruit that followed did far more damage to the Church than any damage Arius had done.

Because the bishops had gone beyond Scripture, they almost immediately found it necessary to declare that the decision of the Nicene Council was inspired by God and was equal to Scripture. In other words, special revelation had not ended with the apostles. After a hiatus of over two hundred years, the Holy Spirit was supposedly again giving special revelation on the same level as Scripture. To this very day, the Roman Catholic and Eastern Orthodox churches expressly declare that the pronouncements of the Nicene Council and the other so-called ecumenical councils have the same authority as Scripture.

As the centuries rolled by, the Church added more and more extra-Scriptural language to the dogma of Christianity. They even added language that was *contrary* to Scripture. For example, four hundred and sixty years later, in A.D. 785, another ecumenical council, which also met at Nicaea, made the following pronouncement:

> "Just as the figure of the precious and life-giving Cross, so also the venerable and holy images, as well in painting and mosaic as of other fit materials, should be set forth in the holy churches of God, and on the sacred vessels and on the vestments. ...

> "To these should be given due salutation and honorable worship [Greek: *proskineo*], not indeed that true worship of faith [Greek: *latria*] which pertains alone to the Divine Nature. But to these, as to the figure of the precious and life-giving cross and to the Book of the Gospels and to the other holy objects, incense and lights may be offered according to the ancient pious custom. For the honor which is paid to the image passes on to that which the image represents, and he who worships the image worships the subject represented in it. ...Thus we follow Paul, who spoke in Christ, and the whole divine apostolic company and the holy Fathers, holding fast the traditions which we have received. ...

> "We salute the venerable images. We place under anathema those who do not do this. ...Anathema to those who do not salute the holy and venerable images. Anathema to those who call the sacred images idols."[4]

Scripture, as well as the early church, had condemned the use of images. Now the Church condemned those who *didn't* use images.

3. Theology Becomes the Essence of Christianity

After Nicaea, the Church came to imagine that the essence of Christianity is theology. It supposed that persons can be Christians simply by giving mental assent to a list of doctrines—without a radical change in their lives.

What's more, the Church was no longer satisfied with the basic theology of the kingdom gospel. Rather, it now focused on fine points of theology that the ordinary Christian would probably not grasp. So Nicaea gave birth to a whole new type of Christian: the theologian or church father. And ever since the emergence of these theologians, the Church has not known a single year of peace free from theological controversies.

The fourth century bishop, Hilary of Pointers, said, "The partial or total resemblance of the Father and of the Son is a subject of dispute for these unhappy times. Every year, nay, every month, we make new creeds to describe invisible mysteries. We repent of what we have done, we defend those who repent, we anathematize those whom we defended. We condemn either the doctrine of others in ourselves, or our own in that of others. And, reciprocally tearing one another to pieces, we have been the cause of each other's ruin."[5]

The fourth century witnessed quite a few church councils, and the fights between theologians became ever more vicious. These theologians invariably ascribed nothing but virtue and pure motives to themselves, but they imputed nothing but evil and guilty motives to their opponents. Nobody was willing to believe that any errors held to by their opponents might be innocent or that their faith was perhaps sincere.

No one approached his brother in love, trying to help him see the truth. Rather, theologians sought only to refute and condemn their opponents. No wonder the secular Roman historian of that day, Ammianus Marcellinus, remarked that the enmity Christians had for each other surpassed the fury that savage beasts have against man.[6]

Within a century after Nicaea, the Church came to believe that simply studying the Bible was no longer sufficient to give someone an accurate understanding of the faith. It was also necessary to study the writings of these new church fathers and the decrees of various church councils. Just because a man was godly and well-read in Scripture, it didn't mean that he was qualified to preach in the church. What mattered was not a man's knowledge of what the *Scriptures* say, but rather his knowledge of what the *Church* says.

As the poison of this "new Christianity" worked its way through every fiber of the Church, eventually the Church declared that no one—no matter how godly they might be—could any longer preach the gospel (whether inside or outside a church building) without official authorization from the Church. Preaching without a license became a crime punishable by imprisonment and even death.

This new law was not necessarily because the Church was deliberately trying to keep people "in darkness." I think the Church's motives were sincere. Unlicensed preachers might end up misunderstanding the Scriptures and thereby mislead people, causing them to forfeit eternal life. But, again, the Church was using human means to try to solve problems, rather than trusting God's methods.

4. Turning the Bible into a Dangerous Book

In its eagerness to adopt extra-biblical definitions and intricate theology, the Church ended up turning the Bible into a dangerous book. The Church imagined that Christians who read the Bible for themselves could not hope to arrive at the "true" doctrine. Such Christians would almost certainly fall into heresy. Christians could no longer listen to what Jesus Himself said in plain language. Instead, they had to believe what the Church instructed them to believe.

Eventually, the Church reached a point where it believed that a person could end up losing his soul by reading and believing the Scriptures. As a result, in 1229, the synod of Toulouse passed a canon law declaring: "Lay people are not permitted to possess the books of the Old and New Testaments, but only the Psalter,

Breviary, or the Little Office of the Blessed Virgin. And these books are not to be in the vernacular language."[7]

The Bible had become a dangerous book. Somehow the words of Jesus and His apostles were no longer safe for uneducated people to read.

23

Was God Changing
The Rules?

In the brief span of less than fifteen years, enormous changes had taken place in Christianity. The kingdom that had been "not of this world" was now closely linked with a kingdom that *was* of this world.

How did such a complete reversal of values take place in such a short period of time? Why didn't the church leaders say something about it? The reason is that the leaders had convinced themselves that *God* was changing all the rules. All those things that the Scriptures said about nonresistance, loving one's enemies, and not being of the world applied to a different time, a different paradigm.

After all, it seemed to most Christians that God was truly blessing the Church through Constantine. It appeared that *He* was the one ushering in these changes. Christians had prayed for an end to the persecution, and all this seemed to be an answer to their prayers. But was all of this really a *blessing* from God—or was it actually a *test* God was allowing Satan to bring against the church? How could the fourth-century Christians know?

There was a fairly easy way the fourth-century church could know: All they had to do was to continue doing things the kingdom way. They simply needed not to deviate one iota from Christ's teachings. "Jesus Christ is the same today, yesterday, and forever" (Heb. 13:1). Until He returns, there are not going to be any changes in the way His kingdom is run. And there won't be any changes in His laws. If Constantine had been sent by God as a blessing, the Church didn't have to compromise in any way. And it didn't have to water down its message. Christians just needed to stay loyal to the kingdom of God, and they would soon find out whether this emperor was a blessing or not.

Muzzling the Gospel

As I have mentioned, Constantine made various bishops and presbyters his counselors. This provided a perfect opportunity to test whether or not Constantine was being sent by God. Those counselors merely had to give Constantine advice without compromise—and then wait and see what his response would be. If Constantine rejected godly counsel or was angered by it, then his program wasn't from God. Faithful men of God had always spoken straightforwardly to rulers. Look at the examples of Samuel, Nathan, Elijah, Isaiah, and Jeremiah. They weren't afraid to tell kings the truth from God.

Or, look at John the Baptist. The Jewish religious leaders had come to him and asked him what they should do. John could have reasoned to himself, "God is really blessing my ministry! Look, now, even the Jewish leaders want to come and hear me preach. Through their support and assistance, I'll be able to reach the whole Jewish nation!" No, John didn't reason that way, did he? Rather, he reproved them for their sins, telling them, "Brood of vipers! Who warned you to flee from the wrath to come? Therefore bear fruits worthy of repentance" (Mt. 3:7,8).

John the Baptist was just as uncompromising with King Herod. Herod viewed John as a genuine prophet of God. As king, Herod was in a position to render enormous assistance to John. But did John cater to Herod, or compromise his message for Herod's sake? Not in the least. The Scriptures tell us: "Herod himself had sent and laid hold of John, and bound him in prison for the sake of Herodias, his brother Philip's wife; for he had married her. Because John had said to Herod, 'It is not lawful for you to have your brother's wife.' Therefore Herodias held it against him and wanted to kill him, but she could not; for Herod feared John, knowing that he was a just and holy man, and he protected him" (Mark 6:17-20).

John could have materially prospered as a prophet with the king's support. But silence would have implied approval, and it would have misled Herod and Herodias. By speaking up, John gave Herod the opportunity to repent. Herod viewed John as a just and holy man. If he truly wanted to serve God, Herod would have heeded John's words. But Herod wasn't willing to carry his cross. And in the end, he became the unwilling murderer of John.

Our King set the example for us Himself. When the rich young ruler came to Jesus, He respectfully listened to the man's testimony. And then Jesus told him, "You still lack one thing. Sell all that you have and distribute to the poor, and you will have treasure in heaven; and come, follow Me" (Luke 18:22). As a result, Jesus lost the young ruler as a disciple.

The Christian leaders in Constantine's day could have done the same thing. They could have told Constantine to divest himself of his wealth and power. They could have reminded him of Jesus' words to the rich young ruler. They could have told him to love his enemies and do good to them. But they didn't.

The First Believing Emperor

Although most people think of Constantine as the first Christian emperor, there was actually a prior Roman emperor who had apparently professed Christianity. His name was Philip the Arabian, and he ruled for a brief span in the century before Constantine. Philip had married a Christian woman, and he believed that Christianity was the true religion. Eusebius tells us:

> "After six years as Roman emperor, Gordion died, and Philip succeeded him. Word has it that he was a Christian and wanted to join with believers in the prayers of the church on the day of the last Paschal vigil. But the bishop of the time

would not let him enter until he confessed publicly and joined those who were judged sinful and were occupying the place [in the church] for penitents. Otherwise, had he not done so, he would never have been received, due to the many charges against him. It is said that he readily obeyed, showing by his actions how genuinely and piously disposed he was toward the fear of God."[1]

The bishops in Constantine's day could have done the same thing. They could have uncompromisingly called Constantine to repentance. Then they would have found out just how genuine his beliefs were!

Ignoring the Warning Signs

There are several warning signs that may indicate a person is undergoing or is about to undergo a heart attack. Some of these signs are uncomfortable pressure or pain in the chest, pain in the left arm, and shortness of breath. Ignoring these warning signs often cost people their lives.

Similarly, the Christians of Constantine's day ignored the warning signs that Jesus had given concerning the kingdom: "Woe to you when all men speak well of you, for so did their fathers to the false prophets. ...Blessed are you when they revile and persecute you, and say all kinds of evil against you falsely for My sake. Rejoice and be exceedingly glad, for great is your reward in heaven" (Luke 6:27; Mt. 5:11,12).

It's human nature to feel we're on the right track when we are popular and people speak well of us. But it's not that way in the kingdom. Something is wrong when the world speaks well of us and wants to be our friend. Sadly, the fourth century Christians seemed to have totally forgotten Jesus' warning.

24

How Christ's Teachings Disappeared

Three hundred years before, Christians had needed to make a radical paradigm shift in order to enter the kingdom of God. But now, because they ignored Jesus' warning sign, Christians were convinced that it was time to make another paradigm shift. They thought God was ushering in a new golden age in which Christians would be free from persecution and could enjoy worldly power and luxuries. But did the New Testament say anything about such a golden age?

Ah, here was the problem. Nothing in the New Testament fit the model of this new supposedly golden age. Therefore, the Church had to dig back to the Old Testament period to find a Scriptural model that would work. So instead of going forward, the Church went *backward* to ancient Israel to find its role model. It was a retro-paradigm shift.

We'll refer to this new model as the "Constantinian Hybrid."[1] It was an attempt to paste New Testament theology and ordinances onto Old Testament morals and lifestyle. And it was an endeavor to combine the kingdom of God with the kingdoms of the world. The secular government would comprise one half of this hybrid, and the Church would comprise the other half. The two halves would make up the whole—the new hybridized "kingdom of God."

Just as the Old Testament kingdom had been co-extensive with the physical boundaries of Israel, so now this new hybridized kingdom of God would be essentially co-extensive with the vast boundaries of the Roman Empire. The kingdom of God would no longer be "within" someone. It would be a tangible, visible empire. Just as the Israelites had gone to war to defend their kingdom and to subdue God's enemies, now Christians were called on to do the same. Christians who wouldn't accept the Constantinian Hybrid were labeled as heretics.

The Role of the Emperor

Israelite kings—like David, Solomon and Josiah—had been intimately involved in the worship and spiritual life of Israel. So, likewise, the Roman emperors would now assume their "rightful involvement" in the worship and spiritual life of the Church. Eusebius wrote: "[Constantine] exercised special care over the church of God. Anywhere in the various provinces where there were some who differed from each other in judgment, he, like some general bishop constituted by God, convened synods of the ministers. Nor did he hesitate to be present and sit with them in their assembly. Rather, he shared in their deliberations, ministering to everything pertaining to the peace of God."[2]

What Happened to Christ's Teachings?

In the first part of this book, we looked at some of the laws of the kingdom. What happened to these laws under the Constantinian Hybrid? Basically, the new Hybrid explained away all of Christ's kingdom teachings—except where His teachings also fit the Old Testament model. Under the Hybrid, if something had been lawful for the Jews, it now was considered lawful for Christians. With that in mind, let's briefly review what the hybridized Church now taught about wealth, oaths, divorce, and nonresistance.

Wealth. There is no Old Testament commandment that forbids someone from storing up treasures on earth. Therefore, under the Hybrid, it was all right for Christians to store up earthly treasures. It was also acceptable for Christians to retain or reach out for positions of earthly power. In fact, the Church now began to teach that God had instituted class distinctions among humans. A member of the nobility shouldn't live and dress as a peasant, and a peasant shouldn't seek to live and dress as a nobleman.

Oaths. Since oaths were lawful in the Old Testament, they were lawful in the new Hybrid. Furthermore, the Church realized that the mobs of people who had flocked into the Church were not truly regenerated. Their word was not trustworthy. So the Church felt obligated to reinstate oaths. In fact, oaths became a central pillar of late Roman and medieval government and society.

Nonresistance. The Old Testament didn't teach nonresistance or loving one's enemy, so now the Church didn't teach it either. In a matter of only a few decades, Christians went from being the meek and defenseless to being the cruel and powerful. As we've discussed, before the rise of Constantine, Christians wouldn't even take up swords to defend themselves against pagan barbarians. Now, they didn't hesitate to slaughter fellow Romans and fellow Christians.

Divorce. When it came to divorce, things were a bit different. That's because the Old Testament had allowed divorce only to husbands and only if a husband had "found some uncleanness" in his wife. Although some Jewish rabbis had interpreted this law quite liberally, the Church interpreted it quite narrowly, allowing a man to divorce his wife only for *porneia*.

In the West, the Church interpreted *porneia* to mean a violation of the Old Testament Levitical laws that forbade marriage within certain degrees of consanguinity or affinity. For example, a man could not marry his sister or his widowed daughter-in-law (Lev. 18:9,15). Since the Old Testament had now become the model for the Church, the Church brought most of these Levitical laws on marriage wholesale into the Hybrid. If a man had somehow entered into a marriage that violated the Levitical laws, he was expected to divorce his wife. (Today, we would refer to this as obtaining an annulment.) It was on this basis that, centuries later, Henry VIII sought to divorce his first wife, Catherine of Aragon—for she was the widow of his older brother.

So this new supposedly golden age ended up looking an awful lot like ancient Israel—but without the Jewish ceremonial and dietary laws. Oaths, the accumulation of wealth, and state-authorized violence were acceptable. However, sexual immorality, divination, and witchcraft were not allowed, for they are forbidden in the Old Testament. Nearly seventeen hundred years later, this same tie to Old Testament morality typically marks churches that have descended from the Constantinian Hybrid.

The people of the kingdom had once turned the world upside down. Now, the world was doing its best to turn the kingdom right side up.

Had God's Plan Been Thwarted?

So does this mean that God's purpose had been thwarted? Were things not working out the way He had planned? Not at all. The whole Constantinian Hybrid had happened just as God knew it would. It was all foretold in Jesus' kingdom teachings and parables.

In two of His parables, Jesus foretold that His kingdom would be quite expansive: "The kingdom of heaven is like a mustard seed, which a man took and sowed in his field, which indeed is the least of all the seeds; but when it is grown it is greater than the herbs and becomes a tree, so that the birds of the air come and nest in its branches." And again, "The kingdom of heaven is like leaven, which a woman took and hid in three measures of meal till it was all leavened" (Mt. 13:31-33).

At the same time, Jesus had made it clear: "Narrow is the gate and difficult is the way which leads to life, and there are few who find it" (Mt. 7:14). He also said, "Do not fear, *little flock*, for it is your Father's good pleasure to give you the kingdom" (Luke 12:32).

Previously, we discussed the fact that the majority of the persons in the kingdom would be weeded out in the end. Jesus knew the Constantinian Hybrid was coming. And He has used it as a test to cull out those who do not truly love Him and His ways.

25

The Golden Age That Never Happened

I've talked quite a bit about the negative aspects of the Constantinian Hybrid. But it would be a mistake to think that there were no beneficial aspects as well. The Church would never have gone for the bait if it had been all bad. So let's take a look at a few of these beneficial aspects.

The most immediate and visible change that the new Hybrid brought was the legalization of Christianity. The state favored Christianity, and it exempted church property from taxes. Furthermore, Constantine made Sunday a legal holiday, making it easier for the population to attend Sunday worship. He also outlawed all occult practices.[1]

The sudden rise of Christianity, particularly in the public sphere, was accompanied by the rapid decline and eventual extinguishment of classical paganism. Although he tolerated pagan worship and declared freedom of worship for all (except heretics), Constantine prohibited state officers from making pagan offerings on behalf of the state. He also withdrew funding for further construction of pagan temples, and he converted some temples into churches.

In the social realm, Constantine promulgated a law that offered public financial assistance to poor families, so that they would not follow the common practice of abandoning unwanted infants to die. He banned the cruel gladiator contests in many cities, shut down lewd theaters, and outlawed prostitution.

Constantine also prohibited concubinage, punished adultery, and made divorce more difficult to obtain.[2]

The Dark Side of the Hybrid

I believe that Constantine truly wanted to improve Roman society and to outlaw the things that were offensive to God. But he was not a reborn Christian. He was still a man "of this world." So the only way he knew how to do things was through the world's methods, which were often cruel and brutal. For example, Constantine made sexual assault and seduction much more serious crimes than they previously had been. That was good. But the penalties he attached to these crimes were unspeakable: burning the accused person alive, having him torn apart by wild beasts in the amphitheater, or pouring molten lead down his throat.[3]

Furthermore, Constantine and his officers continued to routinely practice torture, just as their pagan predecessors had done. In fact, over the years, Constantine degenerated into a cruel, autocratic ruler, who spent public funds like a drunken sailor. To pay for his proliferate spending, Constantine burdened the people with some of the heaviest taxation the Empire had ever experienced.[4]

Lust for Power

As we have discussed, Jesus told us that we must let go—let go of every chain that keeps us bound to the earth. We have to let go of every possession that will cause us to be anxious, every treasure to which our hearts might become attached. And earthly power is just as much a possession as gold and silver. It's just as intoxicating as riches, if not more so. Once people take their first drink of power, they usually want more. Before long, they will do virtually anything to hold on to the power they have. Not only that, if possible, they will try to *increase* their power. That's one reason why the Christians of the first three centuries required high governmental officials to step down from office if they wanted to become Christians.

Constantine loved earthly power, and he was ruthless in his desire to protect this power. For example, he instituted a system of spies throughout the Empire to keep him posted of any criticism, any possible rivals, and any preparations for revolt. If his spies accused someone of disloyalty to Constantine, the authorities dragged the accused person to Milan or Constantinople to face the charges. If insufficient evidence was available, the jailers tortured the accused person until he confessed his "crime." The fact that the accused person was a Christian made no difference.

As I have mentioned, Constantine and his brother-in-law, Licinius, had jointly issued the Edict of Milan in 313. Constantine ruled the Western Roman Empire, and Licinius ruled the Eastern. But Constantine had not really wanted a divided Empire. His ambition was to rule the *entire* Roman Empire. And Constantine feared that Licinius might have the same ambition.

So, in 324, Constantine invaded the territory governed by Licinius. He justified this to the Church on the grounds that Licinius had begun persecuting Christians again.[5] Unlike all previous Roman wars, Christian soldiers actually participated in the killing during this war against Licinius. Constantine asked bishops from the Church to accompany his army and to pray for them during the battle. He also had a huge cross constructed as a battle standard, which his soldiers carried as a talisman that would ensure a victory.[6]

Indeed, Constantine's troops were victorious, and Constantine took Licinius captive. Now he was the sole ruler of the Roman Empire. And he proclaimed that God had brought all of this about:

"Surely it cannot be deemed arrogance in one who has received benefits from God, to acknowledge them in the loftiest terms of praise. I myself, then, was the instrument whose services He chose. I was the one He esteemed suited for the accomplishment of His will. ...Through the aid of divine power, I banished and utterly removed every form of evil that prevailed. This was done in the hope that the human race—which had been enlightened through my instrumentality—might be recalled to a due observance of the holy laws of God. And also so that our most blessed faith might prosper under the guidance of His Almighty hand."[7]

After his victory over Licinius, Constantine made a solemn promise to his sister, Constantia, the wife of Licinius, that he would allow Licinius to pass the remainder of his life in peace and comfort. He even confirmed his promise with an oath. However, within a month, Constantine had Licinius executed.[8] He couldn't afford to have any potential rival around.

But there were potential rivals everywhere. So Constantine didn't stop with Licinius. Before long, Constantine murdered his own son, Crispus. Later, he killed a nephew who he thought might be after his throne. Apparently, Constantine even murdered his second wife, Fausta, fearing she was plotting against him.[9] Yet, the Church looked the other way, never condemning Constantine—or even criticizing him—for any of these murders.

On his deathbed, Constantine bequeathed the Roman Empire to his three surviving sons—Constantius, Constans, and Constantine II—and to his two oldest nephews. All five of these men were Christians. Rome would continue to be a Christian empire! Yet, these five men all shared Constantine's lust for power. So shortly after Constantine died, his son Constantius slew the two nephews who were to be co-rulers, and he massacred virtually every male on their side of the family.

With the two nephews out of the way, Constantine's three sons divided the Empire among themselves. Surely there could now be peace, for these men were blood brothers and Christians!

But the new Christianity didn't behave anything like genuine kingdom Christianity. None of the three brothers was satisfied with having only a third of the Empire. Before long, Constantine II invaded Italy to grab the portion of the Empire that had been given to his brother, Constans. However, Constantine II died in the attempt. This left only two rulers out of the original five. Constans ruled the Western Roman Empire, and Constantius ruled the East.

But even this simple division of power didn't last long. Soon, a general named Magnentius struck down Constans and seized the Western Empire. But he wasn't satisfied with just the Western Empire. Seeking the rulership of the whole Empire, he and his armies attacked Constantius, the sole surviving son of Constantine. This time, Magnentius was defeated, and he fled to Gaul. This left Constantius as the sole emperor.[10]

But where was the golden age that Christianity was supposed to bring to the Empire? There had been more civil wars in the first *fifty* years of the new "Christian" Roman Empire than there had been in the first *two hundred* years of the pagan Roman Empire. The first pagan emperors had ushered in two hundred years of stability, prosperity, and peace—the Pax Romana. The first Christian emperors ushered in a period of endless civil wars, oppressive taxation, and rapid decay of the Empire.

Valentinian

After the death of Constantius, a nephew of Constantine named Julian became the new Emperor. He was one of the few members of his family who had escaped the massacre carried out by Constantine's son, Constantius. He had seen enough of "Christianity" in action and wanted no part of it. So, although he was tolerant of Christians, he tried to revive classic paganism in the Empire. But his efforts failed.

A year after Julian's death, a churchgoing Christian named Valentinian was proclaimed as the new emperor. As a catholic

Christian, Valentinian lived a chaste life, and he initiated many praiseworthy laws. For example, he established a public physician in each of the fourteen districts of Rome to care for the poor. He allowed freedom of religion for pagans, Jews, and Christians of all persuasions.[11] Life under Valentinian should have been the golden age that Christians were expecting. But it wasn't.

Like the Christian emperors before him, Valentinian never lived a day without fearing that someone would stage a coup and take away his precious throne. So, like Constantine, he used spies to try to detect any disloyalty, particularly from those who could become potential rivals. Valentinian measured the industriousness of his governors and magistrates by how many executions they carried out in their tribunals. Spies and political enemies often brought improbable charges against even respectable citizens. Confessions extracted by cruel tortures were treated as solid evidence against the accused. Wealthy families were made destitute, and hundreds of senators, matrons, and philosophers died ignominious deaths in the holds of dank dungeons and torture chambers.[12]

Innocent citizens everywhere lived in fear lest somehow someone would accuse them of treason. Valentinian took the position that suspicion was equivalent to proof if the issue was disloyalty to his rule.[13] A slight or imaginary offense could result in a citizen's tongue being cut out or his whole body being burned alive. One historian made the observation that the words Valentinian used the most were: "cut off his head," "burn him alive," and "beat him with clubs until he expires."[14] He could calmly watch citizens writhing in agony under torture and yet feel no pity for them whatsoever. Nor did he feel this in any way violated his Christian beliefs.[15]

In the end, Valentinian's own uncontrolled temper proved to be his undoing. One of his officers had invited a barbarian king to a banquet, but then treacherously murdered this king at the feast. In response, the murdered king's barbarian tribe retaliated against the Romans by plundering several Roman provinces.

Rather than apologizing for the murder and working towards reconciliation, Valentinian led his Roman armies against the barbarians and extracted a bloody vengeance. When ambassadors from the barbarians came to Valentinian's tent to beg for mercy, Valentinian became so enraged at them that his face became almost purple. He screamed at the envoys at the top of his lungs. However, in his rage, he burst a blood vessel in his brain and died instantly.[16]

The Fall of Rome

One of the most enduring historical myths is that Rome fell because it was steeped in pagan vices, frequent bacchanalian orgies, and bloodthirsty entertainment. I've read many Christian writers who point to Rome as a lesson of what will happen to the United States if it doesn't restore Biblical morality.

But Rome didn't fall when it was ruled by pagans. When Rome fell, the gladiator games had been outlawed, and a strict Old Testament morality had been imposed on the population. What's more, nearly the entire population were Christians.[17]

And to whom did Rome fall? The popular picture paints the scene of hordes of savage, half-naked, Thor-worshipping barbarians pouring over the walls of Rome and slaughtering everyone in sight. But this, too, is a myth. The Germanic peoples who conquered Rome were not savage and uncivilized. They were half-Roman in their culture, and many of them had been allies or even protectors of the Empire. What's more, they, too, were professing Christians.[18]

The golden age that was supposed to blossom forth never materialized. To be sure, the Roman Empire was already in decline when Christians inherited it. Still, the Christians proved to be no better rulers than their pagan predecessors. Rather than turning matters around, the Christian emperors only made it worse. Their oppressive taxes and endless in-fighting accelerated the decline that had begun under the third century pagan emperors—until finally the entire Western Empire collapsed.

The Christians of the early fourth century had essentially traded in the kingdom of God for the kingdom of this world. This has to rank as one of the worse bargains of all time—right alongside Esau's trading his birthright for a mess of stew. But at least Esau got to eat his stew. The Christians not only lost the kingdom of God, but they lost the Roman Empire as well.

The events from the accession of Constantine in 312 to the deposing of the last emperor of the Western Empire in 476 should have given Christians much to think about. The pagan Roman emperors had been victorious in most of their wars, but the Christian emperors weren't. Christ is the Prince of Peace. So why were pagan emperors—even wicked ones like Caligula and Nero—able to maintain the Pax Romana, when the Christian emperors were not? Why had the Empire not only survived—but flourished—under the pagan emperors of the first and second centuries, whereas it collapsed under the Christian rulers of the fourth and fifth centuries?

By 476, it should have been obvious that the Constantinian Hybrid was not of God.

The Pattern of the Hybrid

But the fall of Rome didn't bring the Church to repentance. Nor did it bring an end to the Constantinian Hybrid. In fact, the Church became the dominant institution of the Middle Ages. The societal pattern of the Hybrid continued throughout the medieval period: Sexual sins, witchcraft, abortion, and lewd entertainment were condemned (although, as to sexual immorality, a double standard was allowed to the nobility). Accumulating wealth, making oaths, and killing in war were considered acceptable. That was the pattern in Constantine's day, that was the pattern during the Middle Ages—and that has been the pattern in most "Christian" governments up through our day.

26

Augustine —
Apologist for the Hybrid

The Roman Empire was crumbling. The Church was sinking into the world, instead of turning the world upside down. So the kingdom of God badly needed a Paul or John the Baptist to stand up boldly and challenge the whole Constantinian Hybrid. However, what the Church got instead was the primary *defender* of the Hybrid. His name was Augustine.

Augustine was quite typical of his age, totally accepting the Constantinian Hybrid and the changes it had brought into the Church. He was a very capable apologist for the Hybrid, and unfortunately, there were no gifted spokesmen for the kingdom. So, naturally, Augustine's arguments prevailed.

But Augustine did more than merely defend the Hybrid. He also tried to defend orthodox Christianity against the claims of heretics, such as the Gnostics. His method was to listen to his opponent's position and then counter it by taking the exact opposite position.

To illustrate, let's liken one of the apostolic doctrines to the color green— which is obtained by mixing blue and yellow together. And let's liken the heretical view of that doctrine to the color blue. The heretic has some of the truth, since green is partly comprised of blue. However, the heretic has not grasped the full truth. He has altered the apostolic doctrine by leaving out an essential portion of it—the yellow part.

Now, Augustine's method was *not* to call his opponent back to the fullness of the apostolic doctrine, represented by the color green. No, Augustine would simply swing to the opposite extreme and argue that the matter was not blue at all, but was actually *yellow*. He thereby refused to acknowledge that his opponent had even a measure of truth. And it was quite effective as a means to win arguments.

Augustine may have won arguments, but in the process, he overturned historic Biblical Christianity. Yellow is just as much a half truth of the (green) apostolic faith as is blue.

Let me give you two examples of what I mean.

Augustine Against the Gnostics

Gnosticism had been among the first heresies that Christianity faced. It taught that the material world was evil, having been created by a different deity than the God of the New Testament. In support of their position, the Gnostics pointed to the fact that Jesus' teachings were different from those of Moses. For example, the God of the Old Testament had commanded the Israelites to go to war, but Jesus told His disciples to love their enemies. Logically, many Gnostics accepted Jesus' kingdom teachings, but they rejected the entire Old Testament as being the work of another god. They even denied that the Son of God had actually become man.

The early Christian writers, such as Irenaeus and Tertullian, had already ably defended historic Christianity against the teachings of Gnosticism. These early defenders of the faith argued that there was no new God between the Old and New Testaments. There was only a progression of revelation between the two. The Law of Moses had been a tutor preparing the Israelites for Christ. Jesus' teachings were the ultimate goal for which the Law was preparing the Israelites.

However, these arguments didn't fit the Constantinian Hybrid. As we have discussed, the Hybrid was basically a combination of New Testament theology with Old Testament morality and lifestyle. To acknowledge that the New Testament introduced new and greater moral laws than the Old Testament would mean admitting that the Hybrid was wrong. And that wouldn't do.

So Augustine countered the Gnostics (known in his day as the Manichaeans) by denying their underlying premise. He said the teachings of Jesus were *not* different from those of the Old Testament. Killing was just as lawful under the New as it was under the Old. He wrote: "What is evil about war? Is it the death of some who will soon die anyway, so that others may live in peaceful subjection? This is mere cowardly dislike, not any religious feeling. The real evils of war are love of violence, revengeful cruelty, fierce and implacable enmity, wild resistance, the lust of power, and the like. And it is generally for the purpose of punishing these things, when force is required to inflict the punishment, that, in obedience to God or some lawful authority, good men undertake wars. For they find themselves in such a position as regards the conduct of human affairs that right conduct requires them to act, or to make others act in a certain way."[1]

Yes, but didn't Jesus say to love our enemies and not to resist evil? Augustine had an answer for that: "It may be supposed that God could not authorize warfare because in later times it was said by the Lord Jesus Christ, 'I say unto you that you resist not evil. But if anyone strikes you on the right cheek, turn to him the left also.' However, the answer is that what is required here is not a *bodily* action, but an *inward* disposition."[2] In other words, it's okay to kill someone so long as you love the person you're killing!

Augustine continued, "The Lord commands patience when He says, 'If anyone strikes you on the right cheek, turn to him the left also.' This may be in the inward disposition, although it is not exhibited in bodily action or in words. For when the apostle was struck, ... he prayed to God to pardon his assailant in the next world, but not to leave the injury unpunished at the time. Inwardly, he preserved a kindly feeling, while outwardly he wished the man to be punished as an example."[3]

That kind of logic might win a paper argument, but it's playing games with Christ. According to Augustine, we can perform the same brutal actions as the world. Our actions can be as violent as those of the Old Testament Israelites. We just have to make sure that our inward feelings are nothing but kindness, peace, and love.

Following this line of argumentation, Augustine could rationalize just about anything. For example, Augustine argued that persecuting the Donatists was an act of Christian love, for it brought them back into the fold of the Church: "Is it not a part of the care of the shepherd, when any sheep have left the flock, even though not violently forced away, but led astray by tender words and coaxing blandishments, to bring them back to the fold of his master when he has found them. And he may do this by the fear of the whip, or even the pain of the whip, if they show symptoms of resistance."[4]

What Augustine didn't understand is that in Christ's kingdom the *means* is always just as important as the *end*. Christians don't use evil or violent means in an attempt to obtain godly results. *How* we do something is just as important as *what* we do.

The Just War

Augustine is typically credited as the originator of the "just war" doctrine. Actually, he wasn't. It was the pagan Greek philosophers and rulers who had first formulated a doctrine of the just or righteous war. Augustine merely borrowed what they had taught hundreds of years earlier.[5]

I have seen various lists of the criteria that Augustine said were necessary for a war to be just—and therefore morally upright for a Christian. However, these lists are a bit misleading. Augustine never wrote a treatise on the "just war" doctrine. And he never set forth a list of criteria needed for a war to be just. Instead, various medieval theologians like Thomas Aquinas set forth lists of criteria, saying that these were the conditions laid down by Augustine.

The truth of the matter is that Augustine *did* justify war, as we've seen. And he presented various justifications for war throughout his numerous works. However, Augustine himself never said that *all* of these criteria or aspects had to be met in order for a war to be just. Nevertheless, based on Augustine's writings, the medieval theologians came up with a list of conditions that would make a war just. According to these theologians, it was righteous and just for a Christian to kill another man if:

- The Christian loves the man he is killing.

- The Christian kills only in a war that was the last resort after all other possible solutions had been tried and failed.

- The Christian kills only in a war being fought to redress rights actually violated or to defend against unjust demands backed by force.

- The Christian kills only in a war that is waged under the authority of a ruler.

- The Christian kills only in a war that his side has a reasonable chance of winning.

- The Christian tries to distinguish between soldiers and civilians, and he never kills civilians on purpose.

- The Christian kills only in a war in which the killing is "proportionate" to the end sought.

- The Christian kills only in a war in which the good that is sought by his violence outweighs the evil that the violence brings.

- The Christian kills only in a war in which the winning side never requires the utter humiliation of the loser.[6]

If you are a Christian, these conditions should sound absurd to you. Yet, they may not. That's because most of us have been heavily conditioned by the Constantinian Hybrid and Augustine's defense thereof. So let me help you to see its absurdity.

Under the ancient code of war, it was deemed perfectly lawful and honorable to kill all of the men of the enemy and to sexually assault all of their women. We have seen how Augustine rationalized the killing of men. Now, let's see how these same conditions look if we apply them to the violation of women. Let's say that it is righteous and just for a Christian to violate a woman if:

- The Christian loves the woman he is violating.

- The Christian violates women only in a war that was the last resort after all other possible solutions had been tried and failed.

- The Christian violates women only in a war being fought to redress rights actually violated or to defend against unjust demands backed by force.

- The Christian violates women only in a war that is waged under the authority of a ruler.

- The Christian violates women only in a war that his side has a reasonable chance of winning.

- The Christian tries to distinguish between soldiers' wives and civilian wives, and he never assaults civilian wives on purpose.

- The Christian violates women only in a war in which the violent assault is "proportionate" to the end sought.

- The Christian violates women only in a war in which the good that is sought by this violence outweighs the evil that the violence brings.

- The Christian violates women only in a war in which the winning side never requires the utter humiliation of the loser.

You probably have no trouble seeing the ridiculousness of these criteria when applied to assaulting women. Why is it so hard to see when we're talking about killing men instead of assaulting women? It's because nearly all of us have been conditioned by the Hybrid. We have grown up in a society that accepts and propagates the values of the Hybrid. Remember, under the Hybrid, no condemnation was attached to sins of violence—such as killing and torturing—so long as these acts were done under the authority of the rulers. However, the Hybrid nearly always condemned sexual sins of any kind.

The "just war" criteria are a direct violation of Jesus' teachings. For example, the "just war" criteria say that, to be just, a war must be fought to redress rights actually violated or to defend against unjust demands backed by force. However, Jesus already addressed that very issue. He said not to resist evil. If someone wants your tunic, give him your cloak as well. If someone forces you to carry his load one mile, carry it two. Christians don't wage wars to redress rights; they willingly suffer loss instead. They turn the other cheek. They don't retaliate or fight back, but then say they were actually doing so in love.

Who Decides If A War Is Just?

Nevertheless, let's suppose that if a war meets all of the criteria I've listed above, it would be truly just in God's sight. If that were the case, the next question would have to be: "Who decides if a war meets these criteria?" The Church? The individual Christian? The state? Augustine answers that the state makes the determination. So how do the individual Christians know whether or not the war they're participating in is really just? The answer is, they don't!

Augustine acknowledged this: "There is no power but of God, who either orders or permits. Therefore, a righteous man may be serving under an ungodly king. Yet, he can perform the duty belonging to his position in the State by fighting under the order of his sovereign. For in some cases it is plainly the will of God that he should fight. But, in others, this may not be so plain, for it may be an unrighteous command on the part of the king. Nevertheless, the soldier is innocent, because his position makes obedience a duty."[7]

So, in the end, even the "just war" doctrine is a farce. The individual Christian is supposed to obey even the unrighteous commands of his king, and he is innocent in doing so. As Augustine realized, a person can't give ultimate allegiance to two kings—an earthly king and a heavenly king. So his solution was that so long as we're here on earth, the earthly king receives our absolute allegiance. The only exceptions are if the king commands us to worship false gods or orders us to believe false doctrines not approved by the Church.

However, Augustine's solution is totally unacceptable to Christ. He will not allow us to give superior allegiance to any other person or power. If an earthly king gives us a command that violates Jesus' teaching, it's the earthly king we must disobey, not our heavenly King.

The Constantinian Hybrid tries to relieve Christians of any individual responsibility to Christ. It says that the Church decides what we are to believe and practice. And so long as we obey the Church, we are absolved from any guilt in the spiritual realm. Similarly, the Hybrid says that the secular ruler decides when it is proper to kill, torture, banish, or plunder others. So long as we are obeying our government, then we are innocent before Christ in the secular realm. And ever since, hundreds of thousands of

Christians have killed their fellow man, or even their brothers in Christ, without feeling any moral responsibility for doing so. They were just following orders.

In fact, most "Christian" governments have demanded that their soldiers obey all orders of superior officers, regardless of any concern about the moral uprightness of the order. For example, Christian Russia under the Czars required the following of its soldiers:

> *"Article 87.* To carry out an order received from a superior officer exactly, without considering whether it is good or not, and whether it is possible to carry it out. The superior officer is responsible for the consequences of the order he gives."

> *"Article 88.* The subordinate ought never to refuse to carry out the orders of a superior officer—except when he sees clearly that in carrying out his superior officer's command, he breaks ...["]8

Since these articles were mandated by Christian Russia, we might expect Article 88 to have ended by saying: "except when he sees clearly that in carrying out his superior officer's command, he breaks the commandments of Christ." But that's not the way it read. Rather, it said, "except ... he breaks his oath of fidelity and allegiance to the Czar."[9]

The United States Code of Military Justice requires essentially the same obedience from its soldiers. It requires soldiers to obey all orders from superior officers unless they are "contrary to the Constitution, the laws of the United States, or lawful superior orders."[10]

But is such a code of conduct acceptable before Christ as to His citizens? Not in the least. He made it clear that our absolute obedience belongs to Him. He is our personal King. It doesn't matter what other authorities—ecclesiastical, secular or military—may say to the contrary. What they say is irrelevant, so

204 The Kingdom That Turned the World Upside Down

long as our King has already spoken on the matter. We will stand before the Judgment throne *individually*, not collectively.

Nullifying Personal Responsibility

During Augustine's lifetime, a Christian leader from Britain named Pelagius traveled throughout the Roman world, preaching against the spiritual laxity of the day. He rightfully stressed our personal accountability before Christ. However, either he or his followers went a bit too far. They said (or purportedly said) that we humans can walk perfectly in the commandments of Jesus, without the need of grace.

This went against historic Christianity, which taught that without God's enabling grace, nobody would be ultimately saved. At the same time, Christians had always taught that *we*, too, play a role in our salvation. We have to be willing to let go of the world and to daily crucify our own flesh and its wants. Salvation is a matter of man and God working together—because God wants it that way.

However, in his usual fashion, Augustine countered the Pelagians by going to the opposite extreme. He declared that we humans have no power whatsoever to obey Christ. That we don't even have sufficient free will to *choose* to obey Him. In other words, in reality, we play no part in our salvation. Augustine claimed that our human condition is this way because, before the universe was ever created, God arbitrarily chose who would be eternally saved and who would be eternally damned. There is nothing we can do to change the destiny He already decreed for us before we were born.[11]

But that totally nullifies the whole ethos of Jesus' gospel! What was His purpose for giving us the Sermon on the Mount, if what Augustine taught was true? What was His purpose in warning us that we must build our house on the rock by obeying His teachings? If what Augustine said were true, we have absolutely no power to obey His teachings! So we can't do any of the things He asked of us. Why would He exhort us to build on the rock if that decision had already been made by God before we were born?

Why would Jesus have warned us that 'he who endures to the end' will be saved, if there is nothing we can do to endure? What was the purpose of His parable of separating the sheep from the goats if that separation was already made before Jesus ever came to earth? Why did Jesus denounce the scribes and Pharisees if their actions had already been predestined by God? On what basis did the Pharisees have any guilt if they were simply living out the script God had written for them? What was the purpose of all the other warnings throughout the New Testament? Why preach the Gospel if our preaching cannot make any difference in anyone's eternal destiny?

By swinging to an extreme in order to win an argument, Augustine invented an absurd system that should easily be unmasked by any student of the Bible. The gospel of the kingdom isn't established by proof-texting special passages of Scripture and then ignoring everything else the New Testament teaches. But that's how Augustine created his own special system, by proof-texting a few passages. In contrast, the gospel of the kingdom accepts the *entirety* of the New Testament. It never interprets any part of the Bible in such a way that it nullifies the teachings of Jesus.

The truth of the matter is that Augustine himself didn't believe his own doctrine. If he had, he wouldn't have bothered to reply to the Pelagians. For if Augustine's doctrine is true, what difference does it make *what* the Pelagians taught? Nobody could be harmed by their doctrine. Nobody's relationship with God would be affected. Again, why did Augustine argue that heretics and schismatics should be persecuted? Their errors could harm no one. No one would lose salvation because of them, since everyone's salvation had already been decided before the universe was created.

In summation, under the gospel of the kingdom, the New Testament is an open book that an uneducated Christian can read and obey quite literally. However, under Augustine and the theology of the Constantinian Hybrid, the New Testament became a book dotted with land mines, that only theologically trained minds could interpret correctly.

27

Forgery in the Name Of Christ!

The institutional Church didn't crumble when the Western Roman Empire collapsed. In fact, the fall of Rome only enhanced the Church's power. After the collapse of the Western Roman Empire, the Church became the primary institution of civilization in western Europe. As the Germanic invaders divided the West into smaller "Christian" kingdoms, the bishop of Rome took on the status previously enjoyed by the western Roman emperor. He was now better known as simply "the Pope," and he had become one of the most powerful persons in the West.

As the centuries rolled by, the Roman Catholic Church continued to grow in wealth and in power. Rome remained the principal city of western Europe, but now its chief income came from the Church. Thousands of pilgrims traveled each year to see St. Peter's cathedral in Rome and to look down at the bones of Peter. The good "Christians" of Rome milked these pilgrims for as much as they could. All over Rome, Christians were selling pieces of the cross, bones of saints, and other relics.

In accordance with the Constantinian Hybrid, the Pope now normally ruled in two different capacities. He was the earthly prince of Rome, and he was also the universal bishop of the Roman Catholic Church. In order to justify the Pope's earthly powers, in 750 a papal cleric created a forged legal document that purported to be a donation of earthly kingship from Constantine to the bishop of Rome and all his successors. The donation was to last until the end of the world. This fraudulent document, known as the *Donation of Constantine*, fooled just about everyone in medieval Europe. This bogus document reads in part:

> "Because our imperial power is earthly, we [i.e., Constantine] have decided to honor reverently His most holy Roman Church, and to exalt the most holy See of blessed Peter in glory above our own Empire and earthly throne, ascribing to it power and glorious majesty and strength and Imperial honor. ...

> "By this present document we confer our imperial palace of the Lateran, which surpasses and excels all palaces in the whole world. We also confer a diadem, which is the crown worn on our head, and at the same time the tiara. ...We also confer the purple cloak and crimson tunic, and all our imperial garments. ...

> "To correspond to our own Empire and so that the supreme pontifical authority may not be dishonored, but may rather be adorned with glorious power greater than the dignity of any earthly empire, behold, we give to the most holy Pontiff, our father Sylvester, the universal Pope, not only the above-mentioned palace, but also the city of Rome and all the provinces, districts and cities of Italy and the Western regions."[1]

So the Pope was claiming not only the secular rulership of Rome, but the rulership of all of Italy and the "Western regions" as well.

Making Use of the Forged *Donation*

By 755, a Germanic people called the Lombards had gained control of most of Italy. The Pope feared that they also had their eyes on the city of Rome. Please understand that the Lombards were good "Christians," but that didn't have anything to do with the matter. Catholics had no hesitancy to invade the lands of other Catholics, or to slaughter them. Fearing that the Lombards would take over Rome as well, Pope Stephen journeyed to Gaul to try to convince Pepin, King of the Franks, that he should come to the Pope's aid. The Pope showed Pepin the bogus *Donation of Constantine*, and he urged Pepin, as a good Christian king, to "restore" the Italian cities to St. Peter and his successors, the popes. Falling for the bogus *Donation*, the Franks came to the aid of the Pope, defeated the Lombards, and turned some twenty Italian cities over to the Pope, creating a block of territory thereafter known as the Papal States.

Of course, all of this worldly power and all of the vast tax revenue from the Papal States made the office of Pope something quite desirable to men with less than godly motives. Various factions of powerful families in Rome battled one another to acquire the "throne of Peter." In one year, four different men occupied the papal throne—each of the first three being murdered.

Two Kingdoms, Two Names

In 954, Alberic, prince of Rome, was preparing to go into battle, when he was suddenly struck with a deadly fever. Realizing that he was about to die, Alberic summoned the other noblemen of Rome to the tomb of St. Peter. There, Alberic asked the nobles to swear on the bones of Peter that they would elect his fifteen year old son, Octavian, as prince of Rome upon Alberic's death. He also had them swear that they would make Octavian the next Pope, once the reigning Pope died. The nobles so swore.

So at the age of fifteen, Octavian became prince of Rome. A year later, he also became the Pope. In order to distinguish between when he was acting in his official capacity as the prince of Rome, and when he was acting in his capacity as Pope, Octavian came up with a brilliant idea. As Pope, he took on the artificial name of John XIII. As prince of Rome, he used his actual name, Octavian. He ruled over two kingdoms, so why not have two names? The precedent he set of taking on an assumed name has remained the practice of popes ever since.

Octavian (Pope John) protected his papacy and his princedom by surrounding himself with gangs of armed thugs. He was so incredibly wicked that one historian has called him a "Christian Caligula."[2] He was addicted to drinking, heavy gambling, and every kind of debauchery one could think of. He essentially turned the Lateran Palace into a house of prostitution. His contemporaries brought charges against him that female pilgrims were being violated inside St. Peter's church itself.

Finally, through the aid of the German king Otto, some of the priests and bishops called for a council to bring Pope John to ecclesiastical trial. However, Pope John refused to attend, concealing himself in a safe hideaway. Once the German armies left, the Pope returned to Rome, and vented his rage on those clerics who had testified against him at the council. One priest was flogged to the point of death. Another one had his tongue torn out, a third priest had his hand chopped off, and a fourth cleric had his nose and fingers cut off.[3]

Let's Go After the *Real* Evildoers

Even though a number of the popes were wicked monsters, the Church never excommunicated or punished any of them for their murders and debauchery. The only times popes were removed from office was when rivals killed them or otherwise forcibly removed them.

While ignoring the corruption and wickedness being practiced in its midst, the Church went after "heretics" with a vengeance. It savagely tortured them and threw them into damp, dark horrible dungeons. The Church also slaughtered heretics—often in the most gruesome way possible. Some of the Church's victims did actually hold to doctrinal errors, sometimes enormous ones. Others were good Catholics whose only crime was to question the authority of Rome. Many "heretics" were actually kingdom Christians who were simply trying to obey their King.

One of the German statutes enacted in 1215 is quite representative of the medieval laws passed against heretics:

"Where persons are believed to be heretics, they shall be accused before the spiritual court, for they should in the first place be tried by ecclesiastics. When they are convicted, they shall be taken in hand by the secular court, which shall properly sentence them. That is to say, they shall be burned at the stake. If, however, the judge protects them, or makes any illegal concessions and does not sentence them, he shall be excommunicated, and that in the most severe form."[4]

This statute went on to provide that even a prince who protected heretics or simply failed to prosecute them would also be excommunicated and all of his goods and titles be taken from him.

In 1229, the Synod of Toulouse set forth forty-five regulations on how heretics were to be hunted down and punished. Some of those regulations were:

- In each parish, whether inside or outside a city, bishops must bind [by oath] a priest and two or more laymen of good reputation to diligently, faithfully, and frequently search out heretics in their parishes, individual suspicious houses, subterranean rooms and additions to houses, and other hiding places.

- The house where a heretic is found must be torn down and the property must be confiscated.

- Whoever has involuntarily returned to the Church, through fear of death or for any other reason, must be imprisoned by the bishop.

- All members of a parish shall vow to the bishop under oath that they will preserve the Catholic faith and will persecute heretics according to their power. This oath must be renewed every two years.[5]

Do the "Times" Excuse the Church?

Today, the Roman Catholic Church would acknowledge that the unspeakable horrors the medieval Church inflicted on heretics were wrong. However, Catholics will usually try to excuse the Church's conduct by saying that it was only acting within the norms of medieval society. Society today wouldn't stand for someone being burned at the stake, but medieval society *wanted* this. The Church was just going along with societal norms for the times.

But does this excuse the Church? Not in the least. The values and commandments that Jesus gave us are permanent. They don't change with society. "Jesus Christ is the same yesterday, today, and forever" (Heb. 13:1). Since God's kingdom is not of this world, societal norms that violate Kingdom norms are irrelevant. Nobody would excuse a Christian for worshipping pagan images just because that was the norm of the society in which he lived. Jesus didn't tell us, "Love your enemies—unless the government and church say to torture them."

Part V

When It Was Illegal To Be a Kingdom Christian

28

The Underground Kingdom

In the previous section of this book, we looked at the Constantinian Hybrid in detail—what the hybridized Church believed and how it acted. We also looked at how the "Christianized" state acted. In this final section of the book, we're going to look at how the kingdom of God continued on despite the spiritual fall of the institutional Church.

What Does the Emperor Have to Do With the Church?

Earlier, I discussed the origins of the Donatists. And we saw that their beginnings weren't particularly heroic. They wanted the new perks that Constantine was offering to the institutional Church. And they didn't hesitate to ask the Emperor to intervene in their ecclesiastical dispute.

However, it proved to be a blessing that all of the judicial decisions went against the Donatists. For it forced them to step back and re-evaluate what the institutional Church had become. It opened their eyes to the fact that the Church was no longer a holy body. Rather, it had quickly become a worldly institution that now promoted the rich and the powerful. As a result, the Donatists completely dropped their original desire to win the Emperor's acceptance. As Donatus himself said, "What does the emperor have to do with the church?"[1] So the Donatists now began to refocus their attention on the kingdom of God.

Donatism was limited almost exclusively to North Africa. There, it existed side by side with the institutional or Catholic Church. However, there was a noticeable difference between the two. The Catholics tended to be urban, better educated, and wealthier. The Donatists were primarily made up of the poor. In this, they were quite typical of nearly all of the "kingdom movements" from the time of Constantine until modern times.

Living the Kingdom Lifestyle Within the Church

However, it would be a mistake to think that the only kingdom Christians after the time of Constantine were the ones in groups like the Donatists. To be sure, there were other kingdom churches, such as the Novatianists. But many kingdom Christians remained within the Catholic Church.

Although the Roman Catholic Church followed Augustine in most of his teachings, it did *not* accept his teachings on predestination. As a result, in many places it still taught the need to live obediently to Christ. But rather than completely upholding Jesus' kingdom teachings, the Catholic Church relegated them to the sphere of "perfectionism." The Church taught that only those who wanted to be "perfect" had to literally live by Christ's teaching. To its credit, the Church encouraged such Christian "perfectionism," so long as it remained under the control of the Church. As a result, there were tens of thousands of medieval Christians who lived out Jesus' teachings quite literally.

Many of these Christians—such as Francis of Assisi and Thomas á Kempis—followed a kingdom lifestyle under the auspices of some type of spiritual order or community. They lived out quiet lives of prayer, service, and love. Other kingdom Christians were illiterate rural peasants—far removed from the centers of power and worldly sophistication. Others were urban housewives, living out Jesus' teachings in a family setting.

Of course, there were many persons whose outward life resembled that of kingdom Christians, but who had no genuine relationship with Christ. Some hoped to earn their way to heaven by living an ascetic life. Many were hypocrites and frauds. Still, there was no shortage of genuine kingdom Christians.

The Clash Between the Kingdom and the Church

As I have said, the Catholic Church usually had no objections to someone living a kingdom life—so long as they did nothing to upset the existing religious system. However, when kingdom Christians began preaching the kingdom message—or when they tried to reform the Church—the hammer of the Church came down on them hard.

One example is Arnold of Brescia, an Italian cleric who tried to reform the worldly Church of the twelfth century. He argued that all of the clergy—from the pope down to the village priest—should live like the apostles. He labeled some of the clergy as "moneychangers and dens of thieves." He condemned the papal system for having lost total sight of the true apostolic mission. Arnold preached that the Church should divest itself of all secular power and devote itself exclusively to the gospel of Christ.[2]

The Church's response? The pope had Arnold hung and then burned. His ashes were dumped into the Tiber River that flows through Rome.

About the same time that Arnold was preaching in Italy, a poor village priest was traveling barefoot throughout the towns and villages of southern France, preaching the kingdom of God. His name was Pierre de Bruys, and he attracted a fairly large following among the poor. He taught that church buildings were an extravagant waste. The church, he said, is a spiritual community that does not need buildings to exist. He taught that works done for the benefit of the dead are worthless. He also preached against the Roman Mass and repetitive prayers. He told his hearers that they should not venerate or worship the cross or images. In fact, he encouraged them to destroy any articles of idolatry.[3]

Pierre read the four Gospels to his listeners, and preached the authentic kingdom of God. Unfortunately, some of his followers did not completely embrace nonresistance. They smashed altars and images, burned crucifixes, and destroyed church buildings. Like most of the kingdom teachers of the Middle Ages, Pierre was eventually burned by his Catholic opponents.

One final example of a medieval kingdom preacher was Henri of Lausanne, who traveled throughout northern France during the early twelfth century, preaching the kingdom of God. He not only preached the kingdom message, but he strongly attacked the wealthy clergy. He told his listeners not to attend the Catholic churches. His fiery preaching and condemnations attracted a considerable following among the poor. Finally, however, the Church used the power of the nobility to drive Henri out of northern France.

Henri then traveled throughout southern France and northern Italy, encouraging Christians everywhere to return to the simplicity of the apostles and the early church. Instead of relying on the authority of the church, Henri quoted the New Testament as his only authority. He told Christians that they should confess their sins to one another. It was not necessary to obtain penance and absolution from a priest. Thousands and thousands of the poor responded to Henri's message and focused their lives on Jesus and His kingdom.

Around the middle of the twelfth century, Henri of Lausanne disappeared from the historical record. Whether he was able to keep one step ahead of the heresy hunters and continue preaching, we don't know. We do know, however, that his preaching bore considerable fruit.[4]

Common Traits

Whether they were quiet individuals or members of one of the medieval kingdom movements, kingdom Christians of the Middle Ages generally had two traits in common:

First, by far, the majority of them came from the poor and uneducated classes. No wonder Jesus said, "Blessed are the poor"! They had little stake in this world, so there was little they had to leave behind. Indeed, the kingdom of Heaven *did* belong to them. Removed from all theological sophistry and minutiae, they could see the simple kingdom message that is recorded so clearly in the Gospels. As Jesus said, "You have hidden these things from the wise and prudent and have revealed them to babes" (Mt. 11:25).

Secondly, they took their authority only from the New Testament, particularly from the direct teachings of Jesus. Some kingdom Christians had formal theological training, but most did not. Typically, these kingdom Christians had read or heard Jesus' teachings over and over, and they applied them quite literally.

And that's what kingdom Christianity has always been about.

29

The Waldensians

The Waldensians were the most significant kingdom move-ment of the Middle Ages. This movement began around 1170 in the bustling medieval city of Lyon, France. Here lived a wealthy merchant named Waldesius.* He enjoyed his wealth and loved to be able to move within the power circles of his city. He was a good Catholic, attending Mass each week.

But one day after Mass, Waldesius came upon a minstrel singing a ballad about a fourth-century Christian named Alexis. Alexis was the son of a wealthy Roman senator, and he was a rich, spoiled pagan. However, on the day Alexis was supposed to be married, Christ suddenly broke through to him. Touched to his very soul by his conversion, Alexis left everything—his family, his wealth, and his intended bride. With little but the clothes on his back, he journeyed across Europe to Syria. There he spent most of his life praying and fasting, serving others, and sharing the love of Jesus. He endured poverty and great suffering for the cause of Christ.

Years later—his health broken and his body disfig-ured—Alexis returned to Rome. However, Alexis' family and friends didn't recognize him, as he appeared to be just some bedraggled beggar. So Alexis decided to keep his identity a secret. He accepted a menial job from his father (who didn't recognize him), and he lived in a tiny room under his family's staircase. He lived that way for seventeen years, trying to serve

---

*Or, Valdesius. His French name was Waldes (or Valdes). Some books refer to him as Peter Waldo, but apparently this was not his actual name.

others in the spirit of Christ. When Alexis died, his family found his diary among his few possessions, and then they realized who he really was.

Waldesius was greatly moved by this story, and it triggered a spiritual crisis within him. Troubled in conscience, Waldesius went to a local priest for counsel. He poured his soul out, and the priest listened intently. After several hours of earnest discussion, the priest got the Bible and read to Waldesius chapter 19 of Matthew about the rich young ruler. "If you want to be perfect, go, sell what you have and give to the poor, and you will have treasure in heaven; and come, follow Me" (Mt. 19:21).

Those words resounded in Waldesius' ears as he went home. His wealth was no longer a source of happiness to him. In fact, it seemed like a heavy chain around his neck. In a moment of joy and spiritual delight, Waldesius suddenly decided to throw off the heavy chain of wealth. He *would be* a disciple of Christ! He would enjoy the delights of heavenly treasure!

First, Waldesius used some of his wealth to have parts of the New Testament translated into the common vernacular spoken around Lyon. Then, armed with the Scriptures, he gave all of his remaining possessions to the needy.

"Citizens and friends," Waldesius told the people of Lyon as he gave away his goods. "I am not out of my mind, as you may think. I am freeing myself from the things that were oppressing me. For they made me a lover of money more than a lover of God. This act I am doing both for myself and for you: For myself—so that if ever again I possess anything, you may indeed call me a fool. For you—in order that you, too, may be led to put your hope in God and not in riches."[1]

Waldesius went about the city of Lyon, preaching the simple gospel of the kingdom to everyone. His earnestness and example of faith touched many lives. Soon a small group of like-minded believers gathered with him. They called themselves the "Poor in Spirit." They wanted to take every aspect of Jesus' teaching literally and seriously. They decided to taste the joy of true, uncompromising discipleship for themselves. The kingdom of God had reached Lyon—and it was turning the city upside down!

Waldesius and his disciples had no desire or vision to form a new church. In fact, they had no desire to even challenge or attack the Catholic Church. They simply wanted to live out authentic Christianity within the folds of the Catholic Church and to share their joy with others. They taught no new doctrines, but simply preached the same message that Jesus had preached. Although some wealthy persons and some intellectuals joined the "Poor in Spirit," their membership came predominantly from the poor.

The Poor in Spirit easily could have become a spiritual society within the Catholic Church—if it hadn't been for a couple of their convictions. First of all, they didn't seek the permission of the Church for what they were doing. Secondly, they had no intention of hibernating in monastic seclusion. They wished to remain citizens of Lyon, taking their message to the churches, public squares, and market places.

One of Waldesius' early disciples wrote, "The decision we have taken is this: to maintain until our death, faith in God and in the Church's sacraments. ...We have decided to preach freely, according to the grace given to us by God. This we will not cease to do for any cause."[2] Belittling the doctrines of the Church or challenging its authority were the furthest things from the minds of the Poor in Spirit. In fact, they were encouraging their hearers to attend church more faithfully. How could the Church possibly object to what they were doing?

However, before long, Waldesius and the Poor in Spirit were awakened from their spiritual naivete. The Catholic Church had no objections to the lifestyle of the Poor in Spirit. The Church viewed them as simply following the way of the "perfect." It was a good thing, but not necessary. And the Church had no objections to their doctrines, because they essentially had none.

However, the archbishop was not comfortable with the fact that the Poor in Spirit—untrained at any university and not ordained by the Church—were out preaching on the streets. Ever since the time of Constantine, the Church had tried to maintain a monopoly on preaching. As we discussed earlier, one of the characteristics of the Hybrid was its belief that only those licensed by the institutional Church could safely preach the Gospel. So the archbishop ordered Waldesius to appear before him. He then demanded that Waldesius and the Poor in Spirit quit preaching. Sternly reprimanding Waldesius, the archbishop told him that preaching belonged only to the clergy.

The spiritual lives of thousands now hung in the balance. Waldesius could have played the part of a good Catholic and said, "Yes, your holiness, whatever you direct." He and the Poor in Spirit could have continued to live the kingdom lifestyle under the authority of the Church, and they undoubtedly would have continued to attract new disciples. But Waldesius would not agree to quit preaching. Instead, to the utter shock of the archbishop, Waldesius looked him squarely in the eye and fearlessly replied, "On the contrary, preaching belongs to everyone who chooses to truly live like the apostles of Jesus."[3]

Needless to say, Waldesius had raised the ire of the archbishop, and had put himself in a very dangerous position. But Waldesius still had naive confidence in the Catholic Church. The Third Lateran Council was meeting in Rome at that time. So Waldesius and some of the Poor in Spirit journeyed to Rome to present their case to the Pope himself. The Pope received them cordially and expressed approval of their Scripture translation. He even liked their vision. But he told them that any decision about preaching would have to be made by their local bishop.

One of the delegates at the Council decided he would find out just how qualified these Poor in Spirit were to preach to others. He was a haughty monk from England, named Walter Map. Map called for the Poor in Spirit to appear in front of him and a number of the other delegates. He then asked them, "Tell me, do you believe in God the Father?"

"We do," the Poor in Spirit answered.

"And in the Son?"

"We do."

"And in the Holy Spirit?"

"We do."

"And in the Mother of Christ?"

"We do."[4]

At this last answer, the Council delegates roared with laughter. Waldesius and the others were baffled at what they had said wrong. To a chorus of derision, the Poor in Spirit were dismissed from the Council. The monk, Walter Map, reported: "At this last response a roar of derision went up and they withdrew, confused. And rightly so, because they had no one to guide them. And yet these same people expect to lead others!"[5]

What had they done wrong? Hundreds of years before, the Council of Ephesus had given Mary the title, "Mother of God." So for them to say they believed in the "Mother of Christ" showed they were theologically uneducated. But the Scriptures never refer to Mary as the Mother of God, and the Poor in Spirit were people of the Scriptures. All they knew was the simple gospel of the kingdom—and that was all they needed to know.

When Waldesius and his fellow Christians returned to Lyon, they continued to preach publicly as they had done before. They went out of their way to explain to the local Church authorities that they were not heretics with some kind of new doctrine.

Waldesius even agreed to sign a declaration of adherence to the Catholic faith that had been presented to him by a papal representative. In fact, Waldesius made only one handwritten notation on the papal declaration of faith. His note stated that his call to a life of poverty came as an act of obedience to Jesus Christ—not as an act of "perfection" on behalf of the Church.[6]

Nevertheless, the Church authorities once more commanded Waldesius and the Poor in Spirit to appear before them. And the clergy again firmly ordered them not to preach any more. In reply, Waldesius quoted by memory the words of Peter to the authorities: "Whether it is right in the sight of God to listen to you more than to God, you judge. For we cannot but speak the things which we have seen and heard."[7]

The clergy were furious, and they had the civil authorities permanently banish Waldesius and the Poor in Spirit from Lyon. However, this did not dampen the zeal of these kingdom preachers in the least. Like the apostles, they rejoiced to be persecuted in the name of Christ. So they now traveled throughout southern France, preaching the gospel of the kingdom in the streets and markets. They wrote tracts and organized public debates. And they still spoke favorably of the Catholic Church.

Cross-Pollination

Before long, the Waldensians (as the Church now called them) met some of the disciples of the two kingdom preachers we have previously discussed: Pierre de Bruys and Henri of Lausanne. Waldesius could plainly see that these other Christians were obviously not heretics. Yet, these other Christians voiced strong criticisms of the Roman Church. They attacked Rome for its worldliness, its wealth, and its acquisition of worldly power. They pointed out how veneration of images and prayers for the dead were unscriptural.

This was all new to Waldesius and his disciples. Yet, as sincere Bible students, they pored over the Scriptures. And they soon realized that these criticisms were correct. So now they, too, began to speak out against the errors and sins of the Church.[8]

The Catholic Church was quick with its response. In 1184, the Council of Verona condemned the Waldensians as dangerous schismatics (but not heretics). The same Walter Map who had belittled them with his trick questions apparently had a hand in this. He wrote:

> "These people have no settled dwellings, but go around two by two, barefoot and dressed in wool tunics. They own nothing, sharing everything in common, after the manner of the apostles. Naked, they follow a naked Christ. Their beginnings are humble to the extreme, for they have not yet much of a following. However, if we should leave them to their devices, they will end up turning all of us out."[9]

Once again, people were afraid that the meek and lowly would turn the world upside down. Finally, in 1190, the Church condemned the Waldensians as *heretics*, making them subject to ruthless suppression and death.

Undaunted, Waldesius and his disciples continued to travel across southern France. Later, they crossed the Alps into Lombardy in northern Italy. Here they encountered the followers of Arnold of Brescia, another kingdom preacher we've previously talked about. The insights of these Italian Christians (known as the Lombard Poor) helped the Waldensians to see that the church should have no involvement with the state. In turn, the spirit and zeal of the Waldensians proved to be a refreshing stimulant to the Lombard Poor. So they agreed to join the Waldensians.

The Waldensians brought to this combined movement a strong evangelistic zeal. In turn, the Lombard Poor brought to the movement the stability of community. Together, they were quite a revolutionary force to be reckoned with! But this was an army without any weapons, except the Word of God. Together, they were ready to turn the world upside down!

The Waldensian Insight Into History

Shortly after these two movements joined forces, Waldesius died. However, the movement continued on, for these people were not followers of Waldesius—they were followers of Jesus. After the death of Waldesius, the Waldensians gave further reflection about who they were and what the purpose of their movement was. They could see that the Catholic Church had gone wrong—but when? Studying church history, the Waldensians correctly saw that the turning point had happened in the days of Constantine.

The Waldensians realized that the history of the church could be divided into two periods: the period of the faithful witness (the pre-Constantinian church) and the period of betrayal (the period that began with Constantine). Did this mean that all faithful subjects of the kingdom had disappeared with Constantine? The Waldensians said no. They believed that the poison of the Constantinian Hybrid had not necessarily reached down into each member of the Body of Christ. A faithful remnant had always persevered, down to their very day. The light of the kingdom had been dimmed, but never extinguished.[10]

The Waldensians came to a clear understanding of the nature of the two kingdoms. They could give their ultimate allegiance to the kingdoms of this world, or they could give it to the kingdom of God. But they could not give it to both. So they chose to give it to the kingdom of God.

Waldensian Beliefs

The Waldensians held to no complicated theological beliefs. Their belief system was basically the gospel of the kingdom. Knowing thoroughly the teachings of Jesus, they taught that we humans are capable of making choices. And we are responsible for the choices we make. We each must make the decision to live by the teachings of Christ—and then be faithful to that decision. "No one can be a true Christian," they said, "if he has not truly surrendered his life to the Lordship of Christ."[11] They accurately saw that Jesus' teachings were revolutionary and that they were intended to be lived literally. So they taught against the accumulation of wealth. They also taught against using the sword for either self-defense or war.

In obedience to the words of Jesus, the Waldensians refused to take oaths, even though oaths were a central pillar of medieval society. Furthermore, they held to Jesus' high standard of honesty. And they became quite well known for their honesty. So much so that one poor Catholic man, who was wrongfully accused of being a Waldensian, told his inquisitors: "I'm not who you think I am. I lie. I'm a good Catholic!"[12]

One Waldensian tract said this about true Christianity:

"Many are the false Christians blinded with error, who persecute and hate those who are good, and let those live quietly who are false deceivers. But by this we may know that they are not good shepherds, for they love not the sheep, but only the wool. Scripture says, and we know it to be true, that if anyone is good—loving Jesus Christ—that person will neither curse, nor swear, nor lie, will neither commit adultery, nor kill, nor steal, nor be avenged over the enemy. ...

"This I dare say, and it is very true, that all the popes from Sylvester on, the cardinals, bishops, abbots, and the like, have no power to absolve or pardon any creature so much as one mortal sin. It is God alone who pardons, and no other. This is what pastors ought to do: preach to the people, and pray with them, and feed them with teaching from on high."[13]

The Waldensians were ardent students of the Bible, and over time they eliminated virtually all aspects of the Catholic faith that could not be found in the New Testament. Although they had started out as good Catholics, they eventually taught against such unscriptural practices and doctrines as purgatory, masses for the dead, intercessions of Mary and the saints, veneration and worship of images and crosses, and the supposed sacerdotal power of priests.[14]

Preach the Word!

Although hounded by the papal authorities, and knowing that torture and death awaited them if they were caught, Waldensian evangelists took their simple kingdom message all throughout Europe. Jesus had forbidden His followers from calling anyone by the title of Father. So the Waldensians simply called their itinerant preachers by the name *barba*, meaning "uncle." Their *barbas* normally traveled two-by-two throughout Europe. Usually a younger man teamed up with an older *barba* to learn discipleship first-hand as they traveled together. Often the Waldensian *barbas* were disguised as traveling merchants to escape the Church authorities.

The Crusade Against the Waldensians

For nearly four centuries, the Waldensians had lived like hunted animals, never knowing when the armies of the Church would descend upon them. Various Waldensian communities were obliterated by the sword. One of their last strongholds was in the Piedmont Valley, nestled in the Alps along the border of France and Italy. In 1488 and 1489—only thirty years before the Reformation—the Pope's crusaders descended on Waldensian settlements in the Alps with unspeakable cruelty.

The "holy" Catholic crusaders butchered any Waldensians they could find. They disemboweled parents and then dashed the heads of their children against rocks. They marched fathers to their deaths with the severed heads of their children tied around their necks.[15]

Church historian J. A. Wylie writes:

"These cruelties form a scene that is unparalleled and unique in the history of civilized countries. There have been tragedies in which more blood was spilled, and more life sacrificed, but none in which the actors were so completely de-humanized, and the forms of suffering so monstrously disgusting, so unutterably cruel and revolting. The 'Piedmont Massacres' in this respect stand alone."[16]

By the early 1500s, most of the Waldensian believers had been butchered. Yet, the movement survived these horrible persecutions—although only in limited areas. Still the Waldensians weren't about to quit. The surviving communities immediately began printing tracts, making use of that marvelous new invention: the printing press.

30

The Alternate Stream

Not all medieval reform movements focused on the gospel of the kingdom. Alongside the kingdom stream, there flowed a different stream—the stream of the Augustinian reformers.

At first glance, it would seem that no movement tied to Augustine could be a true reform movement. After all, he was *the* apologist for the whole Constantinian Hybrid. And that is correct. But the Church in Augustine's day had been part of the Hybrid for less than a century. As the years passed, the Church grew even further from Jesus' teaching. Veneration of icons, Mary, and the saints was just beginning in Augustine's day. In his day, there were no papal indulgences and no cardinals. The people of the congregation were allowed to drink of the cup in communion.

So returning to the Christianity of Augustine's day was in itself a major reform. Yet, it was still within the Constantinian Hybrid. It was by no means a return to the gospel of the kingdom.

Augustinian Movements vs. Kingdom Movements

Although they had many points in common, Augustinian reform movements differed significantly from kingdom movements in the following ways:

▸ 1. *Acceptance of the Constantinian Hybrid.* To begin with, all Augustinian reformers accepted the Constantinian Hybrid. They had no objection to the union of church and state. In fact, they invariably sought to accomplish their reforms through the power of the state.

▸ 2. *Rejection of Nonresistance.* Since they accepted the union of church and state, Augustinian reformers did not object to use of the sword. They all recognized that the sword was necessary for the operation and preservation of the state. And since the state was joined to the Church, the Church should not object to its members participating in war, capital punishment, and torture.

▸ 3. *Rejection of Other Kingdom Teachings.* Augustinian movements nearly always took the same form: New Testament theology (supposed!) pasted over Old Testament morals and lifestyle. Augustinian reformers taught that Jesus' kingdom teachings on wealth and oaths did not need to be followed literally. They usually said little about separation from the world. Nevertheless, to their credit, Augustinian reformers usually attacked the additions that the Roman church had made to the gospel after the time of Augustine. However, they invariably accepted most of the changes made *before* the death of Augustine.

▸ 4. *Emphasis on Theology Over Lifestyle.* Another difference between Augustinian movements and kingdom movements was that Augustinian movements typically focused on *theology* as the essence of Christianity. In contrast, kingdom movements focused on *lifestyle*, not theology. Furthermore, the theology that Augustinian reformers focused on was the theology of Augustine. These reformers usually talked about the ultimate authority of Scripture. However, in practice, it was always the Scriptures *as interpreted by Augustine.* Not surprisingly, virtually all Augustinian reformers taught absolute predestination as a major plank of their reform platform.

▸ 5. *Education.* Most Augustinian reformers were university-educated men. In fact, these reform movements usually could boast at least one major university that served as a strong ally. In contrast, most of the kingdom movements were started by laymen, and they usually had no support from the universities.

John Wycliffe

Perhaps the foremost Augustinian reformer of the Middle Ages was John Wycliffe. He served as a professor of philosophy and divinity at Oxford University in fourteenth century England. Wycliffe was popular in the English academic circles of his day, and he had the support of the English royal court.

Like the Augustinian reformers who would follow him, Wycliffe taught against most of the developments in the Catholic Church after the time of Augustine: the doctrine of transubstantiation; the veneration or worship of relics, icons, and saints; and the granting of indulgences.[1]

Wycliffe also rejected the exalted claims of the pope. In fact, he called the Roman church "Satan's synagogue," and he said that the pope was the antichrist. Wycliffe correctly saw that "Peter and Clement, together with the other helpers in the faith, were not popes, but God's helpers in the work of building up the church of our Lord Jesus Christ."[2] Wycliffe wanted the national Church in England to be independent of the pope. He denounced all religious orders in the strongest language, even going so far as to say that nobody could be a true Christian who belonged to one.[3]

In his writings, Wycliffe fiercely attacked the wealth of the Catholic Church. In fact, he taught that neither clerics nor the Church should own any property at all.[4] However, Wycliffe was not ready to embrace the full teachings of Jesus against accumulating treasures on earth. He had no problem with kings and the nobility storing up treasures on earth—he just didn't want the Church to do it. Wycliffe even said that if the Church would not hand over its vast properties to the crown, then the crown should forcibly take them. This, in fact, is precisely what Henry VIII did about 150 years after Wycliffe's death.

Like other Augustinian reformers, Wycliffe totally accepted the Constantinian Hybrid. The only part of it he objected to was the phony *Donation of Constantine* that I have previously mentioned. In Wycliffe's day, this document was still accepted as genuine. Since Wycliffe believed the state was the twin part of the Church, he taught that a secular lord must live in a state of righteousness. He said, "Nobody in mortal sin is lord of anything."[5] In other words, if a ruler is living in mortal sin, he automatically loses his office of rulership, and his subjects no longer have to obey him. This, of course, is directly contrary to what the New Testament teaches. Practically all the Roman emperors lived in mortal sin. But Paul said we were to submit ourselves to them, not *overthrow* them. Wycliffe's teaching laid the groundwork for armed revolution if the Christian body believed the king or any other lord was living in sin (or belonged to the wrong church).

Like Augustine, Wycliffe believed in absolute predestination. He taught that, before persons are ever born, they are already unalterably predestined to either eternal life or eternal damnation. He said this is not a result of God's foreknowledge, but of His arbitrary decree. Wycliffe wrote, "I assert as a matter of faith that everything that will happen, will happen of necessity. Thus if Paul is foreknown as damned, he cannot truly repent."[6]

Unlike the kingdom preachers in France and Italy, Wycliffe wanted to bring about reform through the power of the state. From the beginning, Wycliffe operated within the power circles of England, and the king and other nobles protected Wycliffe from the pope. In fact, Wycliffe's special protector was John of Gaunt, a duke who had enormous influence over the aged King Edward of England.

The Catholic Church declared many of Wycliffe's propositions to be heretical. However, because of his powerful friends, Wycliffe managed to escape burning at the stake. He died a natural death in 1384. Nevertheless, about fifty years after his death, the Church had his body exhumed, burned to ashes, and dumped in a river.

The Lollards

Wycliffe's influence lived on in England through his disciples, who were called Lollards by the Catholics. Wycliffe had always argued the authority of Scripture over the authority of the Church. One of the great accomplishments of the Lollards was their translation of the first English Bible. Although this first English Bible is popularly credited today to Wycliffe himself, the actual translating was done by his disciples and friends.[7]

Initially, the Lollards included many persons of wealth and power in their ranks. Still heavily influenced by the Constantinian Hybrid, in 1394 the Lollards presented a pamphlet to the English Parliament asking it to reform the Church. Yet, their proposed reforms are an interesting mixture of Augustinian and kingdom teachings. They attacked priestly celibacy, holy water, prayers for the dead, pilgrimages to Rome, prayers and offerings to crosses and images, and confession to priests.[8] They called for an end to the practice of the pope or his bishops performing all ordinations in England.[9]

They also attacked the practice of clergymen occupying both governmental and spiritual offices at the same time, saying:

"To have the king and bishop in one person, prelate and judge in temporal causes, curate and officer in secular office, puts any kingdom beyond good rule. This conclusion is clearly proved because the temporal and spiritual are two halves of the entire Holy Church. And so he who has applied himself to one should not meddle with the other, for no one can serve two masters."[10]

So like Wycliffe, the Lollards did not have a complete understanding of the gospel of the kingdom. They wanted secular and religious offices separated, but they still saw the secular and religious powers together constituting the "entire Holy Church." God's kingdom was still married to the state.

Nevertheless, after Wycliffe's death, the Lollards moved further from Augustinian theology and closer to the kingdom gospel. For example, despite their imperfect understanding of the kingdom, the Lollards could see that war was inconsistent with Christianity:

> "Manslaughter in war, or by pretended law of justice for a temporal cause, without spiritual revelation, is expressly contrary to the New Testament, which indeed is the law of grace and full of mercies. This conclusion is openly proved by the examples of Christ's preaching here on earth, for he specially taught a man to love his enemies, and to show them pity, and not to slay them. The reason is this: (generally speaking) when men fight, love is forgotten after the first blow. And whoever dies without love goes down the straight road to hell.

> "And beyond this, we know well that no clergyman can by Scripture or lawful reason remit the punishment of death for one mortal sin and not for another. But the New Testament is the law of mercy. And it prohibits every kind of manslaughter. For the Gospel says: "It was said to them of old, 'thou shalt not kill.'" ...[The crusaders] deserve ill thanks from the King of Peace. For it is by humility and patience that the faith is multiplied. Christ Jesus hates and threatens men who fight and kill, for he says, 'He who smites with the sword shall perish by the sword.'"[11]

As might be guessed, Parliament did not institute these Lollard articles. In fact, within a few decades, the crown and the Catholic Church united in an attempt to completely eradicate the Lollards. The Catholic powers hunted down the Lollards ruthlessly, and many of them were burned at the stake. Others recanted their doctrines when faced with torture and death. The survivors were driven underground. The Lollards continued to meet, but in secret. Their simple meetings emphasized Bible study and preaching of the Word.[12]

After the Lollard movement lost the support of the king and nobility, it began to take on many of the characteristics of the medieval kingdom movements. Their numbers were now almost exclusively made up of tradesmen, peasants, and the urban poor. The Catholic Church could never eradicate them, and so the Lollards were still around when the Reformation reached England.[13]

However, what the Catholic Church could not do, the Reformation did. The surviving Lollards were drawn into the English Reformation and its Augustinian theology. After the time of Queen Mary (1553-1558), they lost their distinctive teachings and their separate identity.

31

The Waldensians Meet
The Swiss Reformers

In the early 1500s, the Augustinian stream that had been a mere trickle during the Middle Ages suddenly gushed forth in Germany through the teaching of Martin Luther. At the same time, it burst out in Switzerland under the leading reformer there, named Ulrich Zwingli. As was typical of Augustinian reformers, both Luther and Zwingli were well educated university men. They were both admirers of Augustine and were well-versed in his writings.

The son of a Swiss magistrate, Zwingli was a prominent patriot, humanist, preacher, and statesman. He was also an ordained priest, serving as a military chaplain for Swiss mercenaries fighting on behalf of the Pope. In 1519, Zwingli was appointed as pastor of the principal church in Zurich, Switzerland.[1]

When he accepted the position, Zwingli was not intending to start a Reformation. Nevertheless, in his preaching, he chose not to follow the interpretations of the medieval Catholic theologians. Rather, he followed his own interpretation of Scripture, which interpretations were heavily influenced by Augustine.

Zwingli was a popular public figure, and the civil magistrates in Zurich did not oppose his preaching. In fact, they even ordered the other priests to preach the Scriptures alone and to be silent about human additions. In 1522, Zwingli preached a sermon that showed that the prohibition of eating meat during Lent had no foundation in Scripture. This touched off a storm that brought Zwingli into open conflict with the Catholic Church and caused considerable commotion throughout Switzerland.

Zwingli asked the magistracy to call for a public debate on the issue of Lent, which they did. In the debate, Zwingli won over both the crowd and the magistracy. With the backing of the state, Zwingli launched a major reform of the church in Zurich. Zwingli's goal became to reform the entire religious, political and social life of all citizens—based on the power of the Scriptures (as interpreted by Zwingli).[2]

Since all of the Swiss Catholic bishops opposed the Reformation, the civil magistracy of Zurich stepped in and assumed the governing and jurisdictional rights formerly carried out by the Catholic bishops. In 1525, the magistracy confiscated all of the property formerly owned by the Church, and it began to control the education of the clergy.[3]

Sadly, Zwingli fully accepted the Constantinian Hybrid. He preached the Augustinian gospel, not the kingdom gospel. Zwingli rooted out those Roman Catholic practices that had been added since the time of Augustine. But like all other Augustinian reformers, Zwingli looked to the power of the state to bring about his reforms. And he had no hesitation to use the sword to further his movement. In fact, he died on the battlefield, serving as the chaplain for his reformed army.[4]

Meeting the Waldensians

South of Zurich, a friend and supporter of Zwingli, William Farel, was preaching Reformation doctrines in the town of Aigle, on the east bank of Lake Geneva. This fiery preacher operated under the protection of the civil government of the canton of Berne, and he successfully persuaded thousands to join the Swiss Reformation.[5]

Meanwhile, news of the Reformation had reached the Waldensians in Italy. So they sent two *barbas* to Germany to learn more about it. The two men the Waldensians selected were quite different in their makeup. The older of the two, who we know only as Giorgio, was steady, mature, and cautious. The other *barba*, Martin Gonin, was young and energetic, but quite impressionable. Together, Giorgio and Martin crossed the Swiss Alps on foot and slowly made their way to the Swiss town of Aigle. They were intending to spend only a night or two and then continue on to Germany. However, while there, they soon heard about William Farel and his Reformation preaching. So they arranged a meeting with Farel, who introduced them to Reformation doctrines. The forceful Farel made quite an impression on the young *barba*, Martin Gonin.[6]

Having learned so much about the Reformation, the two *barbas* decided to report back to their brothers and sisters in Italy, rather than continuing to Germany. The young Waldensian, Martin Gonin, returned to Italy quite enthusiastic about the Reformation. However, the older *barba*, Giorgio, expressed reservations about joining the Reformation. He had heard and seen enough to know that there were significant differences between the beliefs and practices of the Waldensians and those of the Swiss Reformers.[7]

For four years, the Waldensians discussed the matter in their congregations. Finally, they decided to send four new representatives to Switzerland to confer some more. Farel and his fellow Swiss reformers warmly welcomed these four Waldensian representatives. Here were the heroes that had stood nearly alone against Rome for over three hundred years! "You will never have to stand alone again," the Swiss reformers told the Waldensians. "We're here to help you."

The scenario was not that different from what the fourth-century Christians faced when Constantine offered his "help." The same test faced the Waldensians. In the Swiss Reformers, they had found someone practically next door who wanted to embrace them into their fellowship. Perhaps centuries of prayers were now finally being answered. Maybe God was opening a new door for them.

But there was a catch. "There are just a few things that we need for you to change in order to fully fit in to the Reformation," the reformers told the Waldensian representatives. Well, the "few things" turned out to be nothing less than a complete abandonment of kingdom Christianity. The Waldensians listened to what the Reformers had to say and agreed to communicate further after reporting back to the whole body of Waldensians.[8]

The representatives returned to Italy and reported their findings. Soon, there was a three-way split among the Waldensians. The conservatives had heard enough, for they realized that the Reformers were not kingdom Christians. They wanted to remain separate from the Reformers. At the opposite end were liberals like Martin Gonin, who felt the Waldensians should join the Reformation, making whatever changes were necessary to fit in. The last group were the moderates, who wanted further dialogue with the Reformers.[9]

Since the liberals and moderates comprised the majority, they invited William Farel from Switzerland to come and address a church-wide assembly of the Waldensian body. In a meadow near Chanforan, Italy, the Waldensians met to debate their future. The persuasive Farel was able to sway the majority of the body to join the Reformation. At Chanforan, most of the Waldensians agreed to the following positions:

- "A Christian may swear by the name of God without contravention to what is written in Matthew 5, provided that one who so swears does not take the name of God in vain."

- "Oral confession [of sins] is not commanded by God, and it has been determined according to Holy Scriptures that the true confession of a Christian is to confess to God alone."

- "A Christian may exercise the office of magistrate over Christians who have done wrong."

- "All those that have been and shall be saved have been elected of God before the foundation of the world."

- "The minister of the Word of God ought not to itinerate from place to place, except it be for some great good of the church."[10]

For Farel and the Reformers, this was quite a theological coup. The Waldensians had basically agreed to give up practically everything that their movement had stood for. For centuries, they had suffered horrendous persecution from the Catholics rather than discontinue their itinerant preaching. But now they gave it up without shedding a drop of blood. At Chanforan, they even agreed to renounce their practice of voluntary poverty.[11]

The spiritual surrender at Chanforan was capped by the Waldensians agreeing to the commissioning of a new French translation of the Bible to replace the Waldensian translation they had used for centuries.[12]

It was the end of one of the most significant Kingdom movements in Christian history. To be sure, the Waldensians continued on. They became model Reformation Christians, happily taking up the sword in defense of their beliefs. They saw the "error" of having taken so many Bible passages literally. And they are still with us today. But their kingdom witness isn't.

32

The New Zion in Geneva

After the conference in Chanforan, William Farel moved to Geneva, where he became friends with a gifted young preacher named John Calvin. Farel persuaded Calvin to write the foreword to the new Reformed translation that the Waldensians had agreed to use. Farel also convinced Calvin to remain in Geneva and lead the Reformation there. Soon, Geneva became the center of the Swiss Reformation.

Like Zwingli, Calvin accepted the Constantinian Hybrid without reservation. Instead of bringing Geneva back to the gospel of the kingdom, Calvin desired to establish in Geneva a state similar to Israel of the Old Testament. All citizens of the state would *have to* accept the Reformation and attend church. And the state would be actively involved in establishing and maintaining "true" doctrine and godly living. To those who strongly supported Calvin, it was a dream come true.

However, for those who didn't agree with Calvin or his reforms, it was a reign of terror. To maintain discipline over the population, the Geneva reformers established a body known as the consistory. It was composed of all of the pastors in the city, together with twelve presbyters. Citizens who opposed the accepted doctrine of Calvin or who missed church services were called before the consistory for discipline.[1] The consistory went about its task with gleeful enthusiasm. Officers were set over various districts of the city in order to watch over the conduct of the population. These civil officers reported anyone guilty of even the smallest infraction. They questioned children in order to obtain information about their parents.[2]

If any persons were suspected of being opposed to Calvin's rule, the authorities immediately searched their homes for any incriminating evidence. If no solid evidence was found, the authorities typically tortured the suspects to make them confess. Their confessions were then taken as incontrovertible evidence of their guilt. Let me share with you a few examples:

In June of 1546, someone left an anonymous note on the pulpit of St. Pierre's church in Geneva that condemned the Reformed preachers and threatened them with revenge. The city government went into immediate action. They arrested an irreverent freethinker named Jacques Gruet, purely on naked suspicion. They then searched his home. However, they found no evidence linking him to the anonymous note. Nevertheless, when the authorities went through Gruet's private papers, they found a few of them that contained critical remarks about Calvin. That was enough to make Gruet a criminal. So they tortured him hideously until he "confessed" his crime. They then beheaded him.[3]

A few months later, a Reformation preacher named Jean Trolliet spoke against Calvin's doctrine of dual predestination as taught in Calvin's *Institutes of the Christian Religion*. Trolliet pointed out that Calvin's doctrine essentially made God the author of sin. It meant that God was punishing the wicked—even though it was His decision that made them wicked. However, Calvin refused to discuss the issue with Trolliet—or with anyone else. Instead, he haughtily replied that the doctrines in his *Institutes* were put in his brain by God. He then had Trolliet judicially banished from Geneva.[4]

Burning Heretics

Calvin had sent a copy of his *Institutes of the Christian Religion* to a Spanish thinker named Michael Servetus. Servetus was a gifted scientist and geographer. In fact, he was the first person to accurately describe the human circulatory system. A man of many interests, Servetus also wrote some theological works. These works contain both insightful observations and erroneous speculations. By sending Servetus a copy of his theological work, Calvin hoped to "set him straight."

Servetus read Calvin's work, making numerous marginal notes, criticisms, and refutations as he read. Three of the things he criticized were Calvin's teachings on infant baptism and predestination, as well as Calvin's explanation of the Trinity. Although Servetus believed in the Deity of Christ, his understanding of the Trinity was a bit confused and was definitely erroneous on a number of points. Servetus then sent Calvin's *Institutes* back to him—with all of Servetus' comments. Infuriated, Calvin remarked that if Servetus ever came to Geneva, he would never leave the city alive.[5]

However, the Inquisition caught up with Servetus before Calvin did. It arrested him in France (where he had fled) and sentenced him to be burned at the stake as a heretic. Nevertheless, Servetus escaped from prison and headed to Italy. On his way to Italy, Servetus unwisely passed through Geneva. He thought it would be interesting to hear Calvin preach. But Calvin recognized Servetus and ordered his arrest. The authorities then threw him into a horrible dungeon with no heat or light and little food.[6]

At his trial, Servetus was denied the right to have an attorney.[7] The authorities charged him with forty articles of heresy. Most of these articles concerned the Trinity, but others concerned the fact that he denied infant baptism and taught that little children are sinless until they come of age. The criminal indictment also charged Servetus with making insulting remarks about Calvin's theology. The judge would not allow Servetus to explain or defend any of the things he had written.

After hearing the evidence, the Geneva authorities condemned Servetus to be burned to death at the stake for his heretical teachings—even though he wasn't even a citizen of Geneva but was just passing through. William Farel, the man who had persuaded the Waldensians to join the Reformation, accompanied Servetus to the place of execution, loudly berating him the whole time for his heresy.

When they reached the place where Servetus was to die, Farel warned the crowd of observers: "Here you see what power Satan possesses when he has a man in his power. This man is a scholar of distinction, and he perhaps believed he was acting rightly. But now Satan possesses him completely, as he might possess you, should you fall into his traps."[8]

The executioners then chained Servetus to a stake and piled faggots of wood around him, about half of which were green. Because of the green wood, Servetus died a slow, agonizing death—while the crowd watched in amusement.

Although Calvin had recommended that Servetus be executed by some means other than burning, he didn't use his influence to stop the burning. In fact, some months afterward, Calvin wrote, "Many people have accused me of such ferocious cruelty that (they allege) I would like to kill again the man I have destroyed. Not only am I indifferent to their comments, but I rejoice in the fact that they spit in my face. ...Whoever shall now argue that it is unjust to put heretics and blasphemers to death will knowingly and willingly incur their very guilt."[9]

I can't help but wonder what the Waldensians thought of all of these things. A few decades before, they were the ones being hunted down and burned at the stake. Now they were part of a movement that was doing the same thing to others.

What Did the Reformation Gain?

What had the Swiss Reformation gained? To be sure, in the Reformed cantons, it had cleared the churches of the vast majority of Rome's additions to Scripture: Mariolatry, images, saints, popes and cardinals, pilgrimages, and other such unscriptural additions. And that was wonderful. However, Zwingli, Farel, and Calvin did nothing to further the *kingdom* teachings of Jesus.

In fact, Reformed theology was in some ways more antithetical to the gospel of the kingdom than was Rome's theology. As we have discussed, Rome had relegated Jesus' kingdom teachings to the realm of the "perfect." If a Christian wanted to take the extra step of reaching for Christian perfection, then he should live by these teachings. In contrast, Calvin made the kingdom teachings of Christ wholly irrelevant.

Under Calvin's doctrine of predestination, it makes no difference whether a person lives by Jesus' teachings or not. That's because nothing he does can possibly affect the destiny that God has already determined for him. More than that, Calvin—like Augustine—specifically denied that Jesus had introduced any new moral or lifestyle teachings beyond the Old Testament. Writing against kingdom Christians of his day, Calvin said:

> "The only subterfuge left ... is to claim that our Lord requires a greater perfection in the Christian church than He did of the Jewish people. Now this is true with respect to the *ceremonies*. But that there exists a different rule of life with respect to the moral law ... than what the people of old had—this is a false opinion. ...

> "Therefore, let us hold this position: that with regard to true spiritual justice, that is to say, with regard to a faithful man walking in good conscience and being whole before God in both his occupation and in all his works, there exists a plain and complete guide for it in the law of Moses, to which we need simply cling if we want to follow the right path. Thus whoever adds to or takes anything from it exceeds the limits. Therefore, our position is sure and infallible.

"We worship the same God that the fathers of old did. We have the same law and rule that they had, showing us how to govern ourselves in order to walk rightly before God. It thus follows that an occupation that was considered holy and lawful back then, cannot be forbidden to Christians today."[10]

Like the Roman Catholics, Calvin taught that the church and the civil government are simply twin parts of God's kingdom. So it was the *duty* of the state to establish the true faith, protect the church, and compel the citizens of the state to conform their lives to the moral law of the Old Testament. This was expressly stated in the Second Helvetic (Swiss) Confession of 1566:

"We certainly teach that the care of religion belongs especially to the holy magistrate. Let him, therefore, hold the Word of God in his hands, and take care lest anything contrary to it is taught. Likewise let him govern the people entrusted to him by God with good laws made according to the Word of God, and let him keep them in discipline, duty and obedience. Let him exercise judgment by judging uprightly. Let him not respect any man's person or accept bribes. Let him protect widows, orphans and the afflicted. Let him punish and even banish criminals, impostors and barbarians. For he does not bear the sword in vain (Rom. 13:4).

"Therefore, let him draw this sword of God against all malefactors, seditious persons, thieves, murderers, oppressors, blasphemers, perjured persons, and all those whom God has commanded him to punish and even to execute. Let him suppress stubborn heretics (who are truly heretics), who do not cease to blaspheme the majesty of God and to trouble and even destroy the Church of God.

"And if it is necessary to preserve the safety of the people by war, let him wage war in the name of God; provided he has first sought peace by all means possible, and cannot save his people in any other way except by war. And when the magistrate does these things in faith, he serves God by those very works which are truly good, and receives a blessing from the Lord."[11]

When some Christians questioned Calvin on whether it was really right for a Christian to take up the sword in the capacity of a magistrate, Calvin replied, "I ask, if this calling to fulfill the office of the sword or of temporal power is repugnant to the vocation of believers, then how is it that the judges in the Old Testament, especially good kings like David, Hezekiah, and Josiah, and even a few prophets like Daniel, made use of it?"[12]

In other words, in Calvin's mind, nothing had changed with the coming of Christianity. Everything—except theology and ordinances—was just the same as it had been in Israel. Like Josiah and Hezekiah, Christians should try to occupy the office of magistrate so that they could protect true religion with all the powers of civil authority, including the sword.

Yet, Jesus had specifically said that His disciples had not fought to protect Him for the very reason that His kingdom was not "of this world." So in saying that Christians should take up the sword to defend themselves and their church, Calvin was acknowledging that the kingdom he sought to protect *was* of this world. His New Zion was a kingdom of this world, just like all other earthly kingdoms.

33

The Kingdom Banner
Arises Anew

The Swiss Reformers had managed to destroy the kingdom witness of the Waldensians. But they could not prevent others from lifting the kingdom banner anew. One of the very good things that came out of the Reformation was that it fueled the printing and distribution of the Bible throughout Europe. Various Reformation scholars translated the Bible into the vernacular, and the printing press made these translations affordable to the average person.

Europeans who read the Bible for themselves—free of the Augustinian influence of the Reformers—frequently came to embrace the gospel of the kingdom. And so a whole new kingdom movement sprang up spontaneously all across northern Europe.

In Zurich, Switzerland, this new kingdom movement first flowered during the time when Zwingli was preaching. Some of Zwingli's associates were not blinded by the influence of Augustine, and they clearly saw the gospel of the kingdom in Jesus' teaching. They wanted to restore apostolic Christianity, but Zwingli was not willing to go any further with his Reformation than what the city council would allow. So these kingdom Christians began meeting in homes by themselves.

In addition to restoring Jesus' kingdom teachings, these new kingdom Christians also taught the need for a holy, disciplined church—not a state church that included everyone who lived within the state. They also rejected predestination. However, Zwingli proved to be as intolerant and iron-fisted as Calvin later would be. With Zwingli's approval, the civil authorities quickly instituted laws against these kingdom Christians, whom they called Anabaptists—rebaptizers.* One of these laws reads as follows:

> "In order that the dangerous, wicked, turbulent and seditious sect of the Anabaptists may be eradicated, we have thus decreed: If any one is suspected of rebaptism, he is to be warned by the magistracy to leave the territory under penalty of the designated punishment. Every person is obliged to report those favorable to rebaptism. Whoever shall not comply with this ordinance is liable to punishment according to the sentence of the magistracy.

> "Teachers of rebaptism, baptizing preachers, and leaders of irregular meetings are to be drowned. Those previously released from prison who have sworn to desist from such things, shall incur the same penalty. Foreign Anabaptists are to be driven out; if they return, they shall be drowned. No one is allowed to secede from the [state] church and to absent himself from the Holy Supper. Whoever flees from one jurisdiction to another shall be banished or extradited upon demand.[1]

Zwingli and his civil magistrates quickly arrested any Anabaptist teachers or leaders they could find. They threw these Christians into bleak dungeons and fed them only bread and water. If these imprisoned Christians refused to recant their "errors," they were bound with their hands behind them and then drowned in the river—a baptism of death.[2]

In Germany, Austria, and the Netherlands, other leaders and groups of kingdom Christians sprouted up independently of the

---

*This was because they practiced voluntary believer's baptism instead of accepting state-enforced baptism of their infants.

Anabaptists in Switzerland. These other kingdom groups invariably discovered the same gospel of the kingdom, and soon they were all in touch with each other. The Reformers and Catholics labeled all of these kingdom Christians with the name of Anabaptists.

All of the mainline Reformers believed that the primary problem with Rome was its *theology*. That's because all of these Reformers thought that the essence of Christianity itself was theology. However, the Anabaptists correctly saw that the essence of Christianity is *relationship*, not theology. We first have to be born again so that we can enter the kingdom of God. And then we can grow as a branch on the vine of Jesus. Yes, Rome held to many unbiblical practices and doctrines, all of which needed to be corrected. But just making theological corrections wasn't going to solve the underlying problem.

The basic problem was that Roman Catholicism had largely become a mechanistic religion. Everything worked automatically. If a person held to the creed of the Church, partook of the sacraments, and died faithful to the Church (not in mortal sin), he was saved. If a person committed a serious sin, he could mechanically have it expiated by performing the stated penance. This might be a matter of giving alms, going on a pilgrimage or Crusade, paying for an indulgence, or viewing relics of the saints. No change of heart was required. And so his relationship with Christ never changed.

Now, I want to make it clear that the Roman Catholic Church itself did not officially teach that Christianity was nothing more than a matter of mechanically going through a list of steps. The Church certainly taught that love of God and genuine repentance from sin were essential. The problem was (and still is) that there was a considerable gulf between what Rome officially said and what was actually practiced and preached in the typical Catholic community. In practice, Roman Catholicism had largely become a machinelike religion, preaching cheap grace.

It is commonly thought that the Reformation changed all of that. But, instead, the Reformation largely replaced one form of cheap grace (sacraments, indulgences, etc.) with another form of cheap grace—easy believism: Just believe that Jesus died for your sins and that your own obedience plays no role in your salvation and—*voilá*—your eternal life in heaven is assured. The truth is that German Lutherans were little different than German Catholics, except as to theology and forms of worship. To be sure, the Reformed churches in Switzerland did require a much stricter form of Christian living, which they enforced through the civil authorities. Yet these churches still taught the ultimate form of mechanical Christianity: God arbitrarily predestined everyone before they were even born.

The New Birth

Neither Luther, Zwingli, Calvin, or the Roman Catholics put much emphasis on the new birth. In their systems, the new birth was simply part of the whole mechanical process. But for the Anabaptists, it was quite different. A person had to *start* with the new birth, including a personal commitment to the kingdom of Christ. It wasn't just a matter of believing in Jesus as one's *Savior*. He also had to be one's *Lord*. Not just theologically, but as lived out in a person's actual life. As one Anabaptist expressed it:

"Now perhaps some may answer: 'Our belief is that Christ is the Son of God, that His Word is truth, and that He purchased us with His blood and truth. We were regenerated in baptism and we received the Holy Spirit; therefore we are the true church and congregation of Christ.' We reply: 'If your faith is as you say, why do you not do the things which He has commanded you in his Word?' His commandment is: 'Repent and keep the commandments.' ...Faithful reader, reflect that if it had so happened to you as you say, ...you would have to acknowledge besides that the aforementioned birth and the received Spirit are altogether without effect, wisdom, power, and fruit in you; yes, vain and dead. That you live neither after the Spirit nor in the power of the new birth."[3]

The same writer described the type of faith that the kingdom gospel demands: "True evangelical faith cannot lie dormant. It clothes the naked. It feeds the hungry. It comforts the sorrowful. It shelters the destitute. It serves those who harm it. It binds up that which is wounded. It has become all things to all men."[4] As another Anabaptist leader expressed it, "No man can truly know Christ unless he follows Him in life."[5]

As Paul put it, "The kingdom of God is not in word but in power" (1 Cor. 4:20). The essence of the kingdom isn't words—theology—but *power*. And Paul wasn't speaking in that passage about the power to perform wonders. Wonders are like words. They can be part of the kingdom, but they aren't the essence of the kingdom. By themselves, they prove nothing. Jesus knew our inclination would be to follow wonders, so He warned us in advance, "Many will say to Me in that day, 'Lord, Lord, have we not prophesied in Your name, cast out demons in Your name, and done many wonders in Your Name?' And then I will declare to them, 'I never knew you; depart from Me, you who practice *lawlessness*!'" (Mt. 7:22,23).

If Jesus *never knew* these wonder-workers, then it means they were never even on His vine. They lived their entire Christian life in a fantasy world—prophesying and casting out demons in Jesus' name. They thought they had power, but whatever power they had didn't come from Him. What was their problem? Was it that they trusted in their own works? No, Jesus said their problem was that they 'practiced lawlessness.' His kingdom has laws, and if we don't obey His laws, then we practice lawlessness.

This is the very point that the Anabaptists made to their hearers. It doesn't matter how much theology you've figured out correctly. And it doesn't matter what formal steps you've taken to be born again. If you're not living under the power of the Spirit, it's all worthless. Either you never were on Jesus' vine, or you've been lopped off. Someone growing on Christ's vine doesn't practice lawlessness. He doesn't live in disobedience to Christ's laws.

People of the Kingdom

An Anabaptist writer gave this description of the Anabaptists in his day:

"In baptism they bury their sins in the Lord's death and rise with Him to a new life. They circumcise their hearts with the Word of the Lord; they are baptized with the Holy Spirit into the spotless, holy body of Christ, as obedient members of His church, according to the true ordinance and Word of the Lord. They put on Christ and manifest His spirit, nature, and power in all their conduct. They fear God with the heart and seek in all their thoughts, words, and works, nothing but the praise of God and the salvation of their beloved brethren. Hatred and vengeance they do not know, for they love those who hate them; they do good to those who despitefully use them and pray for those who persecute them.[6]

"These regenerated people have a spiritual king over them who rules them by the unbroken scepter of His mouth, namely, with His Holy Spirit and Word. He clothes them with the garment of righteousness, of pure white silk. He refreshes them with the living water of His Holy Spirit and feeds them with the Bread of Life. His name is Christ Jesus. They are the children of peace who have beaten their swords into plowshares and their spears into pruning hooks, and know war no more. They give to Caesar the things that are Caesar's and to God the things that are God's."[7]

These new kingdom Christians quickly found each other and formed local congregations and continent-wide alliances. The Anabaptist movement spread so rapidly that it appeared that it would become a larger movement than the mainstream Reformation.[8] The Anabaptists had no organized missions system. Instead, like the early Christians, all Anabaptists were missionaries, sharing the gospel of the kingdom with everyone they could. Once again, the gospel of the kingdom was turning the world upside down!

But the response from the world was quite swift. It had no desire to be turned upside down. The Reformers feared that if too many people joined this new kingdom movement, they would have insufficient troops to fight the Catholics or the Turks. Both the Reformers and the Catholics wanted a society built within the confines of the Constantinian Hybrid. They had come to believe that if church and state were not joined, all of society would collapse. Therefore, the Anabaptists must die!

Both the Roman Catholic and Reformation churches subjected these new kingdom Christians to the same inhuman tortures that the pagan Romans had once inflicted on the Christians of their day (other than throwing them to the lions). For example, the German authorities executed the following sentence against the Anabaptist leader, Michael Sattler:

> "Judgment is passed that Michael Sattler shall be delivered to the executioner, who shall lead him to the place of execution, and cut out his tongue. Then, they shall fasten him to a wagon and twice tear pieces of flesh from his body with red hot tongs. After he has been taken outside the [city] gate, they shall tear his body five more times in the same manner. After this, he shall be burned to ashes."[9]

And what terrible crimes did Michael Sattler commit to incur such cruel punishment? He simply had taught kingdom Christianity to others. Two of the nine articles of indictment against him were that he taught against oaths and that he preached nonresistance. I wonder if those same Christian authorities would have torn Christ's flesh with red hot tongs and then burned Him alive. After all, He too preached nonresistance and told His disciples not to take oaths.

The persecution against the Anabaptists was actually worse than what the early Christians had faced from Rome. That's because it was far more thorough and relentless. Yet, even with this intense persecution, the Reformers and Catholics were unable to obliterate this new kingdom movement entirely. A faithful remnant of them is still with us. At the same time, the Anabaptists have had their share of shortcomings. For example, as a result of the horrendous persecution from other so-called Christians, most of them eventually lost their zeal to witness to others.

Other Kingdom Christians

The Anabaptist movement was one of the most important movements in the history of Christianity. Not only did the Anabaptists restore the gospel of the kingdom in the sixteenth century, a remnant of them have kept the banner aloft for nearly five hundred years.

Yet, the Anabaptists have by no means been the only kingdom Christians during the past five hundred years. Even though Reformation churches have typically labeled kingdom Christianity as "works Christianity," individual kingdom Christians have still sprouted in the soil of these churches. Nor have kingdom Christians been absent from the Roman Catholic Church either. It's just that it's much more difficult to practice kingdom Christianity in a Catholic or Reformation setting. In fact, no lasting kingdom movements have ever come out of any church that's attached to Reformation theology.

Quakers

Although some Anabaptists reached England, they were never able to establish a permanent foothold there. However, in 1647, a native English kingdom movement arose independently of the Anabaptists. Typical of most kingdom movements, this fresh new movement was started by an unlearned weaver's son named George Fox. From reading the Bible on his own, without any theological training, he discovered the gospel of the kingdom.

With excitement and joy, Fox began enthusiastically preaching kingdom Christianity throughout England. He was so bold in his preaching that sometimes he would interrupt the sermon in the state church and begin preaching to the congregation. On one occasion after doing this, an angry mob of church-goers lynched him. When Fox survived the hanging, they clubbed him until he was unconscious. When he finally regained his consciousness, he stood up, looked at the mob and said in a loud voice, "Strike me again if you like. Here are my arms, my head, and my cheeks." Bewildered, the crowd melted away.[10]

George Fox made many disciples through his preaching, and they called themselves the Society of Friends. Others called them Quakers, the name by which they're best known. Throughout England, and later in the Americas, the Quakers preached kingdom values everywhere they went. Although the church authorities whipped and imprisoned the Quakers, nothing could silence them. In the New World, the Puritans forbade any Quakers to set foot in Massachusetts, on pain of death. But the Quakers continued to witness in Massachusetts, so the Puritans hanged a number of them.

Unlike the Anabaptists and Waldensians, the Quakers emphasized the inner witness of the Spirit over the teaching of Scripture. Believing they had entered a new age of the Spirit, they erroneously taught that baptism and communion are no longer necessary.[11] Over the centuries, their emphasis on the Inner Light of the Spirit led them to greater and greater social activism and less reliance on the Scriptures. Today, the Quakers are an extremely liberal body that focuses primarily on social activism. Only a small remnant of Quakers today hold to the Biblical kingdom gospel.

The Brethren

While the Quaker movement was flourishing in England, a new spiritual movement was sweeping across Germany and northern Europe—Pietism. Hungering for authentic spiritual life, Christians who belonged to the state churches began meeting in small groups to study the Bible and pray. Like the Quakers, the Pietists strongly emphasized the inner work of the Holy Spirit. And, like the Quakers, the Pietists generally viewed baptism and communion as unessential, minor aspects of the Christian life. Unfortunately, unlike the Quakers, most Pietists did not teach a literal obedience to Jesus' kingdom teachings.

In the Palatinate area of Germany in the early 1700s, a young Christian named Alexander Mack had been spiritually awakened by the Pietist movement. Now, most Pietists remained in the state churches (Lutheran, Reformed or Catholic) and held their prayer meetings at times that did not conflict with the state services. However, Mack and his spiritual companions saw the need to separate from the state churches and to return to primitive Christianity. From their Bible reading, Mack and his companions came to see the clear gospel of the kingdom. They rejected oaths, war, the accumulation of wealth, lawsuits, and other such things that conflicted with Christ's teaching.[12]

Calling themselves simply by the name of Brethren, these new kingdom Christians came to be known as the German Baptists or Dunkards. They enthusiastically spread the gospel of the kingdom throughout the towns where they lived. Persecution from the authorities forced them to move from town to town—and eventually to Germantown, Pennsylvania. In his *Autobiography*, Benjamin Franklin describes his encounter with the Dunkards:

> "I think a more prudent conduct [is] in another sect among us, that of the Dunkers. I was acquainted with one of its founders, Michael Welfare, soon after it appeared. He complained to me

that they were viciously calumniated by the zealots of other persuasions, and charged with abominable principles and practices, to which they were utter strangers. I told him this had always been the case with new sects, and that to put a stop to such abuse, I imagined it might be well to publish the articles of their belief, and the rules of their discipline. He said it had been proposed among them, but not agreed to, for this reason:

"'When we were first drawn together as a society,' says he, 'it had pleased God to enlighten our minds so far as to see that some things, which we once esteemed truths, were errors; and others, which we had esteemed errors, were real truths. From time to time He has been pleased to afford us further light, and our principles have been improving, and our errors diminishing. Now, we are not sure that we have arrived at the end of this progression, and at the perfection of spiritual or theological knowledge. We fear that, if we should once print our confession of faith, we should feel ourselves as if bound and confined by it, and perhaps be unwilling to receive further improvement. And our successors, still more so, would conceive what we their elders and founders had done to be something sacred, never to be departed from.'

"This modesty in a sect is perhaps a singular instance in the history of mankind, every other sect supposing itself in possession of *all* truth."[13]

Actually, the Dunkards' non-dogmatic approach to theology (beyond the basics) is quite characteristic of new kingdom movements. When believers first discover the kingdom, their joy for this hidden treasure is so great that they focus primarily on the kingdom and its King. They don't worry much about intricate issues of theology.

Apostolic Christian Church

In eighteenth century Switzerland, after the Anabaptists had virtually disappeared from that country, Samuel Froehlich, a young seminary student, organized Christian fellowships based largely upon a literal interpretation of God's Word. Not surprisingly, this led him to the familiar basics of the kingdom gospel: nonresistance, simple theology, a recognition of the role that obedience plays in salvation, and the rejection of oaths and materialism. Like all other new kingdom Christians, Froehlich and his fellow believers witnessed enthusiastically and their new kingdom movement spread rapidly throughout Europe. These kingdom Christians are still with us today, being known in Europe as the Nazarenes and in America as the Apostolic Christian Church.

Kingdom Sprouts

Most people who read the Scriptures unfettered by prior indoctrination generally come to a knowledge of the kingdom gospel. So it's not surprising to find that new house churches and small fellowships often teach the gospel of the kingdom. In fact, some of the established, conventional churches that are familiar today actually embraced nonresistance and preached more of a kingdom gospel in their infancy. Some examples are the Church of Christ, the Christian Church, the Moravians, and some of the Wesleyan holiness and Pentecostal churches. However, as those movements grew, they established seminaries, acquired respectability, and usually lost most of their kingdom teachings.

Before leaving our discussion of the various kingdom movements through history, I want to make it clear that these kingdom groups didn't hold to the same minute theological beliefs. They all[*] held to the Apostles Creed and the gospel of the

---

[*]With the exception of the Quakers, whose teaching on baptism was weak.

kingdom, including the lifestyle teachings of Jesus Christ. That's what's important to Jesus.

34

The Ball Is Now
In Our Court

As I've said before, what I've shared with you in this book isn't David Bercot's personally concocted theology. It's the *historic* Christian faith. It's what the church of the first few centuries taught, which can easily be demonstrated from the writings of the pre-Constantinian Christians.[*]

Evangelicals Who Worship Mary

If there is nothing else you remember from this book, I hope you'll remember that the essence of Christianity is not theological, nor mechanical—but *relational*. This doesn't mean that there are no necessary theological doctrines, because there are. However, when we enter the kingdom, we enter into an ongoing relationship with our King.

Of course, most churches today acknowledge that as Christians we enter into a relationship with Jesus. But the relationship they describe is not the same one Jesus talks about. The relationship of modern popular theology is usually a fake relationship with a counterfeit Jesus.

---

[*]I encourage you to examine this for yourself. The writings of the pre-Nicene Christians are contained in the set, *The Ante-Nicene Fathers*, which is available from various vendors at an affordable price. In fact, these writings can be read for free on the Internet. Simply do a search for "Ante-Nicene Fathers."

One of the great sins of the Roman Catholic Church is its devotion to Mary. The Mary of Roman Catholicism and Eastern Orthodoxy is extremely popular because Mary is never angry, she never punishes sin, and she has no commandments to give. Her grace covers every sin. And all she wants in return is popular devotion. Devout Catholics imagine that they have an ongoing relationship with this make-believe Mary.

Although Bible-believing Christians criticize Catholics for worshipping Mary, the truth is that most of them worship Mary as well. What? They worship Mary? Yes, they do. But they call her Jesus, not Mary. The popular Jesus of easy-believism is simply a warmed-over version of the Catholic Mary. This Jesus is never angry, He never punishes sin, and He has no commandments. He is all grace, and He loves nothing more than to be praised and worshipped. A relationship with this counterfeit Jesus is no more real than a Catholic's imagined relationship with Mary.

God *Will* Test Us

A crucial part of kingdom theology is the realization that God *will* test us. Our faith will be put to the test to see whether we truly love the real Jesus. That's why James tells us, "My brethren, count it all joy when you fall into various trials, knowing that the testing of your faith produces patience" (Jas. 1:3,4). Paul wrote, "Even so we speak, not as pleasing men, but God who tests our hearts" (1 Thess. 2:4).

This isn't something new that came in with the kingdom. God has *always* worked this way. For example, God gave numerous instructions to the Israelites as tests. He told them not to store manna overnight (except before the Sabbath), but some Israelites tried to do it anyway. He told them *to* store up manna before the Sabbath, but some Israelites didn't listen. (Exod. 16:19-30). God told the Israelites to devote everything from Jericho to destruction, but Achan kept some of the gold for himself.

Beware of "Repealed" Commandments

One of God's basic ways of testing us is to give us a clear command and then allow someone to contradict it later. A good example of this is the episode described in Kings about the Judean prophet whom God sent to confront Jeroboam. The prophet risked his life to fearlessly deliver his message to Jeroboam as He was commanded. God even worked miracles through him.

Recognizing him as a true prophet, King Jeroboam invited the prophet to refresh himself at the king's palace before returning home. But the prophet replied, "If you were to give me half your house, I would not go in with you; nor would I eat bread nor drink water in this place. For so it was commanded me by the word of the Lord, saying, 'You shall not eat bread, nor drink water, nor return by the same way you came." (1 Kings 13:7-10). So far, so good. The prophet from Judah had passed all of God's tests.

But as the Judean prophet was returning home, another prophet of God, who lived in Bethel, chased after the Judean prophet and told him, "I too am a prophet as you are, and an angel spoke to me by the word of the Lord, saying, 'Bring him back with you to your house, that he may eat bread and drink water.' (He was lying)." (1 Kings 13:18). Hmm. This put a new dimension on the test. God had apparently changed His instructions. So the Judean prophet stayed and ate with the prophet from Bethel. What was the result? On his journey back to Judea, a lion attacked and killed the prophet.

It's a sad story, but it well illustrates what Paul said centuries later, "But even if we, or an angel from heaven, preach any other gospel to you than what we have preached to you, let him be accursed" (Gal. 1:8). If God gives us a clear command, He isn't going to later contradict it. That would put His servants in an impossible situation—having to decide whether the countermand had really come from God or not.

Since the time of Moses, there has been only one situation where God *did* alter some of His prior commandments—that was with the coming of the kingdom. But on that unique occasion, God didn't simply send a human messenger—or even an angel—to announce the change. He sent His very own Son, who performed enough miracles to satisfy any skeptic.

Jesus' coming was the final stage of God's purpose for mankind. No angel or human has power to countermand anything Jesus taught. And the Father is never going to contradict His own Son. So until Jesus returns and personally tells us differently, His commandments stand. As I've quoted before, "Jesus Christ is the same yesterday, today, and forever" (Heb. 13:8).

This business of contradicting God's express commandments goes all the way back to the Garden of Eden. God had plainly told Adam, "Of every tree of the garden you may freely eat; but of the tree of the knowledge of good and evil you shall not eat, for in the day that you eat of it you shall surely die." But then the serpent told Eve, "You will not surely die. For God knows that in the day you eat of it your eyes will be opened, and you will be like God, knowing good and evil" (Gen. 3:3,4).

So God said one thing, and then the serpent said another. Most of us would say, "What an easy test!" But, incredibly, our first parents failed it! Eve actually believed the serpent, and Adam went along with it rather than to stand up to his wife when she was in the wrong. But are we Christians any different? We read the plain, clear commandments of Jesus. Yet, when a preacher or Bible commentator directly contradicts Jesus, we choose to believe such a man—rather than Jesus.

So Where Do You and I Stand?

In the course of this book, I've discussed a lot of Christian history. But all of the history in the world does not do us one bit of good if we don't learn from it. Millions of Christians castigate the Roman Catholic Church for its errors. Yet, those self-same Christians fall into the same pit of errors as the Catholics. For, like the Catholics, they too accept the Constantinian Hybrid, and they acquire their worldview through the Hybrid's tinted glasses.

It's reassuring to know that other kingdom Christians through the ages rejected the Hybrid and refused to play by its rules. But their time on the playing field has passed. The ball is now in our court. If every other Christian on earth ignores or explains away Jesus' teachings, this in no way excuses disobedience in you and me. When the Lord has spoken to us directly in the Scriptures, what others say is irrelevant. As the late evangelist, Leonard Ravenhill, used to say, "Jesus is either *absolute*, or He's *obsolete*." There's no middle ground.

I realize that this book has perhaps made you feel uncomfortable. It may even have offended you. Your natural reaction may be to go out and find another book that contradicts most of what I've said about the gospel of the kingdom. And that won't be very hard. In fact, the book right next to where you found mine in your local bookstore will probably say the opposite of what I'm saying.

But rather than doing that, I encourage you to read for yourself the teachings of Jesus. I don't mean proof-texts from Jesus' teachings. I mean the totality of what He taught. Have I misrepresented in any way what He preached? If so, obviously you need to listen to Him, not me. But if I haven't misrepresented Him, I beg you not to toss this book away and forget the things Jesus said. You may have entered into the wedding feast without embracing the gospel of the kingdom—but you won't stay there unless you embrace this gospel.

On the other hand, perhaps this book has struck a responsive chord in your heart. Perhaps you, too, are burning with excitement about the kingdom. Is the kingdom of God to you like the pearl of great price? Does the kingdom bring you such joy that you're willing to let go of everything in order to obtain it? If so, please join me and other modern-day kingdom Christians. Let's do our part in turning the world upside down!

Bibliography

Primary Sources

Barry, Colman J., ed. *Readings in Church History*. Westminster, Maryland: Christian Classics, Inc., 1985.

Calvin, John. *Treatises Against the Anabaptists and Against the Libertines*. Translated by Benjamin Wirt Farley. Grand Rapids: Baker Book House, 1982.

Calvin, John. *Institutes of the Christian Religion*. 2 vols. Translated by Henry Beveridge. Grand Rapids: Wm. B. Eerdmans Publishing Company, 1983.

Eusebius. *Ecclesiastical History*. Translated by Paul L. Maier. Grand Rapids: Kregel Publications, 1999.

Franklin, Benjamin. *The Autobiography and Other Writings*. New York: Penguin Books USA Inc., 1783.

Gee, Henry, and Hardy, John William, eds. *Documents Illustrative of English Church History*. London: MacMillan and Co., Ltd., 1910.

Krey, August C., ed. *The First Crusade: The Accounts of Eyewitnesses and Participants*. Princeton: 1921.

Leith, John H., ed. *Creeds of the Churches*. Atlanta, Georgia: John Knox Press, 1973.

Luther, Martin. *The Bondage of the Will*. Translated by Henry Cole. Grand Rapids: Baker Book House, 1976.

Luther, Martin. *Works of Martin Luther—The Philadelphia Edition*. 6 vols. Translated by C. M. Jacobs. Grand Rapids: Baker Book House, 1982.

Marcellinus, Ammianus. *The Later Roman Empire*. Translated by Walter Hamilton. New York: Penguin Books, 1986.

Randi, James. *The Faith Healers*. Buffalo: Prometheus Books, 1989.

Roberts, Alexander and Donaldson, James, eds. *The Ante-Nicene Fathers*. 10 vols. Grand Rapids: Wm. B. Eerdmans Publishing Company, 1985.

Schaff, Philip, ed. *The Nicene and Post-Nicene Fathers, First Series*. 10 vols. Grand Rapids: Wm. B. Eerdmans Publishing Company, 1983.

Schaff, Philip and Wace, Henry, eds. *The Nicene and Post-Nicene Fathers, Second Series*. 10 vols. Grand Rapids: Wm. B. Eerdmans Publishing Company, 1982.

Simons, Menno. *The Complete Writings of Menno Simons*. Translated by J. C. Wenger. Scottdale, Pennsylvania: Herald Press. 1956.

Secondary Sources

Bainton, Roland H. *Christian Attitudes Toward War and Peace*. Nashville: Abingdon Press, 1960.

Bainton, Roland H. *The Reformation of the Sixteenth Century*. Boston: Beacon Press, 1952.

Cairns, Earle E. *Christianity Through the Centuries*. Grand Rapids: Zondervan Publishing House, 1954.

Chadwick, Henry. *The Early Church*. New York: Penguin Books, 1967.

Chamberlin, E. R. *The Bad Popes*. New York: Dorset Press, 1969.

Christie-Murray, David. *A History of Heresy*. New York: Oxford University Press, 1976.

Dickens, A. G. *The English Reformation*. New York: Schocken Books, 1952.

Dowley, Tim, ed. *Eerdman's Handbook to the History of Christianity*. Grand Rapids: Wm. B. Eerdmans Publishing Company, 1977.

Driver, John. *How Christians Made Peace with War*. Scottdale, Pennsylvania: Herald Press, 1988.

Edwards, David. *Christian England*. Vol. 2. Grand Rapids: Wm. B. Eerdmans Publishing Company, 1983.

Eller, Vernard. *Christian Anarchy*. Grand Rapids: Wm. B. Eerdmans Publishing Company, 1987.

Ellul, Jacques. *The Subversion of Christianity*. Translated by Geoffrey W. Bromiley. Grand Rapids: Wm. B. Eerdmans Publishing Company, 1986.

Erbstösser, Martin. *Heretics in the Middle Ages*. Leipzig: Druckerei Fortrschritt Erfurt, 1984.

Estep, William. *The Anabaptist Story*. Grand Rapids: Wm. B. Eerdmans Publishing Company, 1996.

Gibbon, Edward. *The Decline and Fall of the Roman Empire*. New York: Penguin Books, 1952.

González, Justo. *Faith & Wealth*. New York: Harpers Collins Publishers, 1990.

González, Justo. *A History of Christian Thought.* 3 vols. Nashville: Abingdon Press, 1970.

Grimm, Harold J. *The Reformation Era 1500-1650.* New York: The Macmillan Company, 1965.

Hershberger, Guy F. *The Recovery of the Anabaptist Vision.* Scottdale, Pennsylvania: Herald Press, 1957.

Kraybill, Donald B. *The Upside-Down Kingdom.* Scottdale, Pennsylvania: Herald Press, 1978.

Lucas, Henry S. *The Renaissance and the Reformation.* New York: Harper & Row, 1960.

Schaff, Philip. *History of the Christian Church.* 8 vols. Grand Rapids: Wm. B. Eerdmans Publishing Company, 1910.

Shannon, Albert. *The Medieval Inquisition.* Collegeville, Minnesota: The Liturgical Press, 1984.

Strype, J. *Ecclesiastical Memorials.* London: 1822.

Thomson, John A. F. *The Later Lollards 1414-1520.* London: Oxford University Press, 1965.

Hoehner, H. W. "Maccabees." *The International Standard Bible Encyclopedia.* Ed. Geoffrey W. Bromiley. Vol. 3. Grand Rapids: Eerdmans Publishing Co., 1986.

Tolstoy, Leo. *The Kingdom of God Is Within You.* Lincoln, Nebraska: University of Nebraska Press, 1894.

Tourn, Giorgio, et al. *You Are My Witnesses.* Torino, Italy: Claudiana Editrice, 1989.

Verduin, Leonard. *The Anatomy of a Hybrid.* Sarasota, Florida: Christian Hymnary Publishers, 1976.

Verduin, Leonard. *The Reformers and Their Stepchildren.* Sarasota, Florida: Christian Hymnary Publishers, 1964.

Willoughby, William C. *Counting the Cost.* Elgin, Illinois: The Brethren Press, 1979.

Notes

Chapter 1: Holy War?

1. Raymond d'Aguiliers in August C. Krey, *The First Crusade: The Accounts of Eyewitnesses and Participants* (Princeton: 1921) 250-256.
2. J. Arthur McFall, "The Fall of Jerusalem," *Military History Magazine* (June, 1999)1-6.
3. Krey 252.
4. Krey 253.

Chapter 3: A Different Kind of Kingdom

1. Tertullian, *Against Marcion*, Book IV, Ch. 26; *ANF*, Vol. III, 409.

Chapter 4: Have You Made the Kingdom Commitment?

1. From the Bureau of Citizenship and Immigration Services, at www.immigration.gov/graphics/aboutus/history/teacher/oath.htm.
2. "Florida During World War II, http://www.floridamemory.com/OnlineClassroom/FloridaWWII/history.cfm.
3. *Webster's New World College Dictionary*, *Third Edition* (New York: Simon & Schuster, Inc., 1997) 765.
4. Edward More, "The Solid Rock."
5. Frank Koch, *Proceedings*, quoted by Stephen Covey in *The 7 Habits of Highly Effective People* (New York: Simon & Schuster, 1989) 33.

Chapter 5: Changing Our View of Mammon

1. Clement of Alexandria *Who Is the Rich Man Who Shall Be Saved?* 14; *ANF*, Vol. II, 595.
2. Infoplease: "Economic Statistics by Country, 2001," http://www.infoplease.com/ipa/A0874911.html.
3. Source: Bureau of Census, http://factfinder.census.gov/servlet/BasicFactsServlet.
4. Infoplease.
5. Infoplease.
6. Infoplease.
7. Infoplease.

Chapter 6: A New Standard of Honesty

1. Mike Hertenstein and Jon Trott, "Selling Satan: The Tragic History of Mike Warnke," *Cornerstone*, Vol. 21, Issue 98 (1992).
2. "The Cornerstone Series on Mike Warnke," http://www.cornerstonemag.com/features/iss098/warnke_index.htm.
3. "Cornerstone Series."
4. Bob & Gretchen Passantino and Jon Trott, "Satan's Sideshow: The True Lauren Stratford Story," http://www.cornerstonemag.com/features/iss090/sideshow.htm.
5. James Randi, *The Faith Healers* (Buffalo: Prometheus Books, 1989)105,106,150.
6. Randi 146-153.

Chapter 7: The Kingdom Laws on Marriage and Divorce

1. Testimony of Israel Abrahams before the London Divorce Commission, November 21, 1910, quoted in "Divorce in the Old Testament," *International Bible Encyclopedia* (online) http://www.studylight.org.
2. "Divorce Facts," at http://wheres-daddy.com.
3. "Divorces: 1858-2000" at http://www.statistics.gov.uk.
4. Margaret F. Brinig, "These Boots Are Made for Walking: Why Most Divorce Filers Are Women," *American Law and Economics Review* 2-1 (2000) 126-129.
5. 1 Corinthians 7:10-15, *King James Version*, rendered into contemporary English by the author.
6. Source: Barna Research Group, quoted by B. A. Robinson in "U. S. Divorce Rates for Various Faith Groups," March, 2002, at (http://www.religioustolerance.org/chr_dira.htm).
7. Barna Research Group.
8. Barna Research Group.
9. Source: National Center for Health Statistics. Quoted in "U.S. Divorce Statistics," *Divorce Magazine.com*, at http://www.divorcemag.com/ statistics/statsUS2.shtml.
10. National Center for Health Statistics.
11. Barna Research Group.
12. David Knox and Caroline Schacht, *Marriage and the Family: A Brief Introduction*, (Belmont, California: Wadsworth Publishing Company, 1999). Quoted in "Asian-American Couples," at http://www.uwyo.edu.
13. Source: Institute for Divorce Reform, quoted in *Divorce Magazine.com*

14. "Divorce Rates of All Countries, Compared to the U.S.," quoted at http://www.divorcereform.org/nonus.html.

Chapter 8: Love My Enemies?
1. Adin Ballou, quoted by Leo Tolstoy in *The Kingdom of God Is Within You* (Lincoln, Nebraska: University of Nebraska Press) 10.

Chapter 9: But What If ...?
1. From author's interview with the Weaver family and from "Mountain Man Arrested," *The Sentinel* (Carlisle, PA: May 25, 1988) 1,2.
2. Arthur Kellermann, MD, *New England Journal of Medicine*, 1998, as cited at http://goodsforguns.org.
3. Origen *Against Celsus*, Bk. II, Ch. 30; *ANF*, Vol. IV, 444.
4. Arnobius *Against the Gentiles*, Bk. I, Par. 6; *ANF* Vol. VI, 415.
5. Origen *Against Celsus*, Bk. VIII, Ch. 73; *ANF*, Vol. IV, 667, 668.
6. Ballou, "How Many Does It Take," available at http://www.adinballou.org/HowMany.shtml.

Chapter 10: But Don't the Scriptures Say?
1. W. E. Vine, *Expository Dictionary of New Testament Words* (Grand Rapids: Zondervan Publishing House, 1940) 188.
2. Tertullian *On Idolatry*, Ch. 19; *ANF* Vol. III, 73.

Chapter 12: Life Under Two Kingdoms
1. Tertullian *On Idolatry* Ch. 15; *ANF* Vol. III, 70.
2. "Survey: U. S. Pays Soldiers Less Than $16K," at http://www2.hrnext.com/Article.cfm/Nav/5.0.

Chapter 13: Am I of This World?
1. Dave Moreland, "Dave Moreland's Bozo Criminal of the Day," at http://www.kooi.com/bozo/jan99.htm.

Chapter 14: Does This Make Us Peace and Justice Activists?
1. "Capital Punishment Statistics" at http://www.ojusdoj.gov.
2. Statistics furnished by the Alan Guttmacher Institute and reported at http://www.nrlc.org/abortion/aboramt.html.

Notes 275

Chapter 15: Has Anyone Done This in Real Life?

1. H. W.Hoehner, "Maccabees," *The International Standard Bible Encyclopedia*, Vol. 3 (Grand Rapids: Wm. B. Eerdmans Publishing Company, 1986) 196-199.
2. R. H. Smith, "Pella," *The International Standard Bible Encyclopedia.*

Chapter 16: But Is This Historic Christianity?

1. Hermas *The Shepherd*, Book III, Ch. 1; *ANF*, Vol. II, 31.
2. Tatian *To The Greeks*, Ch. 11; *ANF*; Vol. II, 69.
3. Clement of Alexandria *The Instructor*, Book III, Ch. 8; *ANF*, Vol. II, 281.
4. Tertullian, *Apology,* Ch. 38; *ANF*, Vol. III, 45,46.
5. Tertullian *De Corona*, Ch. 13; *ANF*, Vol. II, 101.
6. Origen *Against Celsus*, Book VIII, Ch. 75; *ANF*, Vol. IV, 668.
7. Cyprian *On Mortality*, Ch. 26; *ANF*, Vol. V, 475.
8. Clement of Alexandria, as quoted in Sermon 55 of Maximus. *ANF* Vol. II, 581.
9. Tertullian *Of Patience*, Ch. 10; *ANF*, Vol. III, 713.
10. Tertullian *Against Marcion*, Ch. 39; *ANF*, Vol. III, 415.
11. Lactantius *The Divine Institutes,* Bk V, Ch. 21; *ANF*, Vol. VII, 158.
12. Lactantius Ch. 24; *ANF*, Vol. VII, 160.
13. Lactantius Ch. 18; *ANF*, Vol. VII,184.
14. Athenagoras *Plea for the Christians*, Ch. 1; *ANF*, Vol. II, 129.
15. Hippolytus (Gregory Dix and Henry Chadwick, trans.) *The Apostolic Tradition* (Ridgefield, CT: Morehouse Publishing, 1992) 26.
16. Canon XII of Nicaea; Philip Schaff, ed. *The Nicene and Post-Nicene Fathers, First Series*. Vol. 10 (Grand Rapids: Wm. B. Eerdmans Publishing Company, 1983) 27.
17. "Epistle of Marcus Aurelius to the Senate," *ANF*, Vol. I, 187.
18. Origen *Against Celsus*, Bk. V, Ch. 37; *ANF*, Vol. IV, 560.
19. Lactantius, Bk. 6, Ch. 17; *ANF*, Vol. 7, 182, 183.

Chapter 18: How to Enter the Kingdom

1. *Webster's New World College Dictionary, Third Edition* (New York: Simon & Schuster, Inc., 1997) 1138.
2. John H. Leith, ed., *Creeds of the Churches* (Atlanta: John Knox Press, 1973) 24,25.

Chapter 21: What Happened to the Kingdom Gospel?
1. Eusebius, *Ecclesiastical History*, Bk. VIII, Ch. 17.
2. Eusebius, *Ecclesiastical History*, Bk. X, Ch. 5.
3. Eusebius, *The Life of Constantine*, Bk. I, Chs. 41 & 42. Philip Schaff and Henry Wace, eds., *The Nicene and Post-Nicene Fathers, Second Series*, 10 vols., Grand Rapids: Wm. B. Eerdmans Publishing Company, 1982, vol. 1, 494.
4. Eusebius, *Constantine*, Bk. II, Chaps. 44 - 46.
5. Lactantius, Bk. V, Ch. 24; *ANF*, Vol. VII, 160.

Chapter 22: The Kingdom of Theology
1. Please see my earlier work, *A Dictionary of Early Christian Beliefs*, where I document this at length under the heading, "Christ, Divinity Of."
2. Socrates, *Ecclesiastical History*, Bk. I, Ch. 9. *The Nicene and Post-Nicene Fathers, Second Series*, Vol. II, 14.
3. Edward Gibbon, *The Decline and Fall of the Roman Empire*, (New York, Penguin Books, 1952) 386.
4. "The Decree of the Holy, Great, Ecumenical Synod, the Second of Nicaea," Philip Schaff, and Henry Wace, eds., *The Nicene and Post-Nicene Fathers, Second Series*, 10 vols. (Grand Rapids: Wm. B. Eerdmans Publishing Company, 1982) vol. XIV, 550, 551.
5. Hilary of Pointers, quoted by Gibbon, 397.
6. Ammianus Marcellinus, *The Later Roman Empire* (New York, Penguin Books, 1986) 239.
7. Colman J. Barry, ed., *Readings in Church History* (Westminster, Maryland: Christian Classics, Inc., 1985) 522.

Chapter 23: Was God Changing the Rules?
1. Eusebius, *Ecclesiastical History,* translated by Paul L. Maier (Grand Rapids: Kregel Publications, 1999) 231.

Chapter 24: How Christ's Teachings Disappeared
1. Leonard Verduin uses this term in his well-known work, *The Anatomy of a Hybrid*, to refer to the church-state hybrid.
2. Eusebius, *The Life of Constantine*, Bk. I, Ch. 44. Schaff, 494.

Chapter 25: The Golden Age That Never Happened
1. Philip Schaff, *History of the Christian Church*. 8 vols. (Grand Rapids: Wm. B. Eerdmans Publishing Company, 1910) vol. III, 33-35.
2. Schaff 107-125.

3. Gibbon 252.
4. Gibbon 380.
5. Eusebius, *Constantine*, Bk. II, Ch. 3; Schaff, 500.
6. Eusebius, *Constantine*, Chaps. 7-9.
7. Eusebius, *Constantine*, Chaps. 24-29.
8. Gibbon 258.
9. Gibbon 380.
10. Gibbon 382.
11. Gibbon 470-472.
12. Gibbon 476.
13. Gibbon 477.
14. Gibbon 478.
15. Gibbon 478.
16. Gibbon 509.
17. Lynn H. Nelson, "The Later Roman Empire," http://www.ku.edu/kansas/medieval/108/lectures.
18. Gibbon 562-619. Also see Vincent Bridges, "Arthur and the Fall of Rome," http://www.sangraal.com/library/arthur1.htm.

Chapter 26: Augustine—Apologist for the Hybrid

1. Augustine, *Reply to Faustus the Manichaean*, bk. 22, ch.74. Philip Schaff and Henry Wace, eds., *The Nicene and Post-Nicene Fathers, First Series*, vol. 4 (Grand Rapids: Wm. B. Eerdmans Publishing Company, 1982) 301.
2. Augustine, ch.75; Schaff, *Fathers*, vol. 4, 301.
3. Augustine, ch.79; Schaff, *Fathers*, vol. 4, 304.
4. Augustine, *The Correction of the Donatists*, ch.7, par. 23; Schaff, *Fathers*, vol. 4, 642.
5. Roland H. Bainton, *Christian Attitudes Toward War and Peace* (Nashville: Abingdon Press, 1960) 33-43.
6. Bainton, 96-98. Augustine, *Faustus*, ch.75; Schaff, *Fathers*, vol. 4, 301.
7. Augustine, *Faustus*, ch. 75; Schaff, *Fathers*, vol. 4, 301.
8. Leo Tolstoy, *The Kingdom of God Is Within You* (Lincoln, Nebraska: University of Nebraska Press, 1894) 306.
9. Tolstoy.
10. Article 92(1)(c) *Uniform Code of Military Justice*.
11. Augustine, *On the Predestination of the Saints*, chaps. 16-19. Schaff, *Fathers*, Vol. V, 506-508.

Chapter 27: Forgery in the Name of Christ!
1. Colman J. Barry, ed., *Readings in Church History*, 235-237.
2. E. R. Chamberlin, *The Bad Popes* (New York: Dorset Press, 1969) 43.
3. Chamberlin 60.
4. Barry 522.
5. Barry 521, 522.

Chapter 28: The Underground Kingdom
1. Tim Dowley, ed., *Eerdmans' Handbook to the History of Christianity* (Grand Rapids: Wm. B. Eerdmans Publishing Company, 1977) 202, 203.
2. Martin Erbstösser, *Heretics in the Middle Ages* (Leipzig: Druckerei Fortrschritt Erfurt, 1984) 80, 81.
3. Erbstösser 83.
4. Erbstösser 85.

Chapter 29: The Waldensians
1. Giorgio Tourn, et al, *You Are My Witnesses* (Torino, Italy: Claudiana Editrice, 1989) 14.
2. Tourn 15.
3. Tourn 16.
4. Tourn 20.
5. Tourn 17
6. Tourn 18.
7. Tourn 19.
8. Tourn 19.
9. Tourn 20.
10. Tourn 36.
11. Tourn 37.
12. Erbstösser 202.
13. Tourn 54.
14. Tourn, 51.
15. Judith Collins, "Heritage of the Waldensians: A Sketch," at http://www.wrs.edu/journals/jour896/waldensians.html.
16. J. A. Wylie, *The History of Protestantism*, 1878, Vol. II, page 485, quoted in Collins.

Chapter 30: The Alternate Stream

1. Henry Gee and John William Hardy, eds, "Wycliffe Propositions Condemned at London," *Documents Illustrative of English Church History* (London: MacMillan and Co., Ltd., 1910) 108, 109.
2. "Council of Constance," Session 15 - 6 July 1415, at http://www.dailycatholic.org/history/16ecume3.htm.
3. Gee and Hardy 110.
4. Gee and Hardy 109, Conclusion 10.
5. Gee and Hardy Conclusion 16.
8. Gee and Hardy 128-131.
9. John A. F. Thomson, *The Later Lollards 1414-1520* (London: Oxford University Press, 1965) 247.
10. Henry Gee and John William Hardy, eds, "The Lollard Conclusions," *Documents Illustrative of English Church History* (London: MacMillan and Co., Ltd., 1910) 128, Conclusion 6.
11. Gee and Hardy 131, Conclusion 10.
12. Thomson 244-21.
13. J. Strype, *Ecclesiastical Memorials*, Part II (London, 1822) 54, 55.

Chapter 31: The Waldensians Meet the Reformers

1. Henry S. Lucas, *The Renaissance and the Reformation* (New York: Harper & Row, 1960) 519.
2. Lucas 520.
3. Harold J. Grimm, *The Reformation Era 1500-1650* (New York: The Macmillan Company, 1965) 188.
4. Lucas 526.
5. Grimm, 321-324.
6. Tourn 66.
7. Tourn 66,67.
8. Tourn 66,67.
9. Tourn 66-69.
10. Tourn 72.
11. Tourn 72.
12. Tourn 69.

Chapter 32: The New Zion in Geneva

1. Grimm 338.
2. Grimm 325.
3. Grimm 342.
4. Rahull Nand, "John Calvin: Not So Tyrannical" at http://oprfhs.org/division/history/interpretations/2000interp/.doc.

5. "The Murder of Michael Servetus" at
    http://www.bcbsr.com/topics/servetus.html.
6. John F. Fulton, *Michael Servetus Humanist and Martyr* (Herbert
    Reichner, 1953) 35.
7. Philip Schaff, *History of the Christian Church*, vol. VIII (Grand
    Rapids: Wm. B. Eerdmans Publishing Company, 1910) 768.
8. Walter Nigg, *The Heretics* (Alfred A. Knopf, Inc., 1962) 328.
9. "The Murder of Michael Servetus."
10. John Calvin, "On the Magistrate" in *Treatises against the Anabap-
     tists and against the Libertines* (Grand Rapids: Baker Bk. House,
     1982) 77,78.
11. "Second Helvetic Confession," Ch. XXX, reproduced in John H.
     Leith, ed., *Creeds of the Churches* (Atlanta: John Knox Press, 1973)
     190,191.
12. Calvin 77.

Chapter 33: The Kingdom Banner Arises Anew

1. Sammlung Simler, quoted in "A History of the Baptists,"
    http://www.pbministries.org/History/John%20T.%20Christian/vol1/h
    istory_10.htm.
2. Simler.
3. Menno Simons, *The Complete Writings of Menno Simons*. Trans. J.
    C. Wenger: *Reply to False Accusations* (Scottdale: Herald Press,
    1956) 96.
4. Menno Simons, as quoted by John D. Roth, "The Mennonites' Dirty
    Little Secret," *Christianity Today*, October 7, 1996, 44.
5. Hans Denk, quoted in "What Is Anabaptism?,"
    http://www.anabaptistnetwork.com/WhatIsAnabaptism.htm.
6. Simons 93.
7. Simons 94.
8. Roland Bainton, *The Reformation of the Sixteenth Century* (Boston:
    Beacon Press, 1952) 101.
9. Thieleman J. van Braght, *Martyrs Mirror* (Scottdale, Pa: Herald
    Press, 1950) 418.
10. Norman Penney, ed., *The Journal of George Fox* (London: J.M. Dent
     & Sons, 1924) http://www.geocities.com/quakerpages/fox17.htm.
11. David Edwards, *Christian England*. Vol. 2. (Grand Rapids: Wm. B.
     Eerdmans Publishing Company, 1983) 341.
12. William C. Willoughby, *Counting the Cost* (Elgin, Illinois: The
     Brethren Press, 1979) 45,46.

13. Benjamin Franklin, *The Autobiography and Other Writings* (New York: Penguin Books USA Inc., 1783) 129.

Free Catalog

When Christians discover the historic faith, they soon realize that today we live in a topsy-turvy spiritual world. A world where truth is called error and where error is called truth. A world where the commandments of Jesus are often ignored, but the commandments and traditions of men are treated as though they are sacred.

If you would like to learn more about kingdom Christianity and the historic Christian faith, please contact Scroll Publishing to receive our free catalog. It features books, cassettes, and audio CDs on:

- Kingdom discipleship
- Cultivating an obedient love relationship with Christ
- What Christians believed before the time of Constantine
- The history of kingdom Christians, such as the Waldensians and Lollards
- The Anabaptists

Scroll Publishing Co.
www.scrollpublishing.com

P. O. Box 122
Amberson, PA 17210
(717) 349-7033
Fax (717) 349-7558